DOT
VERTIGO

DOT VERTIGO
Doing Business in a Permeable World

Richard Nolan

John Wiley & Sons, Inc.
New York • Chichester • Weinheim • Brisbane • Singapore • Toronto

Library of Congress Cataloging-in-Publication Data:

ISBN 0-471-41529-4

Printed in the United States of America.

10 9 8 7 6 5 4 3 2 1

Preface

D ot companies have always given investors a fast and tumultuous ride. We've seen the Nasdaq, which is heavily made up of high-tech companies, go on a roller-coaster ride from the highest peaks to the lowest depths, with some unfortunate firms dropping off the board completely. (See Figure P.1.)

When the dot frenzy began, few understood its complex makeup. The difficulty in pinpointing growth strategies or accurate valuations was made apparent only when the market came crashing down. We all seem to be experiencing dot vertigo. In the past four years I have focused on studying companies in the dot sector as well as the leading incumbents and bricks-and-clicks firms. These included America Online (AOL), Amazon.com, drugstore.com, IBM, Merrill Lynch, Charles Schwab, and Cisco Systems. My goal has been to better understand what we can learn from these companies about management's effective and strategic use of technology within the firm. Technology has moved beyond being just tools to forming a company's actual infrastructure. My interest has always been in determining how companies transform themselves throughout the entire value chain (i.e., senior managers to back-office workers to the customers) to incorporate technology as a strategy rather than just a solution.

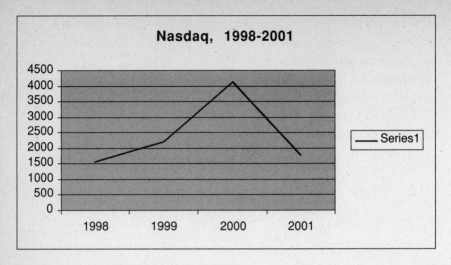

Figure P.1   The Market Roller Coaster

During this time, I discovered that most of the managers had very strong opinions about the role and importance of dot companies—opinions that have seemed to reverse since the slide that began on April 15, 2000. Before that day, the managers viewed dot coms as leading the way to the development of a new agile, real-time-oriented way of managing companies. After April 15, opinions changed. Now the managers I spoke with viewed dot coms as merely a flash in the pan, as "dot nothings"—that is, dot coms became something to be ignored as the managers went back to the traditional approaches to management they had been accustomed to.

This is unfortunate and seems to be a product of the "one minute" management philosophy where complicated market nuances and the evolving business environment can be summed up in a neat package of generalities. My work, for reasons that you will discover in this book, has led me to the conclusion that by their very nature, which is to be permeable and fluid, dot companies have refined traditional business thinking and approaches. Further, I believe that dot companies—and those other companies that incorporate the most robust approaches emerging from these New Economy firms—will continue to be both the leading and the bleeding edge of business.

First, I believe that the Nasdaq alone, intimating an economic collapse, tells an incomplete story. The Dow Jones Industrial Average allows us to take a longer view of events. The Dow index was founded toward the end of the nineteenth century. As we know, it is made up of the 30 leading companies in the United States and roughly reflects how they are doing in creating wealth for their investors.

Some 20 years or so after its founding, the Dow reached 100 on July 3, 1906. Forty-four years later, in 1950, the Dow closed above 200. Sixteen years later, in 1966, the Dow broke 1,000. Twenty-five years later, in 1991, the Dow closed above 2,000. Then a decade of accelerated growth began: On November 22, 1995, the Dow closed above 5,000 (less than four years after reaching 2,000). Less than one year later the Dow closed above 6,000, and four months later the Dow broke 7,000. It continued to climb through 10,000, and that's about where it is today. (See Figure P.2.)

So if we add an additional perspective by looking at the performance of the Dow index, it appears that the U.S. economy has not crashed, nor

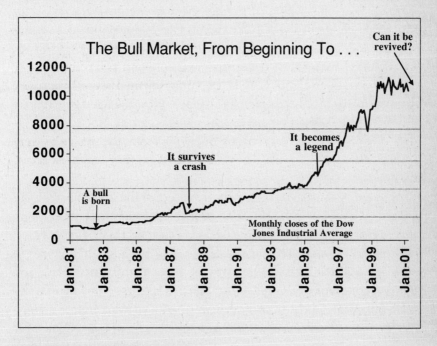

Figure P.2 Tracking the Bull Market

Source: Datastream International. Description adapted from Floyd Norris, "Worries over a Besieged Bull Market," *New York Times* (March 18, 2001).

has the economy fallen into a deep recession in 2001; more accurately, it has reached a plateau. Indeed, one might conclude that the tech crash flushed out those companies with weak management and poor business models, and left as survivors those with both viable business models and strong management teams.

Second, I believe that the role of technology in business has been woefully misunderstood through the years. The role has continued to change dramatically and become more important to the point that today it is extremely strategic. If we follow the learning curve of technology's dominant designs, we see that the data processing (DP) era of mainframes began around 1960 and ran through the early 1980s; the microprocessor era began in the early 1980s and ran through 1995; and finally, the network era of the Internet began around 1995 and still is going on. The network era benefits from the cumulative organizational learning of the previous two eras about use of information technology (IT), resulting in fundamental structural changes to organizational forms from vertical integration to virtual integration. The boundaries of today's organizations are more permeable and less rigid, as I describe in Chapter 1.

Dot-com companies built from greenfield sites—that is, organizations built from the ground up without having to transform from existing structures—like drugstore.com (covered in Chapter 8), rely on a great deal of virtual integration. More importantly, the virtually integrated structures of the dot coms are what many of the more established companies are trying to achieve through a creative destructive process. Also, when we examine the management processes of dot coms as they use technology to connect electronically with their customers and "sense and respond" to customer needs in real time, we see a speed and innovative openness also sought by transforming companies. While many of the dot-com structures and management practices are "bleeding edge," my research indicates that other companies continue to emulate the virtual structures and speed of decision making of dot companies. It is just that large incumbents are not starting from greenfield sites.

Since the mid-1980s, traditional incumbent companies have been consistently making investments in IT amounting to more than 50 percent of their annual capital budgets. These investments have been associated with a myriad of significant benefits. During this time, we have seen companies achieve massive reduction in their workforces while simultaneously either increasing revenues or holding revenues constant, and service levels have continued to increase, too. Take, for example, the steel industry in the United States. Output has remained relatively constant for the past 30 years, but the labor force has been reduced from 600,000 workers to around 200,000 workers. And 30,000 workers in nontraditional steel mills (mini-mills and micro-mills) produce about 45 percent of the steel.

Nevertheless, a counterpoint associated with vertical versus virtual integration is worth making too. The traditional incumbent's workforce is generally much larger than that of the new entrant dot com. For example, in the IT industry, IBM (the incumbent listed on the New York Stock Exchange) has a workforce of about 300,000 compared to Cisco (the more recent industry entrant listed on the Nasdaq) of about 30,000. (There are about 3,000 companies listed on the New York Stock Exchange, and about 4,800 listed on the Nasdaq.) Even more dramatic is the retail drug industry comparison of Walgreens' workforce of more than 1,000,000 (including part-time) versus that of drugstore.com of about 400. As we can see by comparing the two charts, the dot-com collapse affected the Nasdaq-listed companies more than those of the Dow, which is comprised mainly of NYSE-listed companies. Here two points are important. First, the Nasdaq companies have relatively fewer employees. Second, many of the high-tech and dot companies impacted have young, well-trained workers who are relatively readily reassimilated into the overall workforce. Many of the Harvard Business School MBA graduates who went to dot companies have resigned themselves to joining consulting firms (B2C—back to consulting) and investment banking firms (B2B—back to banking).

Third, I think that the impact of dot coms was not so much a wake-up call to incumbent companies about investing in IT as it was a wake-up call about refocusing the strategic investment of IT to the front office—that is, leveraging the Internet to "sense and respond" to customers directly. As demonstrated by Cisco Systems (covered in Chapter 9), replacing obsolete legacy systems with Internet-compatible architecture is a strategic necessity, but IT strategic advantage has shifted from the back office to the very robust front office.

Fourth, I think that we are a bit myopic in too quickly generalizing from our dot-com experience. Chapter 11 identifies five dangerous Internet myths that managers must be careful to avoid in their strategic thinking.

Keep in mind that while there are more than 100 million U.S. Internet users in 2001 (the highest number of any country), there are now more than 22 million Chinese Internet users, up from only 5 million the previous year. If that rate of increase continues in China, there will be more Chinese users than U.S. Internet users. Also, keep in mind the role that the Internet and network era technologies can play and are playing in enabling doing business globally. For managers to think that the Internet will continue to be an American/English-language phenomenon are naive. The Internet is fast becoming a global phenomenon whereby the American influence will remain important, but not dominant.

The dot companies have given us a peek into the future of emerging organization structures and new management approaches. We need to overcome dot vertigo to see clearly the implications. My goal in this book is to provide managers with a more balanced perspective that draws from the achievements of dot companies, and leverage these approaches in all types of firms, creating organizations that are fluid, permeable, and connected.

Introduction

If you've ever experienced vertigo where the landscape is frenetically blurring past you and those points of reference that provided balance in the past are pulled out from under you, you know what executives managing in the current economic climate are going through. Valuation, stock price, and return on investment (ROI) are just a few of the indicators whizzing by managers as their companies are frozen in a downward spiral of falling revenues, loss of market share, and competitive surprises.

Vertigo—that dizzy, confused state of mind where your surroundings whirl about—is disastrous for pilots who suffer disorientation and lose control of their aircraft, and is no less catastrophic for businesses and their investors who are now plunging headlong into an increasingly unpredictable economic landscape. *Dot Vertigo* examines how established bricks-and-mortar firms as well as first-generation Web companies have responded to an onslaught of technology-strengthened competition, and have adapted to meet these competitors head-on. The book introduces the next shift in Internet technology—the I-Net—and demonstrates how it is being used to create permeable businesses. It is an organization's ability to become permeable that determines whether it has a chance for long-term growth and profitability. Permeability refers to the level at which a company's network has so thoroughly and seamlessly permeated the firm, both internally and externally, that the boundaries that traditionally define a firm's activities, strategies, and functions are transparent. *Dot Vertigo* introduces the notion of permeability for executives who must create these companies, and for investors who have committed to their long-term profitability and success. It is the permeable organization that truly reflects the speed, collaboration, and scalability of the network economy.

The key to the permeable organization is the I-Net, which I believe is a quintessential approach to competing, evolving, and doing business in an Internet-driven economy—what I refer to in this book as the network economy. The I-Net represents the pinnacle of this economy, where the operations of the company (reflected by its Intranet) meet the outside world made up of suppliers, partners, and customers (i.e., the Internet).

The Permeable Organization

Dot Vertigo will force investors and managers to rethink their three-year plans, resetting their agendas for the rapidly evolving network economy. While technology is at an advanced stage, business and finance applications are still in their infancy (save for marketing). In this book, I will show why a company's transformation into a networked organization, blue chips and dots alike, is a leading indicator of who will become the winners and losers in the network economy. The characteristic underlying the networked company is permeability; it is this characteristic that will determine which companies are likely to drive greater profitability and shareholder value. *Dot Vertigo* prescribes a new agenda for managers that includes:

- A modern framework for measuring the effectiveness of the company's infrastructure.
- Action steps to becoming permeable.
- Ways to spearhead organizational change to drive the transformation from flat to permeable.
- Specific recommendations for how blue chips can avoid dot vertigo.

- Establishing new metrics and financial indicators reflective of the network economy.
- Recommendations based on the successful approaches of companies such as Merrill Lynch, Charles Schwab, Cisco Systems, IBM, and drugstore.com.

The book is organized in three parts that can be categorized as concept, execution, and lessons. Beginning with a definition of dot vertigo, Part One identifies the symptoms of companies suffering from business disorientation. The incumbents, mostly blue chip companies but languishing Web companies as well, are the most susceptible to online competitors. This is not because they haven't pursued an online presence, but rather because they lack permeability—the ability the Internet offers to become networked. (In the case of Web companies, vertigo results from the lack of a sophisticated business model and fully developed business plan that would enable the company to take full advantage of the Web.) This inability results in lack of shareholder value, plummeting stock prices and market caps, a need to play catch-up, a loss of market share, a complacent culture, the failure to innovate, and reactionary cost cutting, to name just a few factors. Executives and managers who are charged with creating companies that offer increasing value and investors making financial commitments need to revise their own performance measures to incorporate the warning signs of companies suffering from dot vertigo.

Part Two describes the I-Net infrastructure and offers guideposts to managers responsible for reshaping their companies with technology, who have to understand business models characteristic of the network economy, and who must display the skills needed to execute these models effectively. With the foundation laid for emerging business models in a network economy, the chapters in Part Two provide a framework for building and managing a strategic I-Net that will increase the value of the corporation. The infrastructure needed to create an I-Net that is in complete sync with the organization's financial targets and business operations is described as well.

Part Two goes on to identify key performance areas for these new business models and to assign financial and business benchmarks as well as metrics for each. It encourages readers to consider obvious performance areas such as revenue and operating expenses in the light of the network economy, and to identify less obvious areas such as research and development (sometimes the first casualty of cost cutting) and tangible and intangible assets that require a new definition in the dot world.

The final chapters in Part Three draw from extensive case studies that illustrate how to successfully implement an approach that brings business into the networked world. These final chapters bring to life the principles and practices described in the book through real-world examples from companies that are using emerging business models to reinvigorate their organizations, including:

- Drugstore.com's incisive business focus and effective use of partners—a story of equity advantage and an ideal management scenario.
- Merrill Lynch's graceful plunge into the online world.
- Companies as diverse as Cisco and Ford that have derived a value proposition out of being connected with their customers, colleagues, partners, and peers.

Having spent years observing and advising bellwether organizations like Cisco and powerhouses like Schwab, I am convinced that the stage of the network economy all companies must ready themselves for is the permeable stage and the tool to do this is the I-Net. I have benefited from my position not as an industry observer, but rather as an active participant in creating, executing, and analyzing the approaches core to the success of today's most valued companies. I am fortunate to be able to communicate to you in this book what I have learned as an adviser to leading CEOs and their senior teams.

Contents

1

Doing Business in a Permeable World

The permeable organization taps into the speed, potential for collaboration, and organic scalability of the network economy. Designed to let customers directly interact with the company to tailor offerings for individual needs, all business activities and company strategies are transparent in the permeable organization. In contrast, customers of non-networked or non-permeable companies are not given this type of direct access and subsequently settle for standardized products that don't completely meet their needs at inflexible prices that may not be competitive.

The primary approach for doing business in a technology-driven economy is the I-Net, which, as we will demonstrate throughout this book, is the key to building and managing a permeable organization. The I-Net represents the apex of the network economy, where the operations of the company interact with the outside world made up of suppliers, partners, and customers through the Internet. Dot companies are designed for permeability at the outset and built from the ground up, and are the clearest representation of permeable businesses. Like their dot counterparts, bellwether firms such as Cisco Systems and Charles Schwab cast off their internally focused back-office IT systems, and replaced them with outwardly focused I-Nets. But, the question remains, What happens to

1

those managers and their companies who don't recognize the new guide-posts emerging in business? This question brings us back to the title of this book.

Until recently, the condition we know as vertigo was experienced by pilots, divers, and skiers who, in this state, lost sight of the reference points used to orient their movements; the horizon blends with the clouds; the snow blends with the sky; the fog blends with the sea. The illusions caused by disorientation are the most dangerous aspect of vertigo. Pilots experiencing vertigo have been known to blithely fly their airplanes into the ground at cruise speeds. The pilot may sense the plane is turning right when really it is on a straight course. He or she may feel the plane is gaining altitude when it is actually losing altitude. Instruments provide pilots with vital information when flying in low-visibility conditions, and they must rely on technology rather than their senses when experiencing dangerous conditions. If not, the pilot becomes victim to vertigo.

Now managers as high up as the CEO are vulnerable to vertigo—and the results are as catastrophic as those experienced by pilots. Some managers become confused and send their companies on dangerous headings. But others rely on their instruments to get reoriented and successfully steer their companies onto a new course. The purpose of this book is threefold:

1. To alert managers to the symptoms of dot vertigo (so named, since traditional firms are the first to be left disoriented by the business methods of flexible dot companies).
2. To offer a solution to managers who are in danger of suffering vertigo at the hands of networked or permeable companies.
3. To demonstrate how managers can build a permeable business through a supercharged network that is called the I-Net.

It is my belief that the I-Net will become critical to those companies striving to increase levels of innovation and market share while growing their profits and valuations. The next few chapters discuss why the I-Net is the instrument managers will use to do business in an increasingly permeable world, and which companies have successfully adopted its use. The increasing reliance on more powerful and interconnected networks and on the business models that such connectivity creates is a phenomenon that emerged with the advent of the dot company.

Dot companies pioneered a nimble business model by exploiting the Internet and the latest technologies. By using this explosive combination to their competitive advantage, dot companies engaged 50 million customers in less than four years; current numbers are reaching 200 million. Dot companies have triggered enormous industry restructuring, and while in the past 18 months we have seen these companies come and go, it is equally true that an industry is never the same once the dot company has made its indelible impression.

The Big Picture: Technology Is the Engine Driving the Economy

A lot of time has been wasted in the debate about the technology payoff. It is futile for management to engage in this debate. While many academics and industry pundits continue to conduct pseudoscientific research to show that the payoffs of technology are not real, the plain fact is that companies continue to invest in technology.

Today most companies are investing more than 50 percent of their capital expenditures in one form or another in technology. What's more, the technology industry is robust and growing voraciously. As shown in Figure 1.1, a U.S. Department of Commerce report estimates that the size of the IT industry in the United States is close to $1,400 billion.[1] As you read this book the actual number will probably be increasing, and the pattern of double-digit growth in this industry will take it well into the trillion-dollar level during the early part of this decade.

Second, the products and services that the technology industry is producing are driving the economy. Witness the pervasiveness of firms such as Cisco, Schwab, Amazon.com, Yahoo!, E*Trade, and the like in the consumers' consciousness. The Department of Commerce estimates that by 2006 half of the U.S. workforce will be employed by either companies in the IT industry or companies that are intensive users of IT. For most of the decade of the 1990s, the IT industry accounted for about 8 percent of the U.S. gross domestic product (GDP), but contributed on average 35 percent of the nation's real economic growth.

As IT continues to penetrate companies in every industry, it is becoming

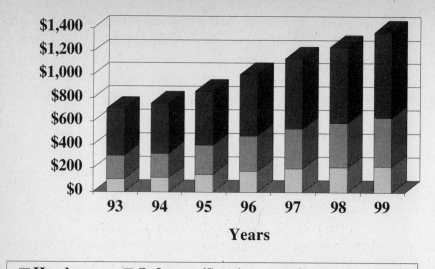

Figure 1.1   Size of U.S. IT Industry (in Billions of Dollars)
Source: Figure 1.1, "GPO Growth in All IT-Producing Industries," The Emerging Digital Economy II, Department of Commerce (June 1999): 17.

more difficult to determine whether a particular company in an industry is more a technology company than it is, say, a bank, a bookstore, or a drugstore. David Pottruck, CEO of Schwab, for instance, considers Schwab to be partially a technology company.

Measuring the Permeable Business

The pre-Internet age business model enabled companies to produce sustained, incremental revenue and earnings growth—what we in management describe as the "march to the northeast corner." Companies considered to be profit drivers accomplished this year after year. Ultimately, this business model led to a handful of large companies in an industry that controlled the majority of that industry's revenue. The companies with the highest revenues and largest industry market share commanded the highest market values.

The main characteristic of these pre-Internet or industrial age companies was control. The drive to control all the factors that influenced a market led to vertically integrated companies, which allowed their management to control raw materials all the way through the production process to distribution of the product.

The high-tech industry, a creation of the network age, spearheaded a different business model where the hallmarks of the company were speed and innovation. Control of too many diverse activities tended to get in the way of these attributes. So vanguard Internet age companies began a trend toward moving away from control and its vertical integration, using technology to virtually integrate the components of the business, connecting the prerequisite partners needed to win in an industry. Technologies—that include but are not limited to the Internet, Enterprise Resource Planning (ERP), and data mining—have enabled the integration and real-time coordination of all of the businesses' stakeholders, both internally and externally. Again, I cite Cisco as a wonderful example of this type of connectivity.

Network-age companies that have mastered virtual integration and melded business boundaries are recognized as having implemented a superior business model. These companies are able to extract value from the marketplace in a more efficient and less complex manner than large, vertically integrated companies. Thus, the market value in network economy companies is no longer correlated with having the highest revenues in the industry. The first company to demonstrate this new business model was Microsoft when its market value grew to rival IBM's market value in 1992 (see Figure 1.2); in 1995 Microsoft's market value broke away from IBM's, and for a time Microsoft had the highest market value in the world.

This shift demonstrates, in part, the impact technology solutions—both as a commercial product and as a business enabler—have had on those nascent companies that we now consider powerhouses. Figure 1.3 further demonstrates this shift by comparing the top 10 ranking for the market value of U.S. companies in 1970, 1980, and 2000. The rankings in 1970 and 1980 are much as you would expect: The list is dominated by a host of industrial companies including General Electric (GE) as well as a handful of oil companies. In 1990 the shift begins to materialize as we see Wal-Mart hitting the list, partially as a result of leveraging its logistic systems to replace Sears' market dominance. Testament to

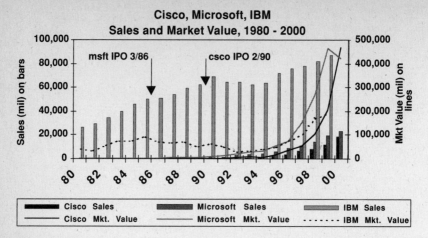

Figure 1.2   Sales and Market Value of Cisco, Microsoft, and IBM from 1980 to 2000
Data source: Compustat.

the power of speed and innovation, IBM falls from the list in 2000, and three other technology companies are included: Microsoft, Cisco, and Intel Corporation. Microsoft and Cisco, while having the first and third highest market values in 1999, also have the smallest revenues of these top 10 firms.

Interestingly, and in support of the practice of following economic patterns, three pharmaceutical companies join the list as we see IT-enabled breakthroughs in biochemistry and the mapping of the human genome. Biotech, pharmaceuticals, and chemical engineering firms continue to dominate the stock market and have become strong performers in an otherwise lackluster initial public offering (IPO) market. Finally, with consolidations in the financial services industry, particularly that of Citibank, Travelers Group, and Smith Barney, Citigroup comes onto the top 10 list. This series of mergers in the financial sector signaled an impressive era of merger and acquisition (M&A) activity that occurred industrywide.

Figure 1.4 further highlights the trajectory of the top 10 highest-valued companies in 2000, and their positions in 1990, 1980, and 1970. GE has sustained the most impressive performance by achieving number 1 in 2000, number 3 in 1990, number 7 in 1980, and number 5 in

Figure 1.3 Top 10 Market Value Companies in 2000 and Their Ranks in 1990, 1980, and 1970 (in Millions of Dollars)

Rank	Company	2000		1990		1980		1970	
		Revenues	Mkt. Value	Revenues	Mkt. Value	Revenues	Mkt. Value	Revenues	Mkt. Value
1	GE	110,832	472,401	57,766	50,095	4,959	13,883	8,727	8,525
2	Exxon	160,883	302,282	105,519	64,449	3,142	34,859	6,554	16,416
3	Cisco Systems	12,154	273,029	70	341	NA	NA	NA	NA
4	Wal-Mart	165,013	236,778	32,602	37,695	1,643	970	44	45
5	Microsoft	19,747	229,150	1,183	8,641	NA	NA	NA	NA
6	Vodafone	12,686	224,929	251	2,441	NA	16,328	NA	NA
7	Merck	32,714	218,060	7,672	34,781	2,734	6,334	748	3,607
8	Nokia	21,088	207,549	6,147	134	NA	NA	NA	NA
9	Intel	29,389	200,457	3,921	7,687	855	1,720	NA	NA
10	Pfizer	16,204	176,962	6,406	13,334	3,029	3,931	870	2,314

Data source. Compustat.
NA—Not available.

Figure 1.4 Changes in Top 10 Companies Ranked by Market Value from 1970 to 2000 (in Millions of Dollars)

Rank	1970			1980		
	Company	Revenues	Mkt. Value	Company	Revenues	Mkt. Value
1	GM	18,752	23,028	IBM	26,213	39,607
2	Exxon	16,554	16,416	Exxon	108,449	34,836
3	IBM	7,504	10,757	Amoco	27,832	23,436
4	Texaco	6,350	9,496	Mobil	59,510	17,163
5	GE	8,727	8,525	Chevron	42,919	17,020
6	DuPont	3,618	6,285	BP	49,368	15,436
7	Gulf Oil	5,396	5,631	GE	24,959	13,883
8	Mobil	7,261	4,762	GM	57,729	13,311
9	Chevron	4,188	4,624	Royal Dutch/ Shell	14,894	13,183
10	BP	4,062	3,950	Texaco	52,484	12,888

Note: Year 2000 data is actually 1999 fiscal year-end data for sales and 12/31/00 market value.
Data source: Compustat.

1970. The shooting star is Cisco, coming from 692 in 1990 and achieving number 2 in 1999. Microsoft has maintained a similar but less dramatic trajectory. Note also that in 1970 revenue and market value of companies show a high correlation, while in 2000, there is not a significant correlation between the two. Cisco has the third highest market value and ranks 290th in revenue; Vodafone is sixth in market value and 277th in revenue. Is this just dated market news? Perhaps some might construe it as such; certainly vertigo-inflicted managers would. However, the perceptive reader understands that these patterns signify those business attributes that create profit-driving companies that form the backbone of an ever-changing economy—the most important attribute being connectivity. Later in this book I'll examine how blue chip com-

	1990			2000		Revenue Rank
Company	Revenues	Mkt. Value	Company	Revenues	Mkt. Value	in 2000
IBM	69,018	64,567	GE	110,832	472,401	9
Exxon	105,519	64,449	Exxon	160,883	302,282	4
GE	57,766	50,095	Cisco Systems	12,154	273,029	290
Philip Morris	44,323	47,932	Wal-Mart	165,013	236,778	2
Toyota	62,566	39,499	Microsoft	19,747	229,150	145
Bristol Myers Squibb	10,300	35,096	Vodafone	12,686	224,929	277
BP	58,990	34,581	Merck	32,714	218,060	72
AT&T	55,977	32,901	Nokia	21,088	207,549	133
Coca-Cola	10,236	31,073	Intel	29,389	200,457	83
Procter & Gamble	24,081	29,998	Pfizer	16,204	176,962	192

panies as well as first-generation dot companies countered competitors and pulled out of vertigo-induced dives by building webs of connectivity that supported and protected the firms.

In addition to market value, the revenue per employee figures for the top 10 in 2000 are all in the high numbers—over $300,000 per employee, with the exception of Wal-Mart, a company that is dependent on a large part-time workforce. Both market value and revenue per employee are telling indicators of an organization's achievements, whether it is dedicated solely to creating wealth or actively participating in shaping its industry. Permeable companies strive to do both. The next sections discuss in greater detail the importance of these two metrics.

Market Value

The U.S. stock market has been shown to be a relatively efficient processor of information about the future prospects of publicly traded companies. Theoretically, the market value of a company represents the collective judgment of the cash that investors think they will be able to realize from their investment in a company; it is the expectations that investors believe they will realize from the returns (profits generated) as a result of the viability of the company's business model and the execution of the business model by its management team. But, for the general business and investment population, market value represents a belief about a company's future.

Now more than ever, the market value of a company is completely dynamic, shifting as new information emerges. The past 18 months have shown us just how dynamic market value is—and how volatile the stock market has become. This volatility has served to weed out those companies that have not been able to increase their levels of performance or strengthen their firms as quickly as their competitors. While the rewards are high for those companies that survive and prosper despite the fluctuations, exactly which companies will reap these rewards remains uncertain. We have seen this uncertainty reflected in the devaluation of Nasdaq companies across the board, impacting even giants of the network age such as Amazon and Cisco. However, volatility only strengthens the argument for creating permeable, highly connected companies that can respond to fluctuations strategically and operationally on a daily basis. It also emphasizes the importance of our second network economy metric: revenue per employee.

Internet bellwether companies have returned the volley of market scrutiny by standing by their business model. Amazon's business approach has been the subject of much debate and analysts' attention, mostly due to the fact that Amazon continues to scale its business—that is, growing in operations and revenue—while maintaining poor earnings. That being said, Amazon is in business today because of its network. Forget about the stock price for a moment and look at the business. Ask yourself, operationally, how are these firms competing? What's their market reach? What are their costs? The reason why firms like Amazon, Google, Yahoo!, and Cisco continue to cause their competitors to suffer dot vertigo is found in their networked infrastructure—the key component of their business model.

Jeffrey Bezos, founder and CEO, describes Amazon's strategy simply: "We intend to build the world's most customer-centric company."[2]

Bezos goes on to explain:

We hold as axiomatic that customers are perceptive and smart, and that brand image follows reality and not the other way around. . . . We're fortunate to benefit from a business model that is cash-favored and capital efficient. As we do not need to build physical stores or stock those stores with inventory, our centralized distribution model has allowed us to build our business to a billion-dollar run rate with just $30 million in inventory and $30 million in net plant and equipment.[3]

In a CNBC interview, Bezos once commented that it's about "prophet" not "profit." With a commitment to networking, connectivity, and seamless service on its side, Amazon and companies like it will continue to counter a fluctuating market, skeptics, and critics.

Delving a little deeper into the Amazon business model to focus on the company's networking capabilities and scalability, let's examine the roll-out from books to everything.

Initially, selling books on the Internet had inherent business advantages. By using a Web-based storefront and keeping only a small inventory on hand, the company could scale with remarkably few fixed assets. Where a traditional bookseller would have to open 1,000 new stores in order to double sales, Amazon could double its sales with minimal expense (just the few new servers needed to handle the extra order load).

Additionally, Amazon turned over its small inventory 150 times a year versus the four-times-a-year turnover that was standard in bricks-and-mortar bookstore, all the while offering a selection many times that of the largest physical bookstores. Further, with the workings of IT systems, Amazon.com got paid immediately with a customer's credit card and didn't have to pay suppliers for 25 days. The result was a significant collapse in the time of the bookselling operating cycle.

In December 1998, Henry Blodget, then with CIBC Oppenheimer, released an analyst report that valued Amazon.com at $20 billion, setting a target share price at $400. Noting Amazon's recent moves into a number of new markets and with a hunch that Bezos was not about to stop, Blodget argued that Amazon was in the beginning stages of "building a global electronic-retailing franchise that could generate $10 billion in revenue and an EPS (earnings per share) of $10 within five years."

Within one month of that report, Amazon broke the $20 billion market value threshold, and, as it turned out, Blodget was right: Bezos was after more than just books. Since announcing its entry into music sales, Amazon has expanded into a new product area every four or five months. The company began offering videos in November 1998 and launched an online auction site in April 1999. In the second half of 1999, Amazon opened a toy and home electronics store. Additionally, the company made strategic investments in drugstore.com, Pets.com, and Homegrocer.com, to enter the online pharmacy, pet, and grocery store arenas. Later, the company announced a home furnishings store.

Figure 1.5 tracks the evolution of the Amazon.com business model and its stock performance. While you've heard this story before, rethink the scenario as it now applies to permeability. With a network at the core of a company's infrastructure, Amazon has remained dominant in the retail market space.

Revenue per Employee

While stock prices are a barometer that many individuals have access to, I have successfully used the revenue per employee metric to measure technology and network investments. I began tracking revenue per employee as a key measure of business performance in the mid-1980s. My logic was that technology enables workers to access massive amounts of information, which, in turn, increases their productivity. A prerequisite to realizing their potential, however, is an IT infrastructure consisting of databases and networked PCs for every employee (a key component of the contemporary I-Net, as you will read in the next chapter).

I made these investments at Nolan, Norton and Company (NNC) in the early 1980s by equipping our consulting staff with portable computers. Soon we began using the computers to communicate among project teams and for preparing and giving presentations to our clients.

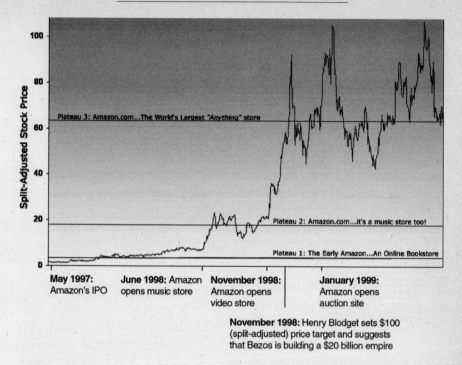

Figure 1.5   The Evolution of Amazon.com's Business Model and Stock
Performance (Stock Price in Dollars)
Data source: Compustat.

One of my more memorable experiences was when making a hypercard
presentation on a projector-equipped Macintosh computer to the then
dean of the Harvard Business School, John McArthur. [Hypercard was
the software product of Apple, and was the first widespread implementation of hypertext. Hypertext involves communicating chunks of information (the idea of a card), and allowing linking to the various cards
from one card to the next.]

John seemed as interested in how hypercard worked as he was in our
technology recommendations for Harvard Business School. We were
able to use these capabilities to present detailed data behind our recommendations as John probed our logic and wanted to learn more about
various aspects of our analysis. Ultimately John and his senior faculty
made the decision to require that all entering MBAs come to HBS with a
PC equipped with a standard software environment. Dean Kim Clark

continued on with this program by equipping the faculty with PCs and building a strategic I-Net for HBS. In this early part of the new millennium, we at HBS believe the I-Net continues to improve the educational experience for our students, and it has provided the impetus for launching an e-learning initiative.

After the acquisition of Nolan, Norton and Company by KPMG Peat Marwick in 1987, I went on to work with KPMG to expand the NNC program into a knowledge management initiative that we called the "shadow partner." The term "shadow partner" captured our vision of using strategic I-Nets and PCs to leverage the work of professionals. The idea of the shadow partner was that the PC should be made so easy to use that the experience would be similar to simply asking one of your real partners a question and getting back a useful response.

Today at the Harvard Business School we introduce almost all the participants in our executive education program to the shadow partner through a team-based exercise. We first introduce the executives to our strategic I-Net, basic concepts of searching on the Internet, and available business databases accessible through the electronic library at HBS. Then we assign a shadow partner case,[4] which the executives work on for the next couple of hours. One version of the case sets up a dot company that enters an industry. During a board of directors meeting, the president comes out and asks the CIO to find out competitive information about the dot company and assess the competitive threat, and presents back to the board two hours later. The presentation and analysis is the deliverable of the team. The faculty reviews the presentations and awards token prizes to the teams with the best analyses and presentations. The results are eye-opening for all involved, and have been said to be equivalent to similar analyses assigned to consultants costing tens of thousands of dollars. This shadow partner exercise has become a seminal event for many executives who have not grown up with computers and the Internet.

With these new metrics as guideposts, a better understanding of the evolution of the I-Net and the impact of networking, let's look at how companies with seemingly savvy management teams fall victim to vertigo.

Symptoms of Dot Vertigo

Dot companies are a phenomenon that has forever changed the practice and principles of business. Companies like Amazon.com are invented and built by a new breed of entrepreneur/managers who have grown up in the world of computers and the Internet. They have a background that allows them to see opportunities in a way traditional managers rarely can.

These new entrepreneurs operate in a different manner. Rather than employ the scientific method of research, hypothesis, and testing before they take action, they are in a constant state of action: try it, learn from it, improve on it, and keep going forward—never look back.

These differences propel the dot company challengers. Capitalizing on the Internet and associated technologies, a worthy industry challenger can be conceived and built in less than one year. Witness garage-born businesses Microsoft and Apple. This quickness catches incumbents off guard and causes a state of dot vertigo. CEOs can learn how to counter-act dot vertigo by being alert to seven symptoms of vertigo: denial or minimizing, maintaining a complacent culture, responding with business as usual, failure to cannibalize your product line before your competitors do, letting egos get in the way, always in catch-up mode, and failure to adopt the new business model for the industry.

Denial or Minimizing

Dot companies, whether they be solely Web-based like Google or a clicks-and-mortar company such as Cisco, surpass unwitting competitors by staying under the radar of the incumbents' senior management teams. Examples of industry stalwarts not recognizing a nascent company in their market or taking competitive threats seriously abound: Microsoft versus IBM, Amazon versus Barnes & Noble, Netscape versus Microsoft. . . . (Interestingly, some companies that initially used this strategy to dominate their market space fell victim to this symptom of vertigo, the strongest example of this being Microsoft.)

Complacency

Complacency and the need to maintain the status quo are real problems for incumbents, especially during times of change—for example, as seen in the recent rise of the strategic importance of IT in business. The culture of the dot company incorporates continuous innovation from the outset; change is inculcated in its modus operandi.

"Business as Usual" Responses

Even once an incumbent recognizes a dot company challenger as a viable competitor, the early competitive responses are often ineffective. Typically, the competitive responses can be characterized as "business as usual." One example is dropping prices with the intention of driving the new competitor out of business.

Competition in many industries has evolved to a few dominant players operating like an oligopoly. When new entrants try to come into an industry, the incumbents drop prices to drive out the new entrant. Once the new entrant is gone, the incumbents raise their prices, and life goes on as before in the industry. Lowering prices rarely works to drive out the dot company. First, the dot company generally benefits from having a lower cost structure than the incumbent due to more reliance on IT and less reliance on bricks-and-mortar resources. Second, the dot company's access to equity markets often provides a source of cash to weather a price war.

Dot companies also prey on incumbents by using technology in a way that is unfamiliar to most incumbent senior management teams—strategically. While incumbents have been using IT for many years, most of their uses can be described as tactical back-office uses and not strategic uses. Thus, responses to strategic uses of IT by incumbents are many times just plain ineffective.

Failure to Cannibalize Existing Products

The innovative use of technology is changing the product development and service processes in every industry. Yet, the incumbents seem consistently tardy in recognizing the impact and acting on it. This slowness to react gives the dot companies a significant advantage.

For industrial age companies, the problem is that change is paced by the annual budgeting process, so even the mechanism for acting slows down the process. These factors govern the cannibalization of the incumbent's products and service delivery systems, which provides even more time for the dot company to implement a better business model. Driving the business model is the IT-enabled capability of being able to connect electronically with individual customers and respond in real time to their needs. In an earlier book, I developed this idea as the emergent strategy in the network age of "sense and respond."[5]

Letting Egos Get in the Way

Old Economy or New, this symptom continues to plague well-established organizations. Simply put, focusing on the trappings of success is sure to force a company to spin out of control. Responding to competitive threats with a show of force is less effective than attacking the actual problem, whether it be innovation, customer responsiveness, or shifting market demands.

One anecdote involves Barnes & Noble's legal retort to a series of rather humorous radio ads by Amazon.com about trying to find appropriate space for Amazon's bookstore, touted to be the largest in the world. B&N took umbrage and litigated the biggest bookstore claim against Amazon.com. Once again, it seems that Amazon.com came out the winner, gaining more publicity and promoting an even bigger buzz[6] about the company. In a publicized settlement, Amazon and B&N settled the lawsuit, agreeing to compete in the marketplace and not in the courts. Not only did Barnes & Noble gain nothing from the litigation, but its senior management team came away looking foolish and desperate.

Always Playing in Catch-Up Mode

Dot companies are built in periods of months. They see themselves in a race for acquiring and holding customers; decisions are made on the basis of expediency as much as on that of "being perfectly right." Incumbents view the fast environment of dot companies as chaos, while dot companies view their environments as a competitive necessity; so incumbents are always playing catch-up.

Amazon versus B&N

It seems that it was not until 1998 that Barnes & Noble realized that it could not effectively respond to the Amazon.com threat within its existing organization. On September 24, 1998, Barnes & Noble announced a public stock offering of Barnes&Noble.com stock, and subsequently partnered with Bertelsmann, its bricks-and-mortar competitor, to build a separate dot company. Around this time, it also tried to buy Ingram Book Group, the leading book distributor used by Amazon.com; the deal was subsequently blocked by the U.S. Department of Justice on antitrust grounds.

By this time, the emergent strategy of Amazon.com was taking on new dimensions. A firm believer in Metcalfe's Law, CEO Jeffrey Bezos had been aggressive about the retention of customers. His marketing strategy included heavy investment in his Web-based bookstore, ad campaigns to generate customer interest, strategic alliances to attract Internet users to the Amazon.com web site, and a continually evolving story to create a buzz on Wall Street. By 2000, Amazon.com had outpaced the incumbent Barnes & Noble. Within a five-year period Amazon.com had built revenue to over $2.5 billion—about 70 percent of Barnes & Noble revenue. The strategy of Barnes & Noble setting up a separate dot company seems to have made good economic sense as reflected in Barnes&Noble.com's market value. Nevertheless, compared to Amazon.com, Barnes&Noble.com still looks like a follower and not a dot company industry innovator.

- The higher cost burden of inventory, accounts receivable, and fixed assets as per revenue dollar of Barnes & Noble compared to Amazon.com will continue to call into question the bricks-and-mortar-oriented business model of Barnes & Noble. Comparison of Barnes & Noble with its dot company only makes the case stronger.
- The higher market value of Amazon.com compared to Barnes & Noble provides Amazon.com with a competitive advantage in making acquisitions, building high-tech distribution facilities, and recruiting the very best people.

Not Embracing New Business Models

Senior managers of incumbents must step out of their traditional way of thinking when considering a new business model. The dot company demonstrates the most salient aspects of the new business models: virtual stores, sense-and-respond strategies, and rapidly falling transaction costs. However, as the dot company scales, the business model expands to include bricks and mortar to form "clicks and mortar." However, it is important to understand that "clicks and mortar" means more than just the coexistence of traditional bricks-and-mortar stores or distribution centers with the virtual stores. Much more is involved. And new business models driven by IT and the Internet are replacing the old business models in every industry. The scenario captured in the box depicts several dot vertigo symptoms in action.

With an understanding of how networked businesses compete and thrive in an evolving technological world, the next chapter delves deeper into the I-Net by defining its components and its impact on the company. Let's return for a moment to our example of the pilot suffering from vertigo. Pilots are instructed and trained to use their instruments. Despite what the pilot's mind might be telling him or her about the plane's trajectory, the instruments are the only tools that offer unquestionable readings and solutions to a pilot who might be suffering from vertigo. For the manager, the I-Net is this critical navigational instrument.

Key Concepts

- I-nets enable permeability and lightning speed.
- Dot vertigo is caused by severely underestimating or overestimating the Internet.
- IT remains a driver of economic and business performance.

2

Keep an Eye on Your Instruments

The I-Net

The key to permeability, an I-Net is the instrument that keeps dot companies on course despite an economic landscape fraught with uncertainty, correction, and change. The I-Net is a fully realized network that integrates a company's Intranet (and Extranet) with the worldwide Internet. It represents the future of how businesses and consumers will use the Web, but more importantly, the I-Net forms the core of an enterprise network designed to make companies permeable.

The ability for a company to coordinate work activities has been directly impacted by all types of computer technology, yet it is this latest generation that has streamlined cycle times and increased productivity. "Internet time" has become a popular—some would say overly hyped—phrase in the modern lexicon, describing a time frame that is instantaneous. While "Internet time" is a catchy sound bite that captures the frenetic pace of modern business, it holds a deeper meaning in the context of this book. This phenomenon—instantaneous execution of business decisions—takes the principles of business and strategic management that have been taught and practiced by generations of managers and implodes them.

The simple reality is that information is power, so the sooner you have that information, the sooner your company can effect critical changes in its business. When you consider that a company can start up and fizzle out in less time than it takes for some firms to generate a sales report, the concept of information being powerful takes on a new dimension.

Cisco Systems has used its I-Net to connect senior executives with real-time (and I mean by the second) revenue and resource data that can be accessed at any time on any day of the week. Access to such critical information impacts everything from how the company presents itself for valuation to how it manages inventory control and innovates product development. Cisco's IT systems literally allow the company to close its books in one day, determining the firm's profitability on a daily basis. Daily access to key performance measures enables Cisco to capitalize on time-sensitive market opportunities, revise tactics, adjust strategies, and redirect operations seamlessly and immediately. This capability has been critical to Cisco's ongoing success and clearly demonstrates both the notion of being permeable and the power of the I-Net.

This chapter introduces the 10 key attributes that characterize the I-Net; four relate to aspects of the organization and six are technological. The cumulative effect of these components is an organization that can execute business strategies and transactions instantaneously or in zero time.[1] The discussions and examples in this chapter will make clear the I-Net's role in increasing a company's IQ, what some call network intelligence.[2] A company's IQ reflects its ability—as embodied in its people, technologies, and knowledge structure—to learn, compete, and prosper. The expediency and depth to which interactions are maintained within and outside of the organization will impact the company's ability to strengthen its intelligence. These interactions involve sharing information, products, and services as well as executing business plans. As such, the I-Net must be robust enough to engage and support the company's employees, customers, and partners while intimidating competitors. The relevance of network intelligence to companies developing strategies and the management team that will take the business into the future was emphasized in a January 2001 *Harvard Business Review* article by Mohanbir Sawhney and Deval Parikh, "Where Value Lives in a Networked World." According to Sawhney and Parikh, information is "static" in the absence of a network. For example, a library book can be borrowed and used by only one person at a time. The usefulness of the information in the book is limited by its accessibility. However, put the book online and an infinite number of users can read it simultaneously, potentially making the information more valuable. The more sophisticated the network, the more useful information becomes to companies and consumers alike. In the current economy, the level of network intelligence reflects how well a company can compete.

The I-Net: The Instrument of the Networked Organization

Four attributes of the I-Net that relate to organizational issues and have an impact on the company's IQ are information transparency, the permeable boundaries of the extended enterprise, knowledge management, and self-directed work. The six technological components are real-time messaging, data warehousing, PC availability, the browser, directory technology, and the web site. With the right talent supporting the firm (i.e., the company's IQ or network intelligence), these technologies provide the framework needed for executing business strategies and performing tasks instantaneously.

Organizational Components

Information Transparency: Information Is Freely Available

We saw in the earlier Cisco example that the availability of information has helped this firm remain a world-class competitor and a real profit driver. When we talk about making information freely available, we refer to the concept of information transparency. A little later in this section you will see how two of the I-Net's six technology components, real-time messaging and data warehousing, make information transparency possible.

Overly emphasizing secrecy is completely antithetical to the idea of the permeable organization and the network economy, particularly when you consider the information-abundant environment of the Internet. How information can be used to redirect the course of a company has a greater impact on business performance than how effectively it can be withheld from competitors. Thus, the emerging policy for the network age is information transparency, whereby information is made freely available to all who might act on it.

Keep in mind that although that concept of information transparency is to enable instant access, companies do not want to saturate their workforce or partners with information that is irrelevant to them. Returning to our Cisco example, financial data is made available 24/7, but only to those who need to act on the information, such as the senior executive team, the CFO, corporate investors, and strategic suppliers.

Boundaries Are Permeable in the Extended Enterprise

The concept of the extended enterprise takes information transparency a step further. Companies that use the Internet to effectively open their Intranets to suppliers and customers are extended enterprises. By providing access to the I-Net's databases, the information transparency is created throughout the supply chain, enabling various players to act on information instantly. Suppliers can schedule and order materials more efficiently; manufacturers are able to reduce order-to-delivery cycle times; and customers receive products faster and can monitor delivery times in a way that enables them to plan better. Vendors can manage customer relationships and even bid on corporate contracts electronically, making the entire supply chain—including the selection process—a more expedient one. KPMG has found that "e-marketplaces promise a fundamental change in the way companies manage their value chains from the sourcing of raw materials to the delivery of finished products." A recent survey conducted by the company revealed that approximately one-third of consumer markets companies are already using vertical industry e-marketplaces, and nearly 70 percent of consumer markets companies look for an online marketplace that allows them to secure lower prices.[3]

The concept of the extended enterprise is central to the permeable organization, stretching the fixed, physical boundaries of traditional organizations to ones that shift to incorporate new ventures or redesign existing elements of the company. Approaches that include strategic alliances and outsourcing add to the ability of a company to remain permeable, extending its boundaries even further. The key idea is that the way we think about the organization becomes much more complex and robust. Managing in the network economy means tending to companies whose boundaries have become etheric, and replaces a much simpler, more linear process of managing employees within a well-defined structure.

Strategic Alliances
Strategic alliances have become an essential part of most corporate strategies and business operations, particularly for those with a Web compo-

nent. Because they are inherently opportunistic, strategic alliances need to be arranged and formalized expeditiously, exploited for as long as they make sense, and disbanded as quickly as they were formed when they are no longer relevant to the business. An effective I-Net ensures that strategic alliances become an integral part of a company's business—strategically and operationally. Constant, expeditious, and frequent interactions are a must for alliances truly to benefit the organization. Working with alliance partners in an environment that operates in zero time makes the relationship particularly dynamic.

For example, a group of small manufacturing companies in eastern Pennsylvania, known as the Agile Web, Inc., enables "the rapid formation of a dynamic combination of companies, selected for each opportunity."[4] The Ben Franklin Institute of Technology in Lehigh helps the individual companies in this select group to define competitive strategies. The companies work together under a set of contractual and ethical guidelines to identify market opportunities, pull together needed competencies, and deliver customer solutions. They make extensive use of electronic data interchange and e-mail in transacting business. After each project is completed the group disbands and a new group based on a different set of capabilities is formed.[5]

Inktomi is a great example of a business based on partnerships. The company provides cache services that allow an organization to use one of Inktomi's servers that are strategically located around the country to speed up the responsiveness of an organization's web site. For example, drugstore.com uses Inktomi so that when a customer orders from anywhere in the United States the transaction is sped up by fast-loading graphics. Oracle is implementing the application service provider (ASP) model whereby it not only sells the logistic software for a supply chain, but it will also run the application on Oracle servers. This relieves the company from having to buy and maintain server capacity.

Outsourcing
Outsourcing has grown by leaps and bounds over the past decade. Savvy organizations capitalize on their relationships with companies, outsourcing necessary, but potentially resource-heavy, business functions such as payroll processing (Automatic Data Processing, Inc.—ADP), logistics (Federal Express), and catering (Marriott Corporation). The Internet can facilitate such relationships by providing a common platform capable of improving

communications and coordination and supporting electronic transactions (i.e., purchase orders, invoicing, and payments) with outsourcing partners.

Knowledge Management

The knowledge management component of the I-Net is central to business value creation. It is the capturing, storing, combining, analysis, mining, and distributing of information resources into forms that can be used to create value. While a considerable amount has been written on knowledge management, much of it has been written about companies without real I-Nets. I-Nets are the essential means for enabling effective knowledge management. Management needs to look to and learn from the pioneers who have both I-Nets and knowledge management, like Cisco, Schwab, and drugstore.com.

Cisco's knowledge management includes knowing each of its customers network configurations. Continued monitoring of the performance of their products in the various customer network configurations provides a base of information resources that are mined to develop performance enhancement products (mostly in the form of software) that can be automatically shipped over the Internet back to customers. Knowledge management at Cisco also is used to detect early warnings of product problems that are fixed before most customers actually incur the actual problems. Many Cisco customers never even know about the problem nor that it has been fixed.

Drugstore.com uses knowledge management to continuously improve the design of their virtual store for personalized shopping. Each time a customer comes to the virtual store, the way that the customer shops the store is watched. This information is carefully mined, and used as a basis for more conveniently laying out the store for the customer's next visit.

Self-Directed Work

Self-directed work transfers the tasks that were once performed by others to the person who most benefits from it. Self-service or self-directed work can be seen in everything from corporate tasks (such as corporate communications, payroll, employee benefits programs, etc.) to activities that help execute the company's strategic intent, which would include interacting with customers, product delivery, supply procurement, order processing, and data management.

At Cisco, the capability to monitor a product's performance electronically enables employees to sense problems and take corrective action before product outages bring down a customer's network. The customer's engineering staff can then access information through the Cisco I-Net and download upgrades or Cisco-engineered solutions. This approach has proven extremely effective for the company; in 2000–2001 Cisco provided over 80 percent of its service electronically, registering extremely high rates of customer satisfaction. In fact, Cisco leads the industry in customer satisfaction. In a foreword he wrote for the book *Digital Revolution*, John Chambers notes that 85 percent of Cisco's orders are done online, amounting to $40 million worth each day.[6]

Technology Components

Real-Time Messaging

The standard time frame for measuring business performance in the pre-Internet economy companies was (and for some companies still is) the 12-month fiscal year. While shorter time periods such as measuring quarterly profits have been added to the metrics over the years, the 12-month standard has been deeply institutionalized into the pace of business. It is this process that reviews and establishes revenue and expense goals for the company including each department within each division. It is also this process that keeps industrial methods alive, crippling the efforts of businesses that wish to become nimble. Remember the Cisco scenario that introduced this chapter; access to information at all times is critical if companies are to remain sensitive and responsive to market fluctuations, changes in customer buying patterns, emerging technology trends, and competitive activity. The ability to disseminate company data at all times is made possible through real-time messaging. This architecture is a key component of an effective I-Net.

Data Warehousing

The data warehouse literally stores and retrieves data that can be gathered from a variety of sources, the Web being a primary one. Once data is stored, the data warehouse then facilitates the management of this information. Data warehousing is among the first steps toward developing a store of corporate knowledge that can be utilized by a strategic I-Net.

The data warehouse and real-time messaging go hand in hand. Data transaction processing techniques update and time-stamp the data so managers are always working with the most current information. The degree of simplification that can be realized by tracking customer orders, supplier shipments, and financial status instantaneously frees up the employees' time; they can then shift their attention to value-adding activities. Amazon's ability to track customer purchases and develop a customer profile based on these purchases that is then used to make product recommendations across various departments is in part due to Amazon's sophisticated data storage and retrieval techniques.

PCs for Everybody

Networked companies must equip their workforces with technology that ties them to the I-Net, whether by PC, notebook computer, or Palm Pilot, if they are in the office, on the road, or at home. It's that simple; committing to the resource needs of the organization is a fundamental in the networked company.

Companies that adopt this mandate must support it with a disciplined, network-oriented administration program that updates and maintains their staffs' PCs. Such a program will ensure that the total cost of ownership (TCO) is managed at appropriate levels. One study estimates the TCO for this effort ranges from \$6,469 to \$9,869 per year.[7] A broad range to be sure, but TCO can be effectively maintained in the lower part of the range or at a lower cost still by standardizing PC software configurations and maintaining version control and updates through the I-Net.

The Browser

The browser was among the first of the Internet's killer apps because its use was so immediate and dramatic that it helped foster the Internet explosion. The browser is intuitive and, once learned, can be applied in a wide variety of applications—and therein lies its power. Adopting a browser as a standard user interface renders a company's entire portfolio of applications accessible across the enterprise, as well as allowing access to most of the Internet's applications. Also, the universal nature of the browser means that workers increasingly come into a company with an established learning curve in this area.

Directory Technology

Interactive work in its many forms—management meetings, conferences, telephone calls, sales calls, group problem-solving sessions, claims processing—involves thousands of people, and the unique combination of forms and people could number in the millions.

Managing information across these relationships through a common directory is essential. Novell, the leading provider of directory technology, characterizes the directory as providing the "digital personas" of the network's users. The personas govern individuals' entry to specific network layers and access to specific resources. Security is incorporated into these digital personas, which are developed not only for employees, but also for suppliers and existing and prospective customers, among others.

Increasingly sophisticated directory technologies enable reporting and priority services to be tailored to individual users and can provide preferred paths to specific web sites and databases that contain information of interest to particular employees or managers. Directory technologies are also important in addressing another key issue: security and privacy. With current directory and encryption technologies, [VCNs (virtual private networks)] can be established for secure communication

---

Dot Victor
Northstar Mortgage: Technology Disintermediation of Large Banks
Northstar is a one-year-old mortgage broker using powerful technology from Fannie Mae and Freddie Mac to originate home mortgage loans. The online technology replaces the mountain of time-consuming paperwork required to obtain a loan approval. The mortgage broker enters a client's income, value of property and house being bought, and its location. The online system goes out over the Internet pulling up information from credit agencies, and applies statistical modeling to estimate the likelihood of a default. Within minutes a decision is returned.

Northstar then finds a bank willing to make the loan and the bank pays Northstar a 1 percent origination fee. This is money that the banks used to keep for themselves when they were often the only game in town for mortgages. In all likelihood, the bank will sell the loan to Fannie Mae or Freddie Mac. In one year, Northstar has originated $120 million in home mortgages. Northstar operations are lean, and brokers are paid on commission. There are more than 25,000 mortgage brokers now originating more than 50 percent of the mortgages—in the early 1990s mortgage brokers originated about 20 percent of the mortgages.[8]

among individuals and groups, which is another important need driving directory technologies.

As more and more companies move their technology systems onto the Internet, the demand for high-capacity directories to uniquely identify people (e.g., employees, customers, suppliers) and network objects (e.g., PCs, routers, data) will quickly outstrip the capacity of rather limited internal directories and require the adoption of new directory technologies. Eric Schmidt, CEO of Novell, predicts that in the not-too-distant future each individual will have his or her own controlled profile residing in a secure directory that identifies the person's available access to I-Nets, web sites, and preferences.

The Company's Web Site: The "Front Door" Receptionist

A company's web site is the portal through which those who interact with the company enter—that is, everybody. Client computers of those who access the company's web site display a version of the company's I-Net home page. Outsiders, such as customers or suppliers, would have digital personas that would determine what information appears via their browsers when they access the company's web site.

Through continuous refinement based on feedback solicited from their various constituencies, companies such as Cisco, Amazon, and drugstore.com have learned to create sophisticated web sites that provide new types and levels of personalized customer service. These companies are using their I-Nets to create greater network intelligence that strengthens the firm's competitive position in the marketplace and among investors and analysts.

Making the I-Net Intelligent

Like planes traveling at Mach speeds, companies must be able to sense and respond to their competitive environments in real time. Decades of automation have left many companies with scattered networks and incompatible computer platforms. Companies that have computerized their business processes over decades without any framework for integrating disparate applications and databases register low in terms of company IQ. Continuing to invest in isolated systems will not lead to the creation of the networked organization that can rely on its instruments and company

IQ for advancements, growth, and profit. To become a permeable or networked organization, companies need to rethink the role of their technology systems and the I-Net, in particular. To be effective, the I-Net must be based on fully integrated technology systems.

The ideal networked organization (what we have in the past called "managing by wire"[9]) is achieved by using an enterprise model that represents the operations of the business integrated into the technical components of an I-Net. Elements of the business—including employees, suppliers, customers, operational processes, transaction systems, expert systems, and databases—and the relationships among these elements are identified in a corporate directory. The I-Net presents information in real time to the executive crew that informs their decisions and translates them into directives for managers charged with re-creating the business based on market changes. This forms the subject of the next section—how sensing and responding to economic and organizational conditions make the company intelligent.

Sense and Respond

A company's IQ reflects its ability as an organization to sense customer needs—that is, capture, share, and extract meaning from marketplace signals—and respond in a timely manner using the unique capabilities of its stakeholders connected by the I-Net. Figure 2.1 depicts three infrastructure components that underlie a company's IQ: connecting, sharing, and structuring information and knowledge.

Connecting

Connecting refers to the degree to which a company's technology platform links its information sources, media, locations, employees, customers, and suppliers. The centralized corporate directory identifies the objects that are connected to the I-Net and is the basis for managing interactions among them, including the assignment of key attributes and access levels.

The all-too-common arrangement of dozens of independent, technically incompatible networks—created in different places, for different purposes, using different technologies—tends to inhibit, rather than promote, information and knowledge sharing.

The Internet has demonstrated the feasibility of interconnecting millions of computers with one another, creating an intricate and practically

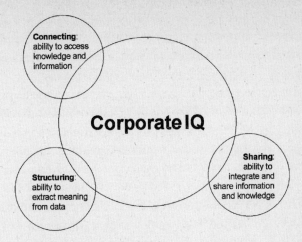

Figure 2.1   Components of Corporate IQ

limitless web of information-based products, services, and activities. All of this is made possible by using a basic set of standards and protocols. Referring again to our Amazon and Cisco examples, these companies can connect and sell products to any customer who has an Internet connection and a standard browser, and the low cost of acquiring a computer, Internet connection, and browser is making connection ubiquitous at the consumer level. Indeed, at the business level, excepting companies that have not yet figured out how to manage the total cost of ownership to appropriate levels, the one-to-one computer-to-employee ratio is a reality.[10]

Sharing

Sharing, to the extent that it enables coordinated effort, is required in order to accrue the benefits associated with teamwork, integration, and scalability. Getting everyone focused on the same issues in a business requires an organizational capability to share and interpret data as well as manage key processes. The added value offered by such integration derives less from the implementation of a breakthrough application than from how the application is executed with respect to the network. This is reflected in a novel extension of Metcalfe's Law by Novell's chairman and chief strategist, Eric Schmidt, who suggests that the value of a corporate network increases exponentially with the number of relationships it enables among employees, strategic partners, customers, and suppliers.[11]

A precursor to sharing is the development of a knowledge structure that categorizes information by its various uses within the company such as professional expertise, functional responsibilities, or troubleshooting.

Structuring

Structuring is accomplished by profiling information, classifying, organizing, and defining relationships and uses for data. When information from previously unrelated sources is structured in a meaningful way, humans become capable of constructing new mental models about their business. Computers—through their phenomenal speed and enormous memory—reveal novel patterns in data that augment a human's extraordinary capacity to recognize and assign meaning to patterns.

For example, using spectral analysis and mathematical equations that model what scientists term the "red shift," a computer can process light signals from a remote galaxy to calculate the distance and size of its parts and display the results in a rotating three-dimensional picture. Presentation in this manner enables scientists to "see" a distant galaxy from the back or side and even to discover, as they did, a huge void passing through it.[12]

A less dramatic example is the use of similarly sophisticated methods to guide new product and service development by mining data for behavior patterns and clues to the wants and needs of customers. This categorization and presentation of data allows for the creation of new mental models and frameworks that can then be used to reinvent the organization as the market demands.

Organizational Learning

Sensing, interpreting, deciding, and acting are essential functions for any adaptive organism. Figure 2.2 illustrates how the permeable business senses the competitive environment, often by electronically connecting with its customers, and invokes processes and procedures for interpreting the information acquired, deciding on a course of action, and then responding. The I-Net provides the infrastructure for capturing and analyzing this information, and then making it available to those who can act on it.

More and more academic work is being done on individual and organizational learning. Chris Argyris has coined and developed important

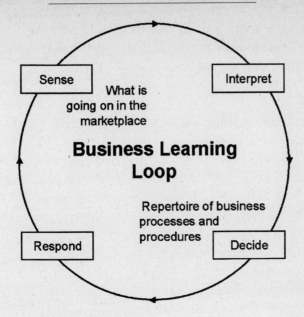

Figure 2.2   Business Learning Loop

ideas about single- and double-loop learning. In his recent book *On Organizational Learning*, Argyris explains:

> Whenever an error is detected and corrected without questioning or altering the underlying values of the system (be it individual, group, intergroup, organizational, or interorganizational), the learning is single looped. The term is borrowed from electrical engineering or cybernetics where, for example, a thermostat is defined as a single-loop learner. The thermostat is programmed to detect states of "too cold" or "too hot," and to correct the situation by turning the heat on or off. If the thermostat asked itself such questions as why it was set at 68 degrees, or why it was programmed as it was, then it would be a double-loop learner . . . . Double-loop learning occurs when mismatches are corrected by first examining and altering the governing variables and then the actions.[13]

Double-loop learning is more easily explained than executed. Embedded company norms such as "Do not confront company policies and objectives, especially those top management is excited about" and fear of telling upper management that a program is failing to meet performance objectives result in filtration as information moves up through the ranks so that by the time it reaches the top it is incomplete. Double-loop learning does not occur in such situations because errors, even if detected, are not questioned.

I-Nets are helping organizations incorporate institutional learning into their architecture and thereby facilitate double-loop learning. The Wal-Mart system for replenishing inventory is a great example of a learning loop. Wal-Mart transmits millions of bits of data from its stores' cash registers to Wrangler daily. The two companies share both the data and a model that interprets it. They also share software applications that translate that interpretation into shipments of specific quantities of jeans in particular sizes and colors. The combination of scanning data, applying decision rules, and executing replenishment shipments is a single-loop learning system. The people monitoring the single-loop learning system performance data, learning from it, and changing the single-loop learning system decision rules based on fashion trends or pricing patterns are engaged in double-loop learning.

Applying the components described in this chapter has varying levels of complexity depending on the organization's technology approach. Chapter 3 describes the evolution of business technology from mainframes through the I-Net, and offers an important context for understanding the structural and cultural shifts that lie ahead for companies looking to become permeable.

Key Concepts

- Real-time "sensing and responding" to customers is a strategic necessity.
- Information and information sharing make the dot corporation intelligent.
- Some companies have a higher "corporate IQ" than others.

3

A little more than five years ago, the Internet remained the domain of only a handful of researchers, technologists, and academics that created specified applications for it. In 2001, the Internet is not only everywhere, it is de rigueur. This technology, seen as disruptive by some, has changed the face of business and society, and will continue to influence our world as advances emerge. The purpose of the chapter is to examine the evolution of the network economy, and from this postulate a business approach, strategies, and tools that will advance this evolution even further. Rigorous and constant reevaluation of the past and present will thwart a host of dot vertigo symptoms. I believe that renowned philosopher George Santayana said it best: "Those who cannot remember the past are condemned to repeat it."

Constraints of the Pre-Internet Age

The industrial or pre-Internet age management model (depicted in Figure 3.1) is grounded in economic theory and took form at the beginning of the twentieth century. Based on economic theory of the time, managers

35

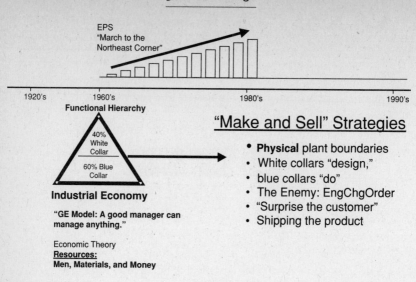

Figure 3.1   Industrial Age Management Model

manage scarce resources to create a profit, scarce resources being described as "men, materials, and money."

The management model consists of organizing resources and applying management principles. The dominant organization of the industrial age is the functional hierarchy. Figure 3.2 details the 13 management principles that guide managers as they operate their organizations. These 13 management principles are internally consistent and work as a system to assist managers in creating sustained business performance.

The top bar chart shown in Figure 3.1 in various forms was commonly presented in the first pages of companies' annual reports. At the Harvard Business School, we refer to this generic bar chart as the "march to the northeast corner." Over time, the successful execution of the pre-Internet age management model enabled companies to build records of annual business performance like incremental increases in profit, revenue, or earnings per share for long runs—15 to 20 years.

Another important concept embodied in the pre-Internet age management model has been attributed to General Electric: "A good manager can manage anything." This mantra refers to a manager's mastery of the 13 management principles (Figure 3.2) and the accounting framework. The

Figure 3.2   Industrial Age Management Principles

1. **Hierarchy Principle**—Organization structured into a three-tier hierarchy: top management, middle management, and production workers.
2. **Functional Principle**—Fixed functions of line and staff based on type of expertise.
3. **Centralization**—Centralized, shared activities carried out by corporate, decentralized operations activities by divisions.
4. **Leadership Principle**—Senior management's role is to set strategy and design organization's structures and control systems for implementing strategy.
5. **Strategic-Orientation Principle**—Driven by production activities.
6. **Task Principle**—Tasks are carried out within functions, and functions are designed to minimize required communications.
7. **Cycle-Time Principle**—Cycle time is the fiscal year.
8. **Worker-Class Principle**—White-collar workers design the way work is to be carried out, and blue-collar workers execute.
9. **Information Principle**—Based on "need to know."
10. **Communication Principle**—Formal and paper-based.
11. **Supervision Principle**—Direct observation of workers.
12. **Reward Principle**—Pay is based on responsibility, loyalty, and seniority.
13. **Span-of-Control Principle**—Span of control of a manager is 6 to 10 subordinates.

Source: Richard L. Nolan and David C. Croson, *Creative Destruction* (Boston: HBS Press, 1995).

accounting framework of balance sheets and profit and loss (P&L) statements permitted managers to set annual production goals that could be translated into low-level departmental budgets. Then during the year through budget variance analyses managers could measure business results financially and take appropriate control actions to ensure effective execution. Companies across industries were managed in similar ways.

For more than 30 years, computers were used in companies to make the hierarchical management model more efficient. However, this model and its associated organizational structure did not maximize the potential of technology, and they have slowly been mutated. Company investments in technology that were made prior to 1995 have resulted in a portfolio of legacy systems that are today out-of-date and obsolete.

Legacy Systems

The Achilles' heel of almost all traditional companies are legacy systems—that is, those information systems that were developed mostly in the data processing (DP) era, but also those systems developed pre-1995. These systems were designed to make the old organization architecture more efficient. Not only were the systems developed in an environment when computers cost millions of dollars compared to thousands today, but these systems effectively set in concrete the old ways of managing through hierarchical organizations.

At the heart of legacy systems are the accounting systems, which provide the basis of control for the business. The first commercial computer applications generally included accounting, as well as automated tasks such as payroll processing and maintaining the general ledger. These applications were often coded in low-level assembler programming languages, although COBOL (from "common business-oriented language"), a higher-level language, rapidly became the preferred programming language for commercial applications during the 1960s. Remarkably, in the late 1990s COBOL remained the most-used language in software and development.[1]

Figure 3.3 shows a typical graphic illustrating an applications portfolio for a functionally organized manufacturing company or a product division of a multidivisional company. The familiar pyramid icon is divided into three hierarchical levels. Within each level, there are functional application groupings such as manufacturing and accounting. Finally, within each functional application at each level there are individual applications representing opportunities for use of the computer.

The applications portfolio evolved by first automating low-level operational support tasks within a function such as inventory control, shop floor control, and scheduling in manufacturing, or plant, cost, and general accounting in the controller function. After sufficient automation of low-level operational support tasks within a function, the organization integrated automated tasks within a functional department such as research and development (R&D) or engineering by automating management control activities such as production operations management, accounting management, and human resources management. More difficult cross-functional automation that supported management control activities

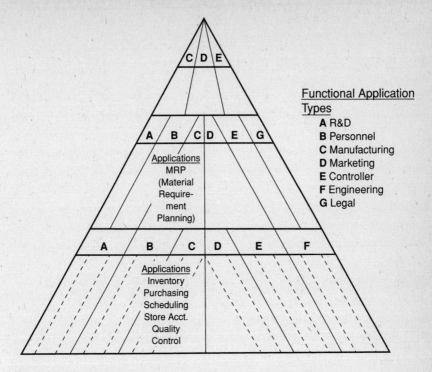

Figure 3.3 Applications Portfolio of a Functionally Organized Manufacturing Company

within the firm laid the groundwork for the third and most difficult level of automation. At this level, automation supported strategic five-year plans through the integration of department profit plans and corporate-wide human resource planning. Throughout this process, the organization moved up the S-shaped curve as it learned more and more about how to apply technology and tap into its potential.

While the product divisions of multidivisional businesses focused on automating tasks from the ground up, the corporate offices focused on tying their divisions together. Indeed, accounting applications of the computer contributed to efficiently managing the complexity of multidivisional command-and-control organizations. In this structure, two main types of accounting control tools play major roles: annual and capital budgeting. The first controlled expenditures aimed at generating revenue during the calendar year, and the second controlled expenditures that generated multiple-year revenues.

Annual Budgeting

The annual budgeting process for the large hierarchical organization is usually based on an incremental growth model of 10 percent to 15 percent growth per year. Once the company became large, the planning process intended to maintain consistent year-to-year incremental growth in revenue and profit. The line item general ledger and the codified hierarchical organization chart formed the foundation of the accounting model. The line item general ledger typically consisted of thousands of objects of expenditures. The organizational chart typically consisted of hundreds of boxes, each associated with a similar group of general ledger accounts. For example, most of the boxes on the organization chart included types of overhead expenses such as paper and office equipment. Before the computer, summarized profit-center accounting was done at a high level and infrequently during the year. After the computer, which largely enabled the process, complex divisional and profit-center accountability evolved.

Accountants categorized the assets and equities of the firm into general ledger accounts and then structured these accounts into a balance sheet, which defined the financial position of a company at a point in time. Another set of accounts referred to as "temporary" accounts recorded in profit and loss (P&L) statements that reflect the inflows (revenue) and outflows (expenditures) of assets intended to generate annual profit. At the end of the year accountants closed out the revenue and expense accounts to their respective general ledger permanent asset and equity accounts, resulting in a profit and loss (P&L) statement and a new end-of-the-year balance sheet. Comparing the beginning balance sheet with the ending balance sheet determined the profit or loss for the company's operations during the year. Technology, first in the form of electromechanical data processing devices and later in the form of computers, enabled this very powerful accounting process to be driven down to the divisional lines of business of the organization for decentralized P&L accountability, as well as accountability for return on investment (ROI). By assigning each box on the hierarchical organization chart a number code, the annual budgeting process could be conducted at very low levels in the organization. The boxes could be assigned a group of expense accounts and revenue accounts, and, for each box, revenues and expenses could be budgeted for activities during the calendar year. Then at any level of the organization chart, the planned revenues and expenses could be summarized and compared with the actual revenues and expenses at a point in time.

Further, managers of the departments, lines of business, regions, and other such combinations could be assigned budget responsibility; budget performance could be summarized by the computer, and managers could be rewarded or penalized for financial performance. During the electromechanical period, most large firms struggled to conduct the annual budgeting process and the closing of the books efficiently. However, the advent of the computer made it easy to do the process monthly or weekly, and in some financial institutions (e.g., Morgan Stanley) in the 1990s the closing of the books was done around the world on a daily basis—almost in real time. Today, Cisco Systems can instantly obtain profitability information, and close its books within a 24-hour period, and it has raised the bar for up-to-date information about business performance expected by analysts and investors in the IT industry.

With efficiently managed computers, organizations routinely produced multitudes of P&L statements by levels in the organization, regions, and even to the detailed level of individual customer profitability. Budgeting processes remain powerful tools for management, and use of computers and networks enables the tools to move from annual and quarterly cycles to daily cycles, as well as broadens the use of probability analysis.

Capital Budgeting

The capital budgeting process was as important as the annual budgeting process in enabling the multidivisional company to achieve consistent financial performance. The capital budgeting process was a methodology for analyzing the financial returns and risks of capital expenditures that spanned multiple annual accounting periods, such as construction of a new building or acquiring a new machine. Organizations used this methodology to work out the inflows and outflows of cash for the life of an expected multiyear expenditure. Then managers applied a variable discount factor that would discount the net value of the flows to the present to equal zero. The discount factor that did this was equal to the expected ROI. Companies used various "hurdle rate"[2] discount factors (typically 15 to 20 percent) to account for risk and to screen potential investments to ensure that the firms used their scarce capital resources most effectively.

While organizations found the computations for capital budgeting during the electromechanical period long, tedious, and expensive, the computer made these computations trivial, and by the 1990s virtually all companies routinely used sophisticated capital budgeting techniques at almost zero cost.[3] Firms extended command-and-control accountability from divisional P&L responsibility to divisional ROI responsibility. In many ways, just as farmers and engineers of the pre-Internet age applied steam engine technology to mechanize the farm and make the farm more efficient, engineers and computer programmers applied computer technology to the traditional command-and-control, multi-functional (M-form) hierarchy to make it more efficient.

This sophisticated use of accounting in the M-form hierarchy enabled managers to control complex operations and to support their goal of consistently increasing revenues and earnings per share (EPS).

The problems raised by legacy systems are threefold. First, legacy systems have the wrong cost. By mapping Moore's Law, we can see that these systems were developed during a time when computers were much more expensive than today's computers. So, systems development has changed, and the features that these legacy systems have are much more limited than those of new systems today. Second, legacy systems have the wrong architecture. Most of these systems were designed for hierarchical organization structures. Vertically integrated functional hierarchy organization structures have mutated into virtually integrated IT—enabled networks. Third, legacy systems have the wrong focus. The focus of legacy systems is internal, back-office transaction automation. The focus of systems in the information age is front-office electronic connections and interactions with customers. It is the front-office technology that should drive back-office IT—not the other way around.

Technology Drives the Internet Economy

Figure 3.4 illustrates the emergence of network economy business models from that of the Industrial age and contrasts key differences between the two. By the early 1980s a critical mass of technology had been assimilated into companies. Yet at that time there was a growing concern that the return from IT investments was not materializing.[4] There were many facets to this problem of IT payoff. One of the most important facets was that the pre-Internet age functional hierarchy was too inflexible to permit the quickening of decision making and customer response that was possible from new IT capabilities. And the functional hierarchy proved hard to change and quite resilient to efforts to change it. It took a crisis to unfreeze the resilient functional hierarchy and the institutionalized management principles, including the annual budgeting process.

The crisis came about in the form of downsizing, also commonly associated with reengineering. With the integration of IT, most companies had a level of slack that allowed them to do the current work with fewer people. When, by serendipity or happenstance, one company in an industry laid off a substantial percentage of workers but did not proportionately reduce revenue, it was seen that the work got done with fewer people by those leveraging IT and changing the way that work was done. This is illustrated in Figure 3.4 with the lower parts of the hierarchy being reduced. Once one company in an industry downsized and began operating with a lower cost structure, the others had to follow in order not to lose market share. So downsizing and reengineering raced through industry after industry in periods of two to three years. The result was a mutation of the functional hierarchy in which shadow networks began "floating" on top of the traditional hierarchies.

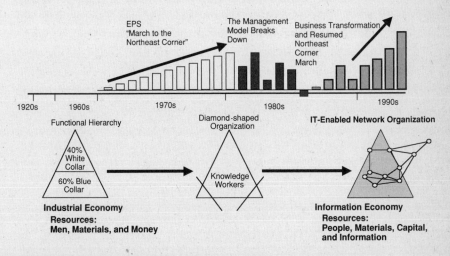

Figure 3.4   Industrial Age Management Model Breaks Down and Information Age Management Model Emerges

Network organizations continued to evolve, becoming more explicit, formal, and refined. Also, most importantly, information as a resource was recognized in economic theory, and a body of knowledge has been evolving for managing resources—including the information resource. And, of course, the dot-com phenomenon came into being to exploit building IT-enabled networks from greenfield sites and building out the front-office technologies to connect and interact with customers. (The term "greenfield site" originated to highlight that it was easier to build a new factory and hire a new work force than convert an existing factory and workforce to a modern factory.) While the academic process of researching, debating, and publishing new management principles is painfully slow, we see these principles emerging in the new dot companies through the necessity of survival and execution of their new business models.

An in-process statement of the new set of management principles is described in the Appendix.[5] These principles are built around IT-enabled network organization structures and, most importantly, incorporate information resource management.

Hierarchies versus Networks

The model for the multidivisional, hierarchical business structure has been institutionalized over many years of industrial enterprise. So ingrained in economic activity is this model that it is hard to imagine work without it. Yet the distinction of the corporate hierarchy is relatively new in the history of the organization, and it is important it be seen for what it is—a mechanism for getting work done in an efficient manner, nothing more. Just as corporate hierarchies grew from the maturation of industrialized energy technologies, today managers are being challenged to apply their increasing mastery of modern technologies to develop new ways to carry out work. This emerging networked structure is a unique hybrid of the hierarchical and Internet age approaches.

Whereas a functional bureaucracy is characterized by a set of fixed relationships, a network is characterized by adjustable relationships to reconfigure resources around a succession of rapidly changing tasks, an attribute that has led some to label it as "self-designing."[6] In effect, a network organization operates as a way for problem solving. Each problem becomes a focal point for the people and resources needed to solve it through a unique set of interconnections. These global interconnections are established by the IT component of the network organization, and operate at speeds unheard-of in functional hierarchies, which arbitrarily route problems through preestablished channels. "The intrinsic ability of the network organization to repeatedly redesign itself to accommodate new tasks, unique problems, and changing environment," asserts Wayne Baker, "enables such organizations to escape the plight of forms such as bureaucracy, which ossify and become incapable of change."[7]

What Makes Up the Organization

The four basic components of an organization are tasks, people, technology, and systems. Each of these components is treated differently in a network organization and a bureaucratic hierarchy.

Tasks

The jobs in a network organization are more abstract and less defined than those in a bureaucracy. In the factories of pre-Internet organizations, jobs were standardized and precisely defined so blue-collar workers on the assembly line could easily be trained to complete their work at acceptable levels of productivity and quality. In information age organizations, work is unpredictable, diverse, and information intensive. The network organization depends on its knowledge workers to attack and solve problems on a day-to-day basis because many tasks cannot be defined in advance due to the complex and dynamic nature of the IT competitive environment. In fact, a host of new job titles have emerged that include the Chief Knowledge Officer, Chief Learning Officer, Chief Change Officer, and the eCFO.

People

While a bureaucracy reduces its dependence on individual initiative by defining formal job descriptions and procedures for handling problems, a network creates an organizational context in which individuals can exercise a great deal of freedom, initiative, and creativity to solve unanticipated problems. Where a bureaucracy narrowly focuses people, a network broadly leverages them. The skills required for successful performance in a network entail such characteristics as interdependent problem solving, curiosity, commitment to quality, need for achievement, and an ability to work well with other people. The basis of networks is knowledge workers, and the orientation is professionals in contrast to managers. The skill sets and mind-sets of knowledge workers are substantially different from those of the middle manager ranks, which filled the multiple levels in the functional hierarchy.

The more traditional middle manager translated top-down goals and objectives and supervised workers in carrying out well-defined tasks required to achieve those goals and objectives. The orientation was more internally focused on production. In contrast, knowledge workers operate within the context of the overall business goals and objectives of the company. They are skilled in problem solving with teams of other knowledge workers in figuring out how best to carry out less well-defined tasks required to achieve broader goals and objectives of the company. The orientation is more customer sensing, and directly shaping production to serve changing customer needs. The knowledge worker is more adept at innovating operations to serve customers more effectively in a faster-changing business environment.

Technology

In functional hierarchies, technologies were introduced to perform physical work in the factories more efficiently and to automate high-volume, routine office work, such as order entry or invoicing functions. In the network organization form, these applications are still important, but the emphasis shifts toward the use of information technology in more robust and sophisticated ways.

The technologies in use in network organizations provide support primarily to knowledge workers. With information technology, work can be done almost anyplace (not just on company premises), at any time (not just 8 to 5), with any set of workers (not just those in the company or in the country).

In traditional functional hierarchies, the revenue per employee generally ranged from $50,000 to $100,000. In contrast, IT-enabled network organizations can have revenue per employee as high as $500,000, and a few like Cisco are approaching $1,000,000.

Risk and reward were much more predictable in the latter part of the industrial economy, enabling rewards systems to be based on achieving annual production and accounting targets. Tasks in a company were also engineered to the point that the relative contributions of people were more determinable. In some cases, tasks were so well engineered that piece-rate incentive systems could be developed to pay people for the precise number of parts a person produced (people more typically were paid for hours worked). A firm like Boeing honed the process into elaborate "work breakdown structures." Unions, in turn, often used these work breakdown structures as the starting point for determining what workers should get paid.

Now simply add to this situation a shift from the known production environment to an unknown production environment—that is, a company wants to connect with its customers and respond to their changing needs rather than just produce a standard product for a long time. The stable environment turns into one of chaos, where there are few anchors for stabilizing it. The answer is not simply more engineering of an already ultracomplex environment, but rather the development of a more flexible system to establish equitable rewards. So companies like Boeing have attempted to risk/profit share with their workers, where workers are incentivized to accept increasing amounts of the risk involved with the company's operations. Clearly, the move toward stock options has been an important initiative here. What is important for the manager to understand is that the basic environment has changed and needs to be dealt with in a fundamentally different manner. The basic distinction is that workers were viewed as providing ubiquitous hourly inputs of labor. Workers were not seen as a relatively important factor in influencing profits. In the new information economy, workers are seen as important influencers of profits. So reward systems such as risk/profit sharing are intended to reflect the role of workers.

Systems

Systems are the structured processes that enable organizations to perform purposeful work. They specify and promulgate goals, define and monitor the execution of tasks, and maintain communications to motivate and monitor performance.

In the bureaucratic hierarchy, systems are generally function-oriented, with major system groups for accounting, marketing, manufacturing, and personnel. Within each functional group, there are well-defined sub-groups. For example, in accounting there are application systems for payroll, accounts receivable, accounts payable, general ledger, and capital budgeting.

As the network organization emerges, these traditional applications are no longer adequate. New management systems must provide the flexibility to enable geographically dispersed workers to work together as teams. During a project, team performance must be measurable so that key resource decisions can be executed. Once a given project is completed, the systems must support the efficient formation of other teams. The systems must also be able to measure and monitor overall productivity and capital formation, even in a dynamic, project-oriented context.

Reward systems must also be altered to pay people for their overall contributions and to motivate them to work in a network environment. Most existing reward systems used in functional hierarchies are locked into the hierarchy and provide incentives that are too limited for making a network organization form successful.[8]

Comparing the Network to the Hierarchy

Networks are webs of interrelationships organized to carry out the tasks of projects. Networks are dynamic and organic, and as the marketplace environment changes they change. This continually evolving organic form versus the more stable pyramid form of the functional hierarchy is at the heart of the differences in how the networks operate.

Multiple Relationships

Multiple direct relationships are the essence of a network. Under the established principles in a functional hierarchy of one boss for every subordinate and a span of control of 6 to 12 subordinates for every manager, the number of direct relationships in a functional hierarchy is the number of people minus one. Accordingly, communication in a functional hierarchy is highly dependent on indirect communications—that is, going through a chain of command. If a message must pass through six levels and the average accuracy of communications is 70 percent, then only $(.70)^{6-1}$—or 16 percent—of the message is accurately communicated. This is the familiar communication problem termed "filtering." (Incidentally, it is also one of the reasons that a traditional hierarchy depends so much on official memos to transmit communications.)

The network organization, in contrast, is based on the concept of allowing direct communication among all organizational members. In theory, there can be $[n \times (n-1)/2]$ direct relationships in an organization of n members. Although the network deals better with the problem of filtering, it creates another problem: the problem of chaos from the possibility of so many people being able to communicate directly. Companies that use e-mail or phone mail systems without usage guidelines often incur the chaos problem where hundreds of messages pile up on the computers of managers, only to be completely ignored.

Of course, the time and energy required for members of an organization to maintain active links with other members would be prohibitive, although information and communication technology can make these links easier and less costly to maintain. Nevertheless, communication chaos is a real problem that must be dealt with if the network organization is to flourish.

No large organization will be purely a network (just as no large organization is purely a bureaucratic hierarchy). All existing organizations are made up of combinations of various structural types. In the transition from hierarchical structures to those that are more networked, we see active, change-oriented networks "floating" on top of the more traditional hierarchies.

Fewer Levels

Networks typically have fewer reporting levels than do functional hierarchies. Network organizations, filled primarily with knowledge workers and supported by computing and communications technologies, do not need armies of middle managers to assemble, process, and report on management control information. Knowledge workers prefer to work more independently as they often resist and resent explicit direction and control from superiors. In fact, the whole concept of "level" is anathema to many knowledge workers, and is considered a hindrance to their productivity.

Variable Span of Control

The conventional wisdom in a bureaucracy is that a manager can effectively manage 6 to 12 subordinates. This number is limited by his or her ability to communicate face-to-face with subordinates and keep track of their activities. When we consider the power of electronic communications and record keeping and new developments like artificial intelligence and decision support systems, relative to the face-to-face communications characteristic of hierarchical organizations, the traditional assumptions governing span of control break down.

Peter Drucker has suggested that we redefine "span of control" as "span of communication" and recognize that information technologies have completely changed the rules of the game in terms of how many subordinates a manager can handle, what kinds of communications are necessary to maintain control over organizational activities, and how teams of professionals work together to solve organizational problems.[9] Over reliance on traditional hierarchical assumptions about span of control can severely constrain an organization's ability to cope with the complexity of change so common in today's business environment.

Functional Specialization

Pre-Internet age bureaucracies typically contain functional hierarchies. The functional organization structure brings together specialists in each area required by the business—such as engineering, manufacturing, sales, finance, and personnel. Clustering specialists by function is based on assumptions of economies of scale and standardization, which in turn create boundaries.

The shortcoming of this approach is that it creates what David Norton has called "functional gridlock."[10] Each function develops its own way of getting the job done, and the total organizational goals are often obscured. Walls build up between functional units, and not only is communication inadequate, but individual careers typically proceed up only one functional ladder. The net results are lack of understanding across functional boundaries and, commonly, mutual distrust.

In network organizations, the information flows freely across departmental boundaries at lower levels as well as senior levels, so the required information gets to the right places more quickly. Networks rely on the knowledge and ideas of organizational members, who directly contact the people they need to work with to get required information or commitments.

Permeable Boundaries

Another feature that distinguishes network organizations from bureaucracies is the nature of the boundaries between networks and their environments, and between parts of the organization itself. In a bureaucracy, the boundaries are clear and well understood; you are either "in" or "out"— there is little middle ground. Relationships with suppliers are generally defined by contracts that spell out in detail not only purchase order specifications, but terms of payment and legal liabilities. Negotiations are typically at arm's length. The objective is to minimize the costs of materials or services to be acquired, consistent with performance requirements.

In a network environment, in contrast, it is often difficult to determine where the buyer organization stops and the supplier begins. While the contractual terms binding supplier and customer are often just as well defined as in the bureaucratic context, the relationship is generally very different. The relationship is seen as a symbiotic one, in which the two parties are mutually dependent on each other.

Electronic media for tasks such as purchase ordering, customer invoicing, and supplier payments intersect boundaries in a network context. While these arrangements have helped to increase responsiveness, improve product deliveries, and reduce in-process inventories, they also introduce new kinds of managerial and organizational challenges.

Professor James Cash of the Harvard Business School suggested the following to me regarding this point: A European commercial airline orders replacement parts by electronic mail from a United States manufacturer, who in turn instantly translates the order into an electronic request for components from a subcontractor in the Far East. The entire transaction is completed in a matter of seconds; yet it involves three corporations on three continents and raises challenging questions about legal commitments, financial obligations, taxation policies, and the issue of exporting jobs from one economic entity to another.

The permeability of network boundaries affects individual roles as well. Networks frequently bring members of two or more organizations into direct contact with each other in the context of joint teams, alliance projects, or customer/supplier projects. For example, typically major automobile manufacturers outsource a significant portion of engineering design work to major vendors, who are networked into the engineering design teams and use the same CAD/CAM (computer-aided design/manufacturing) technologies as the inside engineers, thereby enabling rapid transmittal of design work. In effect, the vendor engineers are part of the manufacturer's network, even though they are located in distant cities and are paid by the vendor.

Successful network organizations encourage and support professional relationships between their knowledge workers and colleagues in other organizations, sometimes even those working for competitors. These networks can be a powerful source of information, ideas, and even future employees or alliance partners, and constitute a very important resource.

Spanning Internal Boundaries

Boundaries between functions, frontline and managerial staff, or segmenting geographic territories may also be crossed more readily at all levels of an effectively functioning network organization. Rather than following the formal, hierarchical command structure, information flows through the organization in branching patterns, with frequent "crosswalks" across functions. Informed decisions can be made and implemented at lower levels, and the pace of decision making and organizational action can be much faster.

Cross-functional networks naturally lead to more complex interpersonal relationships. In a bureaucracy, there are formal procedures for bringing specialized skills to bear on problems and issues. Some specialists are usually viewed as advisers at best, and are often perceived by other specialists as interfering with the real work of the organization.

In a network organization, by contrast, relationships develop among workers with problems and workers with the skills to assist in solving those problems. Knowledge workers develop influence based on their knowledge, expertise, and ability to contribute to solutions, rather than on bureaucratic sources of power such as formal authority, procedural requirements, or budgetary approval. The relationship network is more efficient in bringing together the diverse skills required for solving new problems than any preconceived information path.

Coordination versus Vertical Integration

Network organizations may also have a different orientation toward vertical integration. In the industrial age mind-set, the ultimate objective is to control maximum resources and achieve dominance of the marketplace. The epitome of this perspective was Ford Motor Company's River Rouge plant, where iron ore was unloaded at one end of the facility and newly completed automobiles came out the other. Today, natural resources such as raw materials and energy, while still important, are actively traded in international markets and are no longer considered the source of competitive advantage that they once were. In today's complex, dynamic business environment, strategy points more toward the smaller, flexible network organization buying and selling resources in various markets, rather than the vertically integrated bureaucracy.

After *Fortune* magazine reported in 1988 that Toyota Motor Corporation outsourced 70 percent of its parts and had a profit per car 36 percent higher than General Motors, which outsourced only 30 percent of its parts,[11] the industry was fast to react in extending its organizations to include outsourcing. Today, a virtual network of vendors, raw materials suppliers, and professional services can be assembled more quickly and less expensively than a vertically integrated organization, while also providing greater flexibility for the future. Drugstore.com was built within a year from the time of inception to serving more than half a million customers. This was only possible by leveraging physical distribution through outsourcing, using the established overnight delivery systems, and procuring expertise from key professional service firms.

Diversity

Networks require a different style of operation, or what has commonly been referred to as "culture." First and foremost, workers in a network organization must be flexible. They participate in changing subnetworks to carry out diverse projects, often working on several different projects at the same time. Second, workers must adopt a problem-solving mode of behavior guided by an ethic of doing what's right. In contrast, the familiar bureaucratic response of "not my job" is not the norm in a network organization.

Third, the autonomy of doing what's right must be blended with a mutual respect for the actions and ideas of others. Frequently, there will be overlap in attacking problems with widely different approaches employed. Individuals must resolve most of these conflicts themselves if the network organization is to function effectively. If mutual respect is absent, the conflict of overlapping and multiple approaches for problem solving can lead to breakdowns in the network organization.

Fourth, network organizations require the nurturing of knowledge workers in pursuing professional excellence and functioning as teams. Quality is an important ethic within a network organization culture, creating peer group motivation through its emphasis on doing things as effectively as possible.

These differences in operating style mean a very different role for managers, who consequently require a different set of managerial skills. With many knowledge workers capable of setting their own goals and working with very little direct supervision, the traditional autocratic management style not only is unnecessary, but it can actually be counterproductive in a network structure. Rather, the role of the network manager is to lead, coordinate, facilitate team building, and support the knowledge workers.

These attributes of style are intangibles, and therefore are difficult to manage formally. Nevertheless, our experience indicates that their presence is essential to the migration toward a network organization. In the past, and even still today, we have observed that many companies attempt to achieve this different style under the heading of "culture change programs."

Emerging Hier-Networks

As described by Karen Stephenson and Stephan Haeckel, "Hierarchies and networks are yoked together in the yin and yang of organizational learning."[12] Both hierarchy and networks are essential for economic organization. In the industrial age, hierarchies were formalized and explicitly studied, while informal networks were largely ignored. In the information age, it is important to study and understand both.

Stephenson and Haeckel describe networks as self-organizing structures held in place by relationships of trust. Over time, networks absorb information about what works and what doesn't, and codify the information into rules and procedures. With growth, the networks subdivide and are connected by hierarchy. Over time hierarchies take on a form of artificial intelligence consisting of an entity of repeatable procedures and replaceable parts and people. As a result, the IT-enabled organization becomes scalable.

The institutionalization of rules and procedures hinders innovation and slows change. People in the hierarchies learn to go around the hierarchies and form into networks (e.g., skunk works) to facilitate changing the hierarchy, a mechanism enabling hierarchies to adapt.[13]

The challenge for information age management is balancing the hierarchy and network dimensions of their organizations to facilitate high levels of innovation, while simultaneously enabling their organizations to scale without flying out of control.

Key Concepts
- Blurring boundaries: from vertical integration to virtual integration.
- We've moved from managing physical assets and value to managing intangible assets and value, and from managing constrained innovation to managing unconstrained innovation.
- Legacy systems are obsolete, and must be totally replaced by the I-Net.

4

The Value Economy

Following the Market Leaders

To effectively guide companies into the Internet era, it is critical to understand that the value proposition of products must shift from the physical to the intangible. This pattern of the value evolution is evident in all industries. For example, the value proposition of the automobile has changed from one dominated by physical hardware, and has moved toward a mix of computer software and technology-enabled services such as OnStar in General Motors products. In the high-tech world, industry titans such as IBM, Apple, Microsoft, and Cisco are known for pioneering advanced technologies and creating new markets, but they have also been a part of the sea change that technology has brought to business and consumers over the past 20 years. This chapter gives an overview of the evolution of the value proposition from the pre-Internet era through the network era, and examines the evolving strategies of four market leaders.

IBM Hits A Wall

Early in the Internet age, IBM had a heavy bias to the centrality of the physical product—the computer. The costs of software and services were bundled into the price of the hardware. Customers bought computers that worked; and if problems were incurred, IBM service personnel were there to fix the problems, but the customer did not directly see the cost of the service personnel.

IBM honed to perfection the vertical integration business discussed in the previous chapter and illustrated in Figure 4.1. Between 1956 and 1971 IBM's market share for large computers hovered around 70 percent; by the end of 1984 it had climbed to nearly 80 percent.[1]

IBM not only dominated in market share, but also in 1982 became the most profitable company in the world, beating out other giants such as Exxon, Royal Dutch/Shell Group, and General Motors. Throughout the latter part of the 1970s and for most of the 1980s IBM enjoyed the highest market value in the United States.[2] It remained at number one until 1986, when it slipped to number two behind Exxon.[3] In 1989 IBM dominated the markets for mainframe, mini, and personal computers.

While the cost of hardware was driven down by Moore's Law, the costs of software and services were not. So ultimately the mix in the total cost of computers continued to change, with the demand for hardware diminishing with respect to software and services. (In the 1980s certain software systems exceeded the cost of hardware.)

IBM was beleaguered, like many other incumbent industrial era companies, by the novel challenges of managing fast-changing intangibles such as software and intellectual (as opposed to physical) assets. The company seemed unable to make the transition fully from a hardware to a

Figure 4.1   Vertical Structure of the Computer Industry from 1950 to 1980

- Sales and service
- Applications software (COBOL, FORTRAN)
- Operating system (OS)
- Computer manufacturing and assembly (including peripherals)
- Semiconductor design and manufacture

software focus. It left itself vulnerable to emerging competitors who were not even on the company's radar at the time the onslaught began.

New Economy Titans

Apple Computer, Inc. was founded as a computer company that also bundled hardware and software. However, the significant value proposition of Apple was the Macintosh software, not the hardware. But despite this advantage, Apple Computer seemed uncertain of its status. Jim Carlton, in his book about the company, recounts how its software engineers responded to CEO John Sculley's remark that Apple was really in the hardware business by showing up for work the following day in T-shirts emblazoned with "Apple is a hardware company," along with a list of every software project the company had completed.[4] Mixed priorities such as these are what many think led to Apple falling off the power curve of its early success.[5] Apple's hardware could not keep up with the best in the industry, and this dragged down the value of its superior software.

Microsoft did not make this mistake. Bill Gates was among the first to recognize that the computer was evolving from a hardware- to a software-centric product. Microsoft was founded as and remains a software company that optimizes its software with the latest and best computer hardware in the industry.

While software is expensive to create, once developed its manufacturing cost is extremely low. Thus, the gross margins of successful software companies can result in extremely profitable businesses. The business strategy in a software company is to develop leading software and achieve lock-in with its customers. Once customers are using a company's software, the extended strategy becomes keeping the customer locked in through value-added version upgrades. Of course, the main danger for the software company applying this strategy is that as the basic architecture of its software becomes obsolete it becomes more difficult to continue to incorporate the newest innovations into the software. Another danger is that once a software company introduces a successful product to the marketplace, it relaxes a bit and becomes less innovative and less competitive. An example is Microsoft's rather tardy embrace of the Internet.

Cisco came into the industry as a networked company. The senior management team of Cisco embraced a value proposition focused on the customer by providing network services that emphasized "service." Cisco's initial router product continues to be reinvented around the strategy of providing network services to the customer, and hardware and software are viewed as a platform for network services. Acquisitions are used as a strategy for acquiring network services capabilities.

Building the Company's IQ with Research and Product Development

IBM, like other multidivisional companies, practiced constrained innovation in its product lines. Research and production were separate activities conducted by different people, in different places, with different management approaches. Research occurred far from manufacturing facilities at sites that resembled university campuses more than companies.

Generally the research conducted was both basic research, with no known application but important to advancing innovation in the industry, and applied research, which had more direct application to the products in the industry. When considering new product development, the senior management of the company would review the inventory of research that had been done to determine whether new products or product lines could be drawn from it. Of utmost importance in this decision-making process was the ability to manufacture easily and control product quality and reliability. Thus, the research process was constrained in its direct flow into new products and processes for manufacturing products.

Research by the leading companies in the industry was generally well funded. At the height of its industry dominance in 1989, IBM spent the staggering sum of $6.8 billion on research, not including the $2 billion in software spending that it capitalized.[6] Thirty-eight percent of its research expenditures were investments in software and services. Advanced chip manufacturing techniques were also a top research priority at the time. The productivity of IBM's research was on a par with the best research facilities in the world.[7] Even as late as 2000, IBM produced more patents than any other company.[8]

To understand the IBM constrained process of research for benefiting customers through the incorporation of its research into products and services, it is important to understand the brand image IBM created. Among its principal customers, information systems (IS) managers, a common adage was that "no one gets fired for buying IBM." Computers, then and now, are complex systems. As companies automated manual transaction processes—initially payroll, accounts receivable, accounts payable, and order entry and, later, inventory control and production scheduling—they became highly dependent on the reliable operation of their computer systems. At the time, there were few university programs that trained computer professionals, and companies found it difficult to staff the IS departments that managed their computer systems. IBM filled the gap with large investments in the training of IBM systems engineers who were deployed on-site to ensure that customers' computers were kept running. Legions of systems engineers were dispatched to companies that experienced problems. No company in the industry came close to rendering the levels of capability and support that IBM did.

Its practice of constrained innovation served to preserve IBM's brand image by ensuring that new technologies were released into products in such a way that a steady improvement in cost performance was achieved without jeopardizing stability. Because Moore's Law was not well understood at the time, customers were comfortable with this strategy in the price performance ratio of their IBM computers that continued a path of steady improvement.

IBM's reputation was earned on the basis of reliable products rather than the latest technologies, and the armies of IBM professionals at the ready should a problem arise. Its impressive research capability inventoried important innovations, and its product development group incorporated those innovations deemed to be in the best interest of IBM's business strategy in the next product release. IBM's new product releases invariably surprised and delighted its customers.

Microsoft pioneered the "sense and respond" strategy in the development of its Windows 95 operating system. Rather than try to design the ultimate operating system, Microsoft cobbled together the best version of what it thought the operating system should be and do, then invited 400,000 customers to use it.[9] In return for use of the advanced version, the customers were asked to provide feedback about what they liked, what they did not like, and bugs that they found, and to suggest improvements. Through e-mail, Microsoft and its development team engaged in an electronic dialogue with its customers, with whom, ultimately, Windows 95 was jointly designed. Contrast this approach with IBM's limited customer interaction during product development and its incremental addition of product features based on inventoried technologies that have been previously developed.

Through firsthand experience working with IBM as the supplier of its PC-DOS operating system, Microsoft developed respect for what the large computer company had accomplished, but largely discredited its bureaucratic culture. The Microsoft managers, who developed exceptional software, focused on and valued the competencies of their software development teams. They rarely interfered with their technical professionals. "A good project manager at Microsoft," an employee remarked, "is one who is there to go out and get the pizza during an all-night debugging session."

Microsoft's culture is paced in real time rather than by fiscal years; anything "fixed"—assets, budgets, and functions—is associated with slowness and bureaucracy. Microsoft's software projects are organic, created in response to opportunities, dynamically staffed to reflect changing conditions and needs, and disbanded when their purpose has been achieved.

Innovation is rampant in the technology industry, and no one company can be the leader in all of the innovations in the industry. Accordingly, a "not invented here" phobia where a company rejects innovations or ideas originating in other companies can be fatal to a company's viability. Microsoft initially underestimated the importance of the Internet and set off on a strategy of building a proprietary network called Microsoft Network (MSN).

One of Microsoft's most impressive accomplishments was the quickness and decisiveness with which its management team changed strategic direction from building its MSN proprietary network to embracing the open standards of the Internet. Gates announced on December 7, 1995, that Microsoft, having arrived at a deeper understanding of the Internet's significance, would henceforth incorporate the Internet in everything it did.[10] And that was that! Competitors such as Xerox Corporation and IBM had many opportunities to make similar swift strategic decisions that might have bolstered their competitive strengths, but their industrial age cultures seem to have impeded such decisions.

The Path to Permeability

In the information age, the dominant form of business is the network that maintains and supports melding and organic boundaries. This technological infrastructure is coupled with the organizational shift from vertical to horizontal management. In this section we will discuss those attributes of the networked company as represented by Apple, Microsoft, and Cisco that make them dangerous competitors.

For IBM, Apple's success in mass-producing Macs was a wake-up call. Recognizing that it would take too long for the company to respond to the personal computer opportunity within their traditional organization culture, then-chairman Frank Carey authorized a new PC division to be established in Boca Raton, far from IBM's New York operations. More radical was Carey's approval for the new division to depart from IBM's vertical integration strategy. It was authorized to open up the standards between the various levels shown in Figure 4.1 and outsource the major layers.

The effect of this, as can be seen in Figure 4.2, was to structure the technology industry more horizontally and initiate the open standards movement that fostered much greater competition among many new players. A horizontal structure enabled many specialized players in the industry to coordinate their products for the benefit of customers, and open standards promoted high levels of competition among industries.

Open standards facilitate competition by ensuring new entrants to an industry that larger, established players will not be able to shut them out by changing the interfaces to their products. At least that is the idea.

Sun Microsystems, Inc. was an early advocate of open standards for UNIX operating systems. Sun's powerful workstation computers were used by engineers, Wall Street traders, and others whose work relied on being able to perform intensive computations rapidly. The open standards of Sun's UNIX-based workstations ensured a market large enough to justify the investments required for aspiring independent software vendors (ISVs) to create software products for engineers and traders.

Figure 4.2   The New Horizontal Structure of the Computer Industry

Sales	Retail Stores	Superstores	Dealers	Mail Order	Online

Industry standards linking different levels

Applications	Word	Netscape	Lotus Notes	Excel	SAP	Eudora

Industry standards linking different levels

Application Languages	BASIC	FORTRAN	COBOL	Java	C/C++	Small Talk

Industry standards linking different levels

Operating Systems	Windows	Macintosh OS	UNIX/Linux	IBM/OS2

Industry standards linking different levels

Computer Hardware	IBM	Compaq	Dell	Packard Bell	Hewlett Packard	Sun

Industry standards linking different levels

Chips	IBM	Intel	Motorola	Sun	DEC

But the competition spurred by open standards exerts pressure on the high profit margins of industry leaders, motivating them to retreat from being fully open. The technology industry has coined the phrase "open, but not open" to describe situations in which competitors advocate open standards but employ techniques that discourage customers from switching vendors. Open standards are an inherent source of tension in the high-tech industry; new entrants fiercely support them, but become less fierce advocates once established as incumbents. Even Sun, one of the strongest proponents of open standards, tailored the open version of the UNIX operating system to its proprietary Solaris operating system after the company had established a strong market position.

IBM successfully launched its PC product in 1981. With revenues reaching $4 billion by 1984, had the division stood alone it would have been the 74th largest company in the United States and the third largest computer maker after the rest of IBM (i.e., excluding the revenues from its PC division) and Digital Equipment Corporation (DEC).[11] Innovations

Dot Victor
Sun Taps eBay for New Revenue and Customers

Sun Microsystems discovered a new sales channel and a source of new customers through eBay. Last year, Sun auctioned its servers on eBay, and realized $25 million of new revenue. Twenty-five percent of the eBay customers were new customers to Sun.[12]

and success notwithstanding, the PC division was unable to exert a transforming influence on IBM's traditional industrial age culture.[13] Today the Boca Raton PC division has been closed and the site abandoned, and IBM's market value has been eclipsed by two of the firms that it had treated as allies: Intel Corporation and Microsoft. A subsequent multibillion dollar deal was struck between Dell Computer Corporation and IBM positioning IBM as a components manufacturer and supplier to Dell. Dell, in turn, provides the assembly and order fulfillment for IBM's branded PCs.

The lesson for management is never to underestimate the resistance of the control-oriented industrial age culture to the culture changes required to institutionalize innovation (dot vertigo symptom: complacency).

Changing Role of Business Technology: Creating Greater Value

The internal technology infrastructure of the three market value leaders in the industry—IBM, Microsoft, and Cisco—continued to evolve in sophistication and, of course, along with the increased capabilities of technology over time.

IBM uses IT to facilitate efficiency of the back-office administrative functions. However, the senior and middle managers were not directly involved in IT use until PCs and e-mail became pervasive. Under the more recent leadership of Lou Gerstner, Enterprise Resource Planning (ERP) is being implemented to replace back-office legacy systems with up-to-date technology prerequisite to creating an I-Net. IBM still has a long way to go before it realizes an I-Net, particularly because of its myriad IT systems and entrenched culture.

A management team that is PC proficient and has also built effective back-office systems as the business has scaled leads Microsoft. However, it is Cisco that has emerged as the exemplar in building an effective, strategy-focused I-Net.

Cisco's top management team includes two players not normally found on top management teams. One is venture capitalist Don Valentine of Sequoia Capital, who has served on Cisco's executive team since the company's inception and is currently vice-chairman. The discipline, perspective, and networks a venture capitalist brings can provide a valuable contribution to the effective management of network age companies. The other important player is the chief information officer (CIO). As a full member of Cisco's top management team, CIO Pete Solvik contributes to the strategic decisions implicit in building, and capturing the full potential of, the company's I-Net. In networked companies, it is essential that the CIO function as a peer of the traditional executive team and as a decision maker.

An initial $15 million ERP investment was the largest capital investment Cisco had ever made in its I-Net. That it was followed by a $100 million investment—almost seven times the original investment—speaks to the analogy of I-Net as "factory" of networked companies. To compete effectively and at a pace that mirrors real time, a company looking to thwart dot vertigo must possess the means to allocate resources dynamically, connect electronically with existing and potential customers, sense their needs instantaneously, and respond to customers much more quickly than was ever done in the pre-Internet age. The I-Net is the means to all of these things.

Benefits can accrue when a company's business strategy is integrated tightly with investments in its I-Net. This tight integration of its I-Net with its business strategy has paid back Cisco's investment many times over. In 2000, the estimate is that Cisco is receiving $1.35 billion of benefits per year from its strategic I-Net.

Building the Permeable Organization

There are important benchmarks for the transformation of the business from an industrialized company to a permeable organization. These include a move from vertical to virtual integration, from command and control to sense and respond, and from technology as a tactical resource to technology as a strategic resource; also value is added from the intangible rather than the physical. How have dot companies successfully challenged industry incumbents? Pioneered by Amazon, a dot company's approach in attacking incumbent industry leaders has developed a recognizable pattern. (Later in the book, I'll describe how to avoid falling prey to this approach.)

This section discusses the four elements that comprise a networked or dot company's business approach and how they are being applied to com-

The New Titans: Moving from "Bricks" versus "Clicks" to "Clicks and Bricks"

Amazon.com aggressively entered the retail book industry by advertising itself as the "world's biggest bookstore." This in-your-face advertising claim raised the ire of industry incumbent Barnes & Noble, which brought a lawsuit accusing Amazon of false advertising. According to Barnes & Noble, it was the world's biggest bookstore.

Barnes & Noble's lawsuit seemed to be a rather cumbersome competitive response, leading some to conclude that not only was Barnes & Noble's CEO experiencing dot vertigo, but his competitive response was ineffective, reflecting more of a lumbering giant than a dangerous sleeping giant. Many concluded that dot companies were destined to be the new information age leaders, replacing traditional industry incumbents—that is, "clicks" will win over "bricks." Even the term "being amazoned" cropped up as shorthand to describe dot companies replacing incumbents.

But it isn't exactly happening that way. Instead, emerging contemporary winners like Schwab are leading with "clicks"—that is, building strategic I-Nets that electronically connect with customers—but also pragmatically and creatively integrating "bricks" into their competitive strategies. Schwab describes itself strategically as a "category of one."[14] Co-CEO David Pottruck believes that Schwab's "clicks and bricks" strategy to empower investors through IT and information makes it different from industry incumbent Merrill Lynch, which maintains more than 14,000 financial advisors to directly interact with investors. Schwab's strategy is also different from the pure play Internet brokers that have no physical branches, such as

Schwab has more than 400 bricks-and-mortar branches, mostly in the United States, staffed by salaried and licensed brokers. The primary activities of Schwab branches involve opening new customer accounts and instructing customers on how to use Schwab's sophisticated web site. More than 80 percent of Schwab's transactions are conducted on the Internet through its web site. Indeed, Schwab's winning strategy was made evident when its market value surpassed that of Merrill Lynch in 2000. But Merrill Lynch seemed to be awakened by Schwab's successes, and as this book goes to press Merrill Lynch has regained its market value lead over Schwab.

Drugstore.com's construction of a high-tech distribution center is further evidence of the trend toward "clicks and bricks." Drugstore.com's high-tech distribution center receives real-time customer orders, and is designed to automate the picking and shipping of individual orders. The problem that drugstore.com encountered with its Old Economy distribution center outsourcer is typical of the problem that plagues dot companies that build front-end technology to interface with customers. The drugstore.com outsourcer business was designed to operate on a budget cycle, and set up to pick large orders that were shipped to drugstores where employees unpacked the orders and filled the shelves of physical drugstores.

panies that are both clicks and bricks. (The clicks and bricks phenomenon holds the most promise for incumbents eager to compete in the online world while maintaining their traditional competencies. The box examines how traditional bricks-and-mortar companies are entering the dot world.) The lessons that follow apply especially to this group of competitors.

Line Up a World-Class, IT-Savvy Team

Dot companies line up initial teams with talent that is almost impossible for the incumbent to attract. The teams are mostly comprised of relatively young and accomplished software engineers, and are led by tech-savvy managers. These highly focused teams concentrate on leveraging the Internet to access and serve customers. The exploitation of information resources through the Internet is their secret weapon.

Specialist venture capitalists (VCs) coach the dot company

entrepreneurs, provide seed money, nurture growth through additional rounds of investment, and join boards of directors for those dot companies showing high promise. Venture capitalists provide three essential ingredients that have become known as "smart money." First, they provide seed capital to develop good business plans because dot company ventures are too risky to effectively tap into the traditional sources of capital, banks, and insurance companies. Second, they provide networks for accessing strategic advice, as well as rounding out the management team—that is, the key to managing investment risk. Third, they provide a road to an IPO, which is needed to scale the dot company. This path has recently become even more difficult to travel given the market fluctuations of the past 18 months, particularly as they concern Nasdaq companies. However, from these difficulties have emerged companies with increasingly sophisticated business models and more diligent financial analysis on the part of VCs. At the time of this writing, some companies are delaying their IPOs in order to strengthen their business strategies and processes, as well as sustain the support of the venture community.

Go for the Blind Side of the Incumbent

Traditional industry incumbents have built "make and sell" businesses, in contrast to "sense and respond" businesses. Their emphasis is on building organizations to make products and sell them in marketplaces with pent-up demands—characterized as "production-centric." In contrast, the dot companies effectively exploit the Internet to connect directly with their customers, sense their demands, and respond in real time. For example, drugstore.com takes orders over the Internet and then immediately confirms that the order is received, stock is available, and shipment is on the way. This approach leverages the electronic connection with the customer, and is designed to be "customer-centric" rather than "production-centric."

In addition to its strategic orientation, the dot company can exploit the ubiquity and scope of the Internet through virtual integration. Everyone can come into the company through one door (or portal) via the company's URL (Uniform Resource Locator). People (customers, employees, partners, suppliers) enter the company over the Web; the company recognizes their names, and then builds a unique configuration of the company in real time for the person's interaction. For example, if the person is a customer, a tailored store with boutiques can be presented to the customer to shop based on the customer's interests and past shopping patterns. Drugstore.com has one virtual store that customers can go to using their home computers versus the alternative of physically going to one of the 3,000 or so local bricks-and-mortar drugstores that each of the three incumbents (Walgreens, CVS, and Rite Aid) has in place.

If the name of the person identifies him or her as an employee, the company can be configured in a manner tailored to facilitate the employee doing his or her job. For example, a customer service employee can be presented with information about products purchased by a customer while talking to that customer.

Build the Company with Your Customers as Partners

Surprising incumbents is essential to the execution of dot company business models, but building the business with your customers is similarly important. Here is a subtlety that is often missed. Industrial age companies have mastered an approach of designing a complete set of detailed specifications before building a product or the factory in which the product will be built. The dot company approaches product design by getting something together quickly, sometimes offering it for free, and then engaging customers in a dialogue about preferences and additional features they would like to have. So in one sense, dot companies partner with their customers in developing products and ways to deliver the product.

The objective of the dot company is to acquire a critical mass of customers and partner with them in building a product or service that specifically meets their needs. Of course, the more customers with whom the dot company can build a relationship, the better information it has for designing and building the new product and service and adding new features, as well as achieving economies of scale for efficiency.

Aggressively acquiring customers through "buying"[15] them and therefore sacrificing short-term profits became a common practice among dot companies. With the dot company shakeout in early 2000, investors

---

Dot Victor

- Gateway Computer uses the Internet by serving customers who prefer to shop online.
- Gateway supports its "beyond the box" diversification strategy by making it easier to offer a range of new products and services, including software peripherals, training, and Internet service.
- Gateway uses the Internet to serve the business market by offering an extranet for online procurement, and offering small business services including training, HR, and web site operation.[16]

---

seemed to question this practice and the viability of some dot company business models that were especially aggressive in acquiring customers by sacrificing profits. Nevertheless, the approach to acquire a critical mass of customers is still an integral part of dot company business models, as is customer partnering. The race goes on as importance of customer acquisition parallels the success of establishing dot company brand names on the Internet.

Keep Learning and Change Instantaneously

While the IPO was certainly viewed as a milestone for dot companies, the shakeout of 2000 has confirmed that it is not a guarantee of business viability. Business viability is dependent on how the business model is executed and expanded (scaled) to maintain competitive advantage. First, the company must figure out how to continue to leverage innovation. Second, the company must maintain its flexibility to respond adequately to fast-changing market conditions. Third, the company must round out its management team with experience and functional excellence. Fourth, the company must be wary of waking the incumbent sleeping giants in the industry.

With an understanding of the following execution imperatives and what it means to focus your company around a value proposition, let's look at what it will take to instill the importance of technology into senior management.

Key Concepts

Execution imperatives:

- Creatively destroy industrial age management principles while creatively constructing information age management principles.
- Know where you are at all times by being able to close your books in real time.
- Use scarce resources only when you cannot use information resources.
- Make sure that your organization is Internet-ready before you try to use it.
- Remember that new network technology plus new network organization = 10× results; new technology alone = disappointing results.

5

Instilling the Critical Nature of Technology into Management

When answers are needed concerning the strategic importance of networked technology, many executives come up short. Very often this is the case because they generally lack the background to understand the details of adopting an enterprise technology. In order to build a networked organization that is centered on an effective I-Net, managers must command a clear understanding of these issues. The purpose of this chapter is to introduce the key concepts that managers need to know about computers, information, and information resource management to engage effectively in strategic discussions about using technology in their firms. Understanding these concepts is critical if companies are to thwart dot vertigo.

Key Ideas

It is clear that hierarchical management principles constrain the strategic use of technology, and modern business approaches thrive on its use, optimizing performance through information resource management, speed, and connectivity. What must be drilled into the minds of management daily is that we live and work in a network era where technology has become and will remain strategic, and the value of these networks increases exponentially as the Internet grows. Failing to internalize these realities leads to dot vertigo symptoms of not embracing new business models, letting egos get in the way of change, and always being in catch-up mode.

While it's a given that there are troglodytes among us, it is vital to acknowledge that computers can be used for everything and, as such, should be included in every strategic discussion. Computers, networks, and enterprise technologies must be viewed as tools that can readily access myriad information sources. This realization is underscored by the decreasing cost of computers accompanied by increasing advances in speed, power, and functionality. Finally, managers must admit that legacy systems are obsolete and in fact make them vulnerable to dot competitors, and they must embrace new forms of information and knowledge management. The dot vertigo symptoms of failing to cannibalize the company's product line, denial, complacency, and reacting with outdated approaches (or "business as usual") can be avoided by committing to the belief that technology is a strategic enabler.

The following sections make cogent arguments to support these points.

Technology and Strategy

The stages theory of information technology (IT) holds that the assimilation of the computer, and, more broadly, information technologies has required bold experimentation and lengthy periods of organizational learning. The theory characterizes organizational learning as a series of S-shaped learning curves, each of which comprises four distinct stages (see Figure 5.1). Stage 1, initiation, is characterized by limited investment and constrained experimentation aimed at proving technology's value to an organization. The steep segment of the S-curve reflects stage 2, contagion, which is a period of intense organizational learning as the technology proliferates throughout the organization in a relatively uncontrolled manner. Ultimately, a degree of inefficiency is reached sufficient to generate demand for slowing growth to a more manageable rate leading to stage 3, control. The learning curve is flattened and a balance of managed controls and growth is achieved through accumulated learning in stage 4,

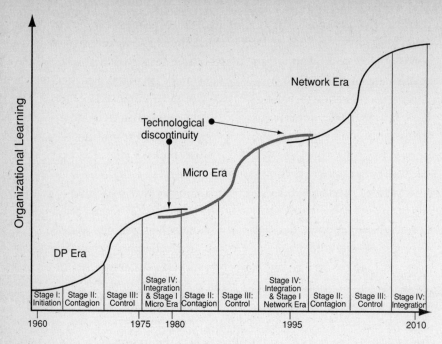

Figure 5.1   The Stages Theory of IT Growth

integration. Mastery of the dominant design of the technology is reached in this stage, providing a foundation for major improvement in the dominant design and the next order of magnitude of progress (i.e., the next set of S-curves).

Later in this chapter, I will review the stages of dominant design of computer and information technologies. This discussion elucidates the growing pervasiveness of technology in business over the past few decades and instills the critical nature of technology into managers who are reinventing their companies to compete in the network era.

Networks Are Increasingly Valuable

The more computers there are, the more valuable they are to us. George Gilder proposed "Metcalfe's law of the telecosm,"[1] whereby interconnecting n computers results in a potential value of n squared.[2] The idea applies to telephones and fax machines, as well as to computers. The increasingly widespread use of the Internet by business can be attributed to its potential value as projected by Metcalfe's Law. As reported by Nielson Media Research and CommerceNet, Internet growth has reached unprecedented levels. In the United States and Canada alone, there was a jump from 58 million users age 16 and over in September 1997 to 79 million in June 1998.[3] Internet users reached more than 50 million in less than 5 years, compared with cable television, which took 10 years; television, which took 13 years; and radio, which took 38 years to reach a similar user penetration.[4]

Moreover, "the total bandwidth of communications systems,"[5] according to Gilder, "will triple every year for the next 25 years." Gilder also predicted for the first decade of the twenty-first century an all-optical network thousands of times more cost effective than electronic networks.[6] We seem well on our way to realizing Gilder's prediction.

The combination of expanding bandwidth together with the attractive underlying economics of computers and telecommunications promises to reduce the cost of processing and transmitting massive amounts of information around the world year after year into the foreseeable future. Standards and protocols have facilitated the movement of data, fax, voice, graphics, and video on the same digital transmission medium, a boon to organizational activities that gave rise to the term "digital convergence."

Computers Are a Part of Every Strategic Discussion

The first thing managers need to realize is that computers can improve performance in all aspects of business. Computers are general information-processing machines. Unlike other machines, computers are programmable and have the capability to "compare and branch," which is equivalent to having logic to make decisions. As such, computers can be programmed to be used for almost anything, and indeed have been.

Computers are blindingly fast and operate at speeds measured in nanoseconds—that is, billionths of a second. For perspective, there are as many nanoseconds in one second as there are seconds in 30 years. Thus, once a software program is developed for a computer to carry out a task such as placing an order for a product, the computer can check customer credit, see if the ordered product is available (if not, the computer can place the order in the factory), and then calculate when the product will be delivered to the customer, plus a thousand other things all while the customer is on the telephone, or, more likely, typing the request on his or her PC. With generality of use and speed, computers have penetrated deeply into business, and have become embedded in almost every product imaginable. For example, computer chips are embedded in the brakes of automobiles and constantly monitor the driving conditions for lockup of brakes on slippery surfaces. When lockup occurs, the ABS (antilock braking system) takes control of the braking function and pulsates the brake in a manner that is more effective in stopping the automobile. There are more than a trillion powerful computer chips embedded in products such as the automobile throughout the world, carrying out millions of tasks to improve the performance of products, services, and business processes in the economy.

Computers Enable Information Resources

Computers have caused an explosion of information resources in the economy. Before computers, the world's information store increased relatively slowly, taking centuries to double in size. Today, estimates are that the world's information store is doubling every seven years.

Not only have computers contributed to this explosion of information, but also networks of computers operating at real-time speeds have made information accessible to people at their fingertips throughout the world. Information access has changed from a cumbersome physical process of going to files or libraries to real-time access over millions of globally interconnected computers searching databases at electronic speeds. A professional with a computer and Internet connection can access information resources about anything, from anywhere, and get results in seconds or minutes. In addition, like networks, the information resource increases in value with its use.

Computers Are Cost-Effective and Powerful Strategic Enablers

As I mentioned earlier, the cost of computer and network technology, and therefore information, has dropped like a rock, with advances in functionality and power increasing. Gordon Moore, chairman emeritus of Intel Corporation, observed that the technology for cramming transistors onto a fixed-size silicon chip doubles approximately every 18 months. Roughly, this means that the power of computers doubles every 18 months, holding cost constant. If you hold computer power constant, the cost of a unit of computer power halves every 18 months. The new economics occasioned by Moore's Law is reflected in innovative and ever more varied, but lower-cost, products and services; indeed, it is difficult to imagine a product or service that could not be cost-effectively improved by a computer.

Dominant Designs and Paradigms for Use

Three principal dominant designs of computer and IT have emerged to date: mainframes and minicomputers; microcomputers; and networked client and server computers (i.e., I-Nets).[7] Figure 5.1 characterized the assimilation of these dominant designs as three S-shaped organizational learning curves.

DP Era: "Automate"

The period from about 1960 to 1980, during which the dominant design for IT was large, centrally located mainframes and, later, distributed minicomputers, is termed the data processing (DP) era. During this time, IBM, with greater than 70 percent market share for mainframe computers, was the undisputed market leader.

Though of a radically different order, the mainframe computer seemed to be but the latest instance of industrial age ingenuity. Like an industrial age machine, it was a hulking thing, its workings audible in clicks and whirrs, visible in spinning disks and panels of flashing lights. People called it a machine and put it in the "machine room."

It is not surprising in light of this interpretation of the earliest practical manifestation of information technology that management should have initially used it, as it had ever more sophisticated machines before it, to reduce or, ideally, eliminate the human labor component of work. To automate labor-intensive business processes it was necessary to rigorously redefine them in such a way that they could be transformed into sets of programmed instructions that could be executed by a computer. Early candidates for such transformation were low-level clerical processes (e.g., payroll, inventory, and personnel records).

Continuous learning led to a deeper understanding of the capabilities of computers, manifested, in time, in such novel concepts as management information, decision support, and computer-aided design systems.

Micro Era: "Informate"

The transition to the microcomputer (micro) era began in the late 1970s and early 1980s; it picked up momentum in 1981 with IBM's launch of its PC, which legitimized the personal computer as a business tool. With its character-based disk operating system (DOS), the PC was more akin to a "baby mainframe" than to a contemporary personal computer. It lacked the now-familiar graphical user interface (GUI); DOS operated more like a mainframe operating system than, say, Windows 2000; and the BASIC (Beginners' All-purpose Symbolic Instruction Code) programming language used to execute tasks was more closely related to COBOL than to Excel or Word. Primitive as they were, the early microcomputers began to relegate mainframes to the background.

Although IBM, sustained by its size and earlier dominance, remained the leading computer company until the early 1990s, it was not the incumbent IBM, but a new entrant, Apple Computer, Inc., that changed the IT industry during the micro era. Apple's Mac personal computer incorporated a robust, GUI-based operating system together with applications software that enabled users to perform useful work largely independent of any IS organization and for the most part without recourse to technical support staff.

The notion that computers could become effective partners, and not just supplant workers, was the significant insight of the micro era. Slow to assimilate this insight, even as it incorporated new products and services into its product line, IBM ceded its market share dominance in product lines such as microcomputers, microcomputer software, and networking products. By the mid-1990s newer entrants such as Microsoft, Intel, and Cisco, while earning considerably less revenue than IBM, exceeded IBM's market value.[8]

Network Era: The Internet

The network era was ushered in, around 1995, by the slow-to-catch-on client/server computing paradigm most often manifested as a local area network (LAN). The Internet had achieved sufficient popularity by this time to demonstrate that millions of computers could be hooked up and communicate with one another, and that the key to doing so was open standards.

It is worthwhile to delve into the network era and the importance of the advent of the Internet at this point. The Internet is an engineering feat that enables millions of computers to interconnect throughout the world. This engineering feat is analogous to AT&T providing "universal service" in the United States.

At the end of the nineteenth century the telephone industry was about where the IT industry was at the beginning of the network era. Entrepreneurial activity had led to the springing up of multiple telephone companies, all vying to make their standards the industry standard. The chaotic result is illustrated by the photograph shown in Figure 5.2 looking up Wall Street in New York.[9]

Multiple lines representing multiple telephone service companies were strung from building to building along Wall Street. Several telephone handsets had to be purchased to communicate among the different systems.

Theodore Vail, CEO of AT&T, stepped in and proposed that in exchange for becoming a regulated monopoly, AT&T would invest and engineer a U.S. telephone system providing "universal service"—that is, affordable dial tone service to every household in the United States. In order to provide universal service, AT&T owned and controlled the entire end-to-end telecommunications system from the standard black handset in the home to the complex telephone switching equipment. The United States ended up benefiting from this arrangement in having the best and cheapest telephone service in the world. It was not until 1984 with the deregulation of AT&T that this system was changed to a more competitive industry.

Computers were on a path similar to the situation shown in the photograph of Wall Street. However, the U.S. government again contributed to bring an engineering order to the IT industry with the advent of the

Figure 5.2   State of U.S. Telephone Industry at the Beginning of the Twentieth Century—View Down Wall Street in New York City

Source: Henry M. Boettinger, *The Telephone Book: Bell, Watson, Vail and American Life 1876–1976* (New York: Riverwood Publishers, 1977).

Internet. Under U.S. government funding, the Internet was designed and implemented beginning in 1969. During the early development, the Internet was limited to government and educational institutions. By 1995, the Internet protocol (IP) and standards had been proven to be scalable in interconnecting millions of computers around the world. That year, with the suffix ".com," the Internet was made available to business. As a result, we now have a dominant design in the network era that enables companies and people throughout the entire world to interoperate through the use of their affordable personal computers.

The design principle of simplifying the network continues to operate through concepts such as the "thin client, " whereby much of the software that generally resides on the PC, or client, is shifted to centralized servers residing on the network. Once a thin client accesses the network, the needed software to carry out various tasks is obtained from the network computers or servers.

Bill Raduchel, chief technology officer (CTO) of America Online and previous Sun chief strategy officer, explains:

> If you have a typical Windows PC today you probably have between one and one-and-a-half gigabytes of files on your system and you probably have less than 100 megabytes in user data. Therefore, you have 10 to 15 times as much environment as you have things that are specific to you. Yet you have to manage and take care of that entire environment that is not unique to you.[10]

Each time a computer is loaded with any piece of software, a unique instance or environment is created, making that computer different from any other. Even two computers with exactly the same operating system and set of software applications can be unique if the software is installed in a different order.

Raduchel elaborates:

> When I take a generic piece of software and I configure it and install it I have created an instance of it. Each instance is unique and the problem you live with in the world is there are literally millions of instances. So the way you eliminate cost while increasing reliability is you eliminate the need to have unique instances.

It is just impossible to debug in this environment. The reason that people do not try to track down a lot of Windows errors is that with 225 million instances of Windows the fact that it failed in one instance does not mean a thing, because it may not fail in any other instance. By the time I figure out why it failed I have spent far more money than it is worth—it is more cost effective to tell you to re-boot your computer and start over. Whereas, if everybody in the world was running one instance and there is a failure, it pays for you to go and fix it because you can fix it and get economies of scale.[11]

Java was introduced by Sun Microsystems to cope with this problem. A key feature of Java—that a user downloads to the desktop only the application that is needed—reduces both the amount of storage space a client needs and the number of unique instances that must be managed. The number of paths as well as the number of unique instances also drives up costs.

Again, Raduchel explains:

How many paths can I have through the network? Well, I can have M routes times N desktops. At Sun we have 10,000 servers and 45,000 desktops. That means in principle I have 450 million possible connections that I have to support across the network. Therefore, it costs me a lot to have a network. The U.S. public switch telephone network has 20,000 nodes on it. The Sun internal network has 55,000 nodes on it. If you understand why computing is complicated, it is because we are substantially larger in the number of nodes than the entire U.S. public switch telephone network. What we are trying to do is reduce the number of instances so that it is proportional to D, where D is the number of device types that you have, which is probably on the order of less than 100 for even the largest enterprise and conceptually could be less than 10.[12]

Sun estimates TCO (total cost of ownership) for "data-less thin clients" that execute applications and access data stored on servers to be $2,500 per unit.[13]

A company that embraces open standards in its intranet in order to connect it selectively to the Internet enjoys revolutionary new economics and opportunities to extend its enterprise outward, thereby changing the competitive landscape forever.

Technological Discontinuity

The overlaps in the S-shaped curves of the stages theory represent characteristic periods of "technological discontinuity" that are observed between eras.[14] These occur when growth of a mature dominant design directly conflicts with the vibrant growth of a promising new design. Management and IT workers who have mastered the existing technology struggle to retain the power implicit in their knowledge against those who are pressing for the adoption of a novel, and hence unfamiliar, technology. A familiar one throughout history, this struggle is inevitably won by the new. Ironically, those who win the struggle in one round often lose it in the next. Given the rapid evolution of technology, IT management and workers are faced with "a diet of continual change."[15]

So far I've discussed the relevance of the I-Net, its components, and methods for soliciting management's support in creating a permeable organization. In the next few chapters I will examine how incumbents, dot companies, and clicks-and-bricks companies have used the network as part of their infrastructure and achieved significant levels of performance and profitability as a result.

Key Concepts

Execution imperatives:

- Think of your organization as dynamic and organic, and as a set of interchangeable components (not functions).
- Replace static accounting control management with dynamic coordination management.
- Act on the fact that now millions of computers can be connected globally and can interchange messages in real time.

6

Merrill Lynch Takes Aim at Charles Schwab

The New Competition

The commoditization of equity trading has continued to undermine the business models based on generating revenue from trading transactions. The pervasiveness of the Internet and availability of information have continued to undermine the views of stockbrokers, bankers, and other so-called financial experts as authority figures. Pressures on time continue to make one-stop shopping for financial services more and more appealing. All of these trends are resulting in the convergence of financial service firms and a search for the new financial services business model. The competition can be seen in the battle between Merrill Lynch and Charles Schwab.[1] Both are pursuing revenue and growth through customer asset growth, but they are using different strategies.

Merrill Lynch versus Charles Schwab

Merrill Lynch is the biggest traditional broker as well as a late entrant to online trading. Charles Schwab is the largest discount online broker. While competing in different segments of the retail brokerage industry, Merrill's and Schwab's target markets have continued to converge.

In 2000, two-thirds of Merrill's net revenues came from customer com-missions, 20 percent from investment banking fees, and 15 percent from the company's own trading profits. By contrast, Schwab received half its revenues from commissions, and another 20 percent came from service fees from Schwab's mutual fund supermarket.

Central to the emerging strategies of both Merrill and Schwab is asset gathering. There is an estimated $100 trillion of investable household as-sets in the United States, with Merrill holding around $1.7 trillion and Schwab $0.9 trillion of these assets.

Merrill Lynch

Charles Merrill founded an investment firm in 1885 with a vision to make financial markets available to everyone. He and his firm have been cred-ited with this accomplishment and are known for "bringing Wall Street to Main Street."

Merrill Lynch was an early leader in using new technologies. With its leading computer applications portfolio in 1977, Merrill Lynch launched its innovative CMA (cash management account), which challenged banks for cash deposits. CMA provided services for cash management, credit card accounting, and brokerage services. The CMA capstone was consolidated statements for customer's cash man-agement transactions, along with a higher interest rate for cash bal-ances than provided by banks. To remain competitive, banks successfully lobbied to overturn regulation that capped interest rates that they could pay. Deregulation of U.S. financial institutions still continues today.

In 2000, Merrill Lynch had revenues of about $35 billion and $1.7 tril-lion of customer assets, and had accumulated 6.6 million customers. A well-trained cadre of Merrill Lynch financial advisers were paid an aver-age compensation of $300,000 a year to assist Merrill Lynch customers in dealing with their financial affairs.

Online trading had not been in the picture for the firm until recently. As late as February 1999, Merrill Lynch exhibited five out of the seven symp-toms of dot vertigo: denial, complacency, business as usual, failure to canni-balize their own products, and not embracing new business models. At that time, John "Launny" Steffens, vice-chairman and head of U.S. Private Client, is reported to have said: "The do-it-yourself model of investing, centered on

Internet trading, should be regarded as a serious threat to Americans' financial lives."[2]

But just four months later, Merrill Lynch rolled out a new strategy that involved the Internet. Called Integrated Choice, the strategy was a one-stop source of financial services where customers self-selected the range of products and services they wanted. We'll discuss later that this was a calculated move to impede Charles Schwab's efforts to dominate the individual investor market. (See Figure 6.1.)

Sensing new competitive pressures, Merrill Lynch had reversed its initial position and responded by offering ML Direct. This service provided online trading and matched Schwab's competitive pricing for as little as $29.95. Previously, the average cost of a trade at Merrill Lynch was about $250. Not only was Merrill Lynch's pricing aggressive, but additional services included customer access to IPOs, Merrill Lynch research, and electronic bill payment services.

ML Direct customers could also access a Merrill Lynch representative 24 hours a day, seven days a week. Customers could call for information, advice, and transactions using a toll-free telephone number. The Merrill Lynch representatives were trained, licensed, and paid on the basis of salaries, not commissions.

Merrill Lynch's new strategy provided three ways to obtain services from their cadre of financial consultants: traditional (account fee and regular commissions), fee-based, and fee-based discretionary. Customers opting for the traditional brokerage relationship paid a fee-for-service based on the existing commission structures. These customers continued to receive services including cash management account (CMA), checking, and a Visa credit card. In addition to the commissions, an annual fee of $100 was levied for these services. About half of Merrill Lynch's customers continued to use the traditional arrangement.

For an annual fee charged as a percent of assets starting at a minimum of $1,500, customers could establish an Unlimited Advantage account. Unlimited Advantage account customers received personalized service from a financial consultant, a personalized financial plan, unlimited trading by telephone, online, and person to person, as well as the Merrill Lynch services including CMA, bill paying, and a credit card (Visa).

Finally, customers who wanted to delegate their investment decision

Figure 6.1   Merrill Lynch's Integrated Choice Strategy

Products: "By mouse, by phone, by human being"

Merrill Lynch Direct	➤ $29.95 per trade for online equity trades
	➤ Self-directed investment channel
	➤ Access to Merrill Lynch's award-winning research
	➤ Thousands of mutual funds from more than 90 fund families
	➤ Participate in e-IPOs
	➤ Cash management services, including checking and Visa card
	➤ Tools and resources of Merrill Lynch Online
Investor Services	➤ Personalized client service from teams of registered investor service consultants (ISCs)
	➤ 24/7 on-demand access to account information, financial guidance, and most ML products/services via an 800 telephone number
	➤ Scheduled, proactive follow-up from ISCs to help clients understand their current financial situation, plan for the future, and invest with confidence
	➤ Access to Merrill Lynch's award-winning research
	➤ Tools and resources of Merrill Lynch Online and other automated features
Traditional Relationship	➤ Personalized services from a financial consultant
	➤ Financial Foundation report with periodic updates
	➤ Cash management, checking, and bill payment capabilities
	➤ CMA Visa Signature card and rewards program
	➤ Mortgage, insurance, and trust services
	➤ Access to Merrill Lynch's award-winning research
	➤ Tools and resources of Merrill Lynch Online
Unlimited Advantage "One fee equals total access."	➤ Personalized services from a financial consultant
	➤ Virtually unlimited trading by telephone, person-to-person, or online for most investors in most securities
	➤ Financial Foundation report with periodic updates
	➤ Cash management, checking, and bill payment capabilities
	➤ CMA Visa Signature card and rewards program
	➤ Reduced origination fee on eligible home financing
	➤ Cost benefits on insurance and trust services
	➤ Access to Merrill Lynch's award-winning research
	➤ Tools and resources of Merrill Lynch Online 2000

(Continued)

	Pricing: Simple annual fee, minimum fee $1,500 First million: % equity/mutual funds, .3% fixed income/cash equivalents Next 4 million: .75% equity/mutual funds, .25% fixed income/cash equivalents Next 5 million: .50% equity/mutual funds, .20% fixed income/cash equivalents Over 10 million: customized pricing
Fee-Based Discretionary Services	➤ Money management by a professional money manager ➤ Products included: ML Consults, Mutual Fund Advisor, Strategic Portfolio Advisor, Strategy Power, Personal Investment Advisory ➤ Range of services specific to each product. All included discretionary portfolio management, services from a financial consultant, Financial Foundation report, custody services, client profiling in addition to product-specific services ➤ Pricing as a percent of assets based on asset size and specific product
Unique Services:	
Global Investor Network	➤ Merrill Lynch exclusive "financial plug-in" offers daily global research commentary ➤ Exclusive access to Merrill Lynch daily research call ➤ Video and audio market coverage from around the world ➤ Syndication onto portals
E-commerce	➤ Convenient online shopping ➤ Four million products, several hundred merchants ➤ Select merchant discounts ➤ Triple reward points using CMA Visa Signature card ➤ Online rewards, redemption, and point balances ➤ Access to Merrill Lynch Online Business Center ➤ Auctions through uBid
Visa Signature Points	The CMA Visa Signature Rewards program is the only high-end travel rewards program linked to an investment account. Program offers unrestricted travel on any airline, anytime, with no blackouts and restrictions. Points can also be used for hotel stays, car rentals, restaurants, and retail certificates as well as a wide range of premium special events
Bullhorn	Free e-mail notification service on a variety of topics

Source: "Merrill Lynch: Integrated Choice," by Professor V. Kasturi Rangan and Research Associate Marie Bell, Harvard Business School case 9-500-090, published February 29, 2000, and revised March 14, 2001.

making could do so either through a Merrill Lynch financial consultant or through one of hundreds of independent professional money managers with whom Merrill Lynch maintained relationships.

The Merrill Lynch strategy was aggressive and was intended to make Merrill Lynch the money manager of choice, the adviser of choice, and the credit card of choice with billions of Visa transactions per year. Additionally, Merrill Lynch strove to be the online portal of choice through Merrill Lynch Online/Merrill Lynch Direct. (The services offered under ML Online and ML Direct are indicated in Figure 6.1.) While challenging to execute their new Integrated Choice strategy, Merrill Lynch was always impressive in its management of IT. IT at Merrill Lynch involved an annual expenditure of more than $2 billion, and an IT internal staff of more than 6,000 supplemented with more than 2,000 outside contractors from various IT service firms. Once Merrill Lynch decided to integrate online trading and services into its strategy, several hundred IT internal staff and contractors were dedicated to the execution of the strategy, enabling Merrill to launch the new strategy within a year.

Charles Schwab

Based in San Francisco next to Silicon Valley and on the opposite coast from Merrill Lynch, Schwab was launched in 1975 by Charles Schwab. Schwab seized the opportunity to start the world's first discount brokerage firm after the Securities and Exchange Commission (SEC) abolished fixed-rate commissions on brokerage trades. Schwab's decision to pioneer the discount brokerage concept was driven by his objection to the conflict of interest inherent in the traditional full-service brokerage business due to broker commissions. The term "churning" had cropped up to describe brokers buying and selling customers' stocks and hence generating income for themselves, which was not always good for their clients.

Schwab's strategy was to empower the individual investor by offering unbiased products and services at discounted prices. Unlike full-service brokerage firms, Schwab did not actively manage portfolios, make investment recommendations, offer proprietary research, or offer actively managed proprietary products. Rather, it offered a wide variety of third-party investment alternatives and provided generalized investment advice. To ensure that there were no conflicts of interest between brokers' incentives and customer interests, Schwab paid its brokers a salary plus bonus, as opposed to commissions on trades.[3]

In 1983, BankAmerica (now Bank of America) bought Schwab for $57 million. An ensuing four-year clash between the entrepreneurial culture at Schwab and the more conservative culture at Bank of America led Charles Schwab to execute a $280 million management buyout of the firm in 1987. Schwab went public later that year in a transaction that valued the firm at $450 million.

The culture conflict between the incumbent and the new entrant has become almost commonplace in industry. In a merger attempt, if the management of the two different types of firms is not fully aware of the challenge involved in integrating the two cultures in innovative ways, integration failure becomes unavoidable and ultimately drags down both firms.

By 2000, Schwab dominated the discount brokerage market with revenue of $3.9 billion, 7.4 million customers (4.2 million were online cus-

---

Overcoming Dot Vertigo: Schwab Cannibalizes Its Telephone Trades with Internet Trades

In response to increased competition from lower-cost stock trading on the Internet in late 1997, Schwab faced a decision of cannibalizing its retail trading business (about $80 per trade) by offering significantly discounted Internet trading ($29.95 per trade) to its entire customer base, accompanied by the full complement of Schwab customer service options. At a time when Schwab's business was healthy and growing, this decision was projected to cost Schwab more than $100 million in short-term profits, having a very negative impact on its stock price. After much soul-searching, Charles Schwab and David Pottruck (co-CEOs), made the decision to do so on January 15, 1998. As it turns out, the decision to cannibalize was brilliant as demonstrated by the results.

By the end of 1998:

- One million new accounts were gained (40 percent of total accounts).
- Revenue was up 19 percent; profits were up 29 percent.
- Stock was up 15 percent.
- For the first time Schwab's market value edged higher than Merrill Lynch's market value.

tomers), $944.1 billion of client assets, and a market value of $44 billion. Schwab operated more than 372 domestic branch offices in 47 states. While the branches initially played an important servicing role, over time a significant percentage of routine customer service requests (e.g., quotes, balances, positions, trades) had migrated to the telephone and online service channels. As a result, the branches had more time to focus on opening accounts, assisting customers with more complex transactions, and providing customers with investment coaching. In fact, while 40 percent of all trades were made at branches in 1991, that figure had dropped to less than 5 percent by the end of 1997, resulting in a 50 percent reduction in the cost of processing trades. During this period, more than 80 percent of the trades became online trades.

However, branches continued to play an important role in new account generation, even for customers who wanted to trade exclusively online. Schwab estimated that around 90 percent of its new online accounts were opened in a branch.

Susanne Lyons, president of Schwab's retail client services division, explained:

Customers want to kick the tires before opening an account. They want to see that there's a *real* building with *real* people who look reputable before handing over a check.[4]

Co-CEO David Pottruck added:

Our branches distinguish us from the other online brokerages. Our customers have higher average balances than customers of the pure[5] online brokerages do, and that's in part due to our branch system. People aren't going to put a $500,000 check in the mail; they just don't do that. New customers that come into our branches want to hand a real person their money, look that person in the eye, and know something about how that person is going to serve them. They want to have a sense of the company's commitment to them, and our branch personnel provide that.[6]

To service its customers by phone, Schwab offered both an automated phone service and access to live customer service representatives.

Schwab's automated TeleBroker phone service enabled customers to place trades, check account status, and get quotes without talking to a customer service representative. To provide live customer support, Schwab operated four 24-hours-a-day, 7-days-a-week regional customer service centers located in Indianapolis, Denver, Phoenix, and Orlando. Customer service representatives were fully equipped with online computer terminals that enabled them to access account information and place orders online.[7]

Schwab's modular IT architecture was based on the premise that all front-end customer channels should access back-end systems. Therefore, a key task of any application development project was to determine how to build a front-end system that could utilize existing back-end systems. The corporate projects IT group would then have to determine how to scale the back-end systems to handle the growth in front-end applications.[8]

The company also had eight middleware servers that served as the conduit between all front-end applications and the corporate databases residing on the mainframes. One of the primary roles of the middleware servers was to validate a user's identity before granting access to the mainframe system. The final component of the back-end system was a series of about 50 Web servers that served two primary functions: communicating with customers over the Web and conducting value-added processing of data obtained from the middleware servers and mainframes.

Schwab: "Investor Empowerment"

Schwab's strategy is to empower the investor with information to make financial decisions as well as avoid conflicts with its business interests and those of its customers. Thus, Schwab brokers are salaried to ensure that the brokers are not put in a position to churn customer trading to generate monies for themselves.

The Internet has played an important role in enabling Schwab to pursue its strategy. As co-CEO David Pottruck has said, technology is the "very air that we breathe at Schwab." The firm has been able to maintain its margins while reducing prices, and credits its effective management of technology for this achievement. Pottruck also considers the company's focus on managing revenue per employee important in achieving

Schwab's strategy.[9] The preferred approach is to have the fewest but brightest employees that you can have; and, for these employees, maximize the investment in technology to the highest practical level to increase the work that the employees can accomplish.

Merrill Lynch: "Integrated Choice"

Industry leader incumbent Merrill Lynch is striving to leverage its IT and force of financial consultants. In 1977 Merrill Lynch attacked the industry with IT by introducing its cash management account (CMA) product. The end result was to change financial services by setting off consolidation among the disparate segments. Merrill Lynch never slacked off in its industry-leading IT investments.

The success of Merrill Lynch's broker delivery system caused the firm to pause in immediately adopting online trading and incorporating the Internet into its business model. The obvious concern was rapid cannibalization of its transaction-based business model, resulting in a negative financial impact on broker compensation. However, once Merrill Lynch accepted online trading and the reality of the Internet, it moved aggressively in developing its Integrated Choice strategy. This strategy is based on the belief that the majority of investors want expert financial consulting in effectively making their financial investment decisions. As part of its strategy, Merrill Lynch is continuing to invest in training its 17,500 financial consultants and equip them with the best research and computer-based tools.

Business Performance Results

We can track the business performance of these two capable and fierce competitors through their battle for market value. As seen in Figure 6.2, Merrill Lynch led in market value right up until the advent of online trading and the Internet.

During that time, Schwab closed in on and then exceeded Merrill Lynch's market value. Once Merrill Lynch responded with its Integrated Choice strategy, it once again led the industry with the highest market value. The competition is still being played out, and both companies now seem to have promising information age business strategies.

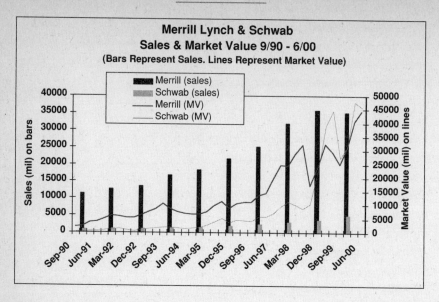

Figure 6.2   Merrill Lynch and Charles Schwab Market Value Updated
Source: Compustat.

Other Battles in Financial Services

No industry has been more deeply penetrated or impacted by technology than the financial services industry. Just a short time ago there were more than 20,000 commercial banks in the United States; today there are about 8,000. Only a few years ago, the industry was heavily regulated and consisted of highly defined industry segments, clear business models among the companies in the various segments, and hard boundaries defining what activities were conducted inside the companies and what ones were outside.[10] Banks took in money in the form of savings and demand deposit accounts, and sold money in the form of loans. The business model was straightforward: Manage the spread between what interest rate you buy money for and what interest rate you sell money for. The difference is your gross profit. Make sure that you have enough collateral from the borrower to minimize the risk regarding loan repayment.

Then the computer came upon the scene, and the industry began to unravel—first slowly, and than at a dizzying speed causing widespread dot vertigo.

Millions of investment transactions take place day after day. While we may take for granted the execution of these transactions, they have been made possible only through an extremely complex web of technology investments and networks developed by companies and governments over the past 50 years. Today, we are the benefactors of these investments. This infrastructure also provides the basis for the various players in the financial services industry to continue to compete by exploiting the shared financial services network that has been built. The result has been radical restructuring of the financial services industry and the development of new business models enabled by technology. This section examines how electronic communications networks (ECNs) have affected the New York Stock Exchange (NYSE), looking specifically at the OptiMark trading system.

New York Stock Exchange versus ECNs (Electronic Communications Networks)

The *Economist* reported that one of the biggest online threats to traditional exchanges is likely to be the OptiMark trading system.[11] OptiMark is one of a dozen or so ECNs (electronic communications network) that have cropped up in the past three years. ECNs have captured 30 percent of all Nasdaq trading, and in the process have reduced commissions from between 6.25 and 18.75 cents a share to 0.075 cent.

The forces driving these changes are familiar information age drivers: IT, deregulation, and globalization. New competitors like the ECNs enter the market, squeeze margins, cause the incumbents to scramble, and lead to a new order in the industry. Some envision that the new order will result in the ability to trade stocks globally 24 hours a day, 7 days a week.

"It's not clear to anybody what the end game will be," says Merrill Lynch's CEO David Komansky. "No one wants to be left out, so we have to cover all the eventualities. The main reason we invested in ECNs is to cover all of our bets."[12] In addition to its seats on the major exchanges, Merrill owns stakes in five ECN trading systems, Morgan Stanley Dean Witter has invested in four, and Goldman Sachs, six. Investors have also invested in ECNs: Fidelity Investments owns a piece of the REDIbook ECN (along with Donaldson, Lufkin & Jenrette, Charles Schwab, and Spear Leeds).

Charles Schwab purchased CyBerCorp for $488 million—an ECN with electronic trading technology and brokerage services in Austin, Texas. CyBerCorp CEO Philip Berber, a former developer of military software, successfully adapted defense technology to the trading environment, bringing to market an intelligent order routing and direct access technology that swiftly searches multiple ECNs and primary exchanges for the best price for a stock trade.[13]

The Incumbent: The New York Stock Exchange (NYSE)

The New York Stock Exchange has a rich and proud history originating with investors coming together under a tree on Wall Street to trade stock in companies. In 1817 the New York Stock Exchange was formalized, and in 1886 it achieved its first 100 million shares traded in a day. By 1992, the average shares traded on the NYSE exceeded 200 million traded shares. Today, more than a billion shares are traded on a daily basis.

IT has played an important role in enabling the NYSE to achieve the volumes that it so efficiently processes every day. Specialists for NYSE stocks were created in 1871—now often referred to as "market makers." Every stock on the NYSE is assigned to a specialist that is responsible for bringing the buyers and sellers together. In 1928, the trading floor was established in which open outcry bids for selling and buying were conducted on the NYSE trading floor at the specialists' trading stations.

In 1929, the central quote system was established, and in 1933 the Securities Exchange Act was passed, delineating the competitive boundaries among the financial institutions of banks, brokers, and insurance companies. The advent of the computer began impacting the exchanges at an early point. In 1964, the SEC established the IT-based ticker system, which became the Security Industry Automated Corporation (SIAC) Consolidated Quotations System. In 1975, the Consolidated Tape System was introduced. The Consolidated Tape Association is a mutual organization run by all regulated exchanges in the United States, which in turn sells its combined data.

In 1977, the Consolidated Quotations System began providing online bid and ask quotes for NYSE securities also traded on other exchanges. The objective of the CQS was to enhance competition by allowing traders to find the best exchange for a desired trade. In 1978, the Intermarket Trading System (ITS) was implemented to link the major exchanges by computer to enable the display of quotes on all markets and the execution of cross-market trades. In 1984, the NYSE introduced the SuperDot system allowing member firms to send buy and sell orders electronically directly to the NYSE floor.

Trading Stock

In the primary market, investment bankers market a firm's securities to the public. An IPO (initial public offering) brings the stock of a newly formed company to the market. Once securities are issued in the public market, investors trade the stocks among themselves in secondary markets. Secondary markets include national exchanges like the NYSE and the Nasdaq, over-the-counter (OTC) market, and direct trading between two parties. The NYSE is jointly owned by a group of qualified members who purchase "seats" on the exchange, which in turn allow them to trade on the floor of the exchange. Each stock traded on the NYSE is allocated to a specialist, who is a licensed broker responsible for trading the stock at a designated trading post on the floor of the exchange. Specialists aggregate buy and sell orders for a particular stock, and they intervene in the market, buying or selling to reduce price volatility and provide liquidity.

The specialist on the NYSE floor has sole access to the exchange's limit order book, which is highly valuable information about the supply of and demand for shares. This knowledge is probably the main source of the specialist's profits as the specialist can use this information to buy and sell stock for the specialist's own inventory.

Floor brokers receive buy and sell orders for stocks, and meet at the trading posts of the specialists where an outcry bidding process is conducted for buying and selling the stock. The NYSE is the last major stock exchange to retain the open outcry process. The other exchanges use screen-based trading whereby the buy and sell orders are listed on a computer screen, and trading is conducted through the computer.

The exchanges have implemented sophisticated IT systems to facilitate the huge volume of trades that are done each day. For example, the NYSE uses SuperDot for electronic order routing, which enables NYSE member firms to transmit buy and sell orders directly to floor brokers. The IT installed allows, for example, the NYSE specialist for America Online to trade 20 million shares on a typical day. On a fast day, the specialist may trade up to 40 million shares—that is more than the entire exchange averaged daily 20 years ago.

Unlike the NYSE system of IT-enabled intermediaries or specialists bringing buyers and sellers together, ECNs use IT to go further by eliminating specialists and instead matching trades electronically and automatically. One out of every eight Nasdaq trades goes through the ECN Island. Island has only a five-person customer support team to monitor the 200 million shares that pass through its low-tech line of Compaq servers and Dell PCs every day.[14]

Globalization and IT

IT and the Internet continue to be strong forces toward globalization of the financial services industry. However, as shown by Figure 6.3, the national exchanges still predominantly list the public companies in their industries.

The low number of company listings outside an exchange's country has a lot to do with the lack of global standards for public information about companies and their business performance. In the United States, public companies are required to report their business performance using GAAP (generally accepted accounting principles) and supply audited financial statements to investors. Also, the exchanges like the NYSE have listing requirements that must be adhered to by the companies whose

Figure 6.3   Stock Exchanges and Listed Companies

Exchange	Number of Companies Listed on Exchange	Number of Companies Headquartered in Exchange Country	Number of Companies Headquartered outside Exchange Country
New York Stock Exchange	3,020	2,630	390
Nasdaq	4,830	4,400	430
London	2,790	2,290	500
Frankfurt	8,610	930	7,680
Tokyo	1,930	1,890	40

Note: Estimates are for 2000, and are rounded to the nearest 10.

stock is traded on the exchange. As a result, there is relatively consistent and complete business information on publicly traded companies in the United States, which helps facilitate the trading of the stocks.

Internationally, there is a wide variance on reporting business performance standards and on regulatory enforcement of standards. This wide variance is an impediment to globalization, but it is slowly changing toward acceptance of international standards. Also, the globalization of the Internet is making more information available on the business performance of companies, which is contributing to the trend toward more globalization in the financial services industry.

An ECN Challenger: OptiMark

In 1995, Bill Lupien, a former exchange specialist and Instinet Corporation CEO, invested almost $5 million of his own money to start his company, OptiMark Technologies Inc. Lupien has been a force behind two of the biggest electronic alterations of the overall structure of U.S. equity markets—the creation in 1978 of the Intermarket Trading System (ITS) that links all of the nation's exchanges and the establishment of Instinet as a pioneer ECN and significant market force in the 1980s.

OptiMark aims to solve the problem of investors who want to buy or sell a large chunk of shares. This problem is that as soon as people in the market get wind that a big trade is under way, they adjust their prices to take advantage of it. So big buyers and sellers are often unable to trade at the market price. The subsequent deterioration of the actual price from the original market price can be as high as 3 percent of the trade—big money for a large block trade by a large portfolio manager. These block trades account for about 50 percent of the dollar trades on the exchanges.

Traditional exchanges try to minimize the leakage of information by breaking up the order into smaller chunks. But the experience is that the information still leaks and impacts price. OptiMark's solution is to combine online ordering with total anonymity and secrecy and to execute the order with lightning speed using a supercomputer. Investors enter into the computer what they want to buy or sell, and how much more than the prevailing market price they would be willing to pay or receive for various-sized lots of shares. They then rank these lots of shares in order of preference. The computer then finds the best available combination of price and quantity—which will often be at a better price than the investor specified—by matching up orders from other investors. The trade is completed automatically, and only then made public.

OptiMark could make floor traders redundant for big trades. OptiMark has received funding from a number of major financial institutions, including Goldman Sachs, Merrill Lynch, and Dow Jones, totaling more than $150 million.

How OptiMark Works

Figure 6.4 diagrams how the OptiMark system works within the overall IT infrastructure of the exchanges. First, investors enter their buy and sell orders in a form that represents their willingness to buy and sell a particu-

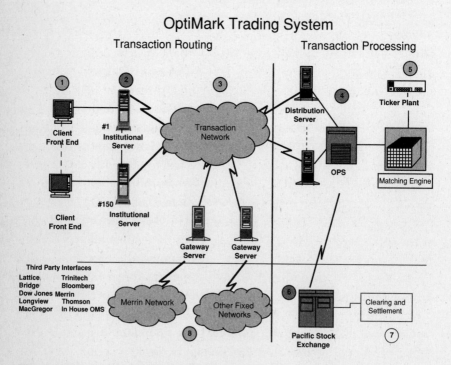

Figure 6.4 The OptiMark Trading Process

Source: "OptiMark: Launching a Virtual Securities Market," by John J. Sviokla and Research Associate Melissa Dailey, Harvard Business School case 9-399-005, published July 10, 1998, and revised August 24, 1998.

lar stock at various prices and quantities. OptiMark gains access to the ITS (Intermarket Trading System) through one of the major regional exchanges, the Pacific Exchange. The ITS electronically ties the seven major exchanges[15] together. The OptiMark supercomputer fires the order into the ITS system, which in turn routes the order to the exchanges. If there is a match, the OptiMark system instantly fires an electronic order to take the bid.

OptiMark reached an agreement with Nasdaq to integrate OptiMark's automated order matching system into the electronic stock market's trading network. Under the OptiMark/Nasdaq integration, broker-dealers act as agents for investors who want to route orders directly to OptiMark. While allowing individual and institutional investors to trade directly with each other, it is hoped that the OptiMark system will increase the market's liquidity and reduce trading costs for all Nasdaq participants.[16]

Issues and Competitive Responses

The NYSE viewed hooking up the OptiMark system through the Pacific Exchange to the Intermarket Trading System as a back-door entry into the buy and sell orders of the NYSE that threatened to inappropriately drain off volume. The other exchanges were worried, too. In June 1998, the American Stock Exchange, the Chicago Stock Exchange, the Boston Stock Exchange, the Philadelphia Stock Exchange, and the Chicago Board Options Exchange (CBOE) all joined with the NYSE in voting against a proposal that would have incorporated OptiMark into the ITS. However, an agreement was reached among OptiMark, the NYSE, and other exchanges that resulted in OptiMark trading its first stock in January 1999. After initially fighting against allowing OptiMark access to the shared ITS of the exchanges, the New York Stock Exchange (NYSE) responded to the competitive threat by announcing its own version of OptiMark technology for big trades, called Institutional Xpress.

OptiMark reached a peak of trading about 1.5 million shares a day, and began a slow decline. Entering the profiles by brokers seemed to be too complicated. Layoffs and low volume led to the demise of OptiMark as a viable ECN. However, OptiMark technologies have changed the economics and the structure of the market.

Other Challengers: eBay and Yahoo!

Dick Grasso, CEO of the NYSE, fears other unexpected challengers more than the familiar ones of Nasdaq, foreign exchanges, and ECNs. He claims that the NYSE will be challenged by e-commerce firms such as eBay or Yahoo! that have become experts at data mining and manipulation.[17] Thus, Grasso wants to regain ownership of its share-price data by withdrawing from the Consolidated Tape Association. He is also looking for new ways to make money out of other data that the NYSE collects, including its limit order book, which includes all uncompleted orders to buy or sell at a prespecified price and which is now available only to the floor specialists.[18]

Technology Changes Everything

The restructuring of the financial services industry depicts an industry restructuring in which there has been an overall industry investment in shared networking technology even before the advent of the Internet. The Consolidated Tape System and the Consolidated Quotation System are shared IT systems that new entrants like ECNs can tap into and become a change force almost overnight. Coupled with the Internet, the IT infrastructure provides a foundation for highly innovative new entrants like OptiMark to bring increasingly sophisticated technologies into the industry. While OptiMark was unable to survive as a viable ECN, its technology has been incorporated by the various players to provide more efficiency for the industry as a whole.

The competition between Merrill Lynch and Schwab is an excellent example of how a strong incumbent that has been a leader in the use of IT can be challenged by a new entrant. Schwab, built more recently from a greenfield site, has been able to rethink the role of physical branches and lead with a "clicks and bricks" strategy, moving ever so close to providing the same services as the full-service broker.

Stepping back from the specific competition of Merrill Lynch and Schwab, we can gain a broader perspective of the convergence of financial companies as they strive to provide full one-stop financial services to customers. We can also see a general trend toward a better understanding of data and the ability to capture the value of data resources in the emerging business models. This broader perspective is important to maintain as companies move from limited "make and sell" strategies to technology-enabled "sense and respond" strategies.

The next chapter examines how IBM overcame its case of dot vertigo and has emerged as a dominant player in the e-business world.

Key Concepts
- The Internet defies management understanding in terms of speed and capabilities.
- The more successful the executive, the more vulnerable to underestimating the impact of the Internet on the business.
- The dot-com phenomenon is only the first round of new Internet competition.

7

Overcoming Dot Vertigo

The Case of IBM

One of the most encouraging stories of overcoming dot vertigo is Lou Gerstner's; with his top management team he succeeded in transforming IBM.[1] In 1993, after most people had dismissed IBM's position as an industry juggernaut, the company looked outside the firm for a new CEO. Gerstner became the first CEO to be hired outside of IBM. John Akers, the previous CEO, had presided over IBM's first and largest losses, which between 1991 and 1993 were close to $3 billion—losses that were propelling IBM toward bankruptcy if not curbed. Prior to Gerstner's appointment, Akers was considering spinning off product units into independent, stand-alone businesses.

With no end in sight to IBM's losses, the board conducted a desperate search, contacting a number of potential CEOs to succeed Akers. The position seemed less than ideal to prospective candidates: IBM appeared too steadfast and set in its ways to undertake the transformation needed to jump-start earnings. Despite the condition of IBM at the time, and the reticence of his peers, Lou Gerstner accepted the job.

Gerstner's role in dramatically improving IBM's performance serves as an example to other leaders of incumbent firms who need to transform their companies, rather than merely making incremental strategic changes. The strategies and tactics spearheaded by Gerstner at IBM provide other executives with a road map for organizational transformation.

Prior to Gerstner joining the firm, IBM had plenty of people within the company as well as outside advisers telling them about the problems and what needed to be done. In 1986, my consulting firm, Nolan, Norton and Company, was commissioned by IBM to do a study on the changing economics of the computer industry. The study showed that the hardware business was commoditizing and that the services business was poised to expand dramatically with attractive margins. As a consultant, I was invited to meet with John Akers' top management team, to whom I presented benchmarks indicating IBM had more than twice the number of employees to produce the equivalent revenues of their competitors.

Healthy debate ensued, and I was left with the impression that the management team members were well versed on IBM's problems, but were uncertain just how to effectively turn the situation around.

Gerstner's Transformation

Upon his arrival, Gerstner made an immediate impression on the company's senior managers.[2]

Sense the Customer

As recalled by Bill Etherington, CEO of IBM Canada, Gerstner's involvement in a sales meeting shortly after coming to IBM demonstrated how things would change under the new CEO:

> We ran customer conferences for key CIOs, and in the spring of 1993 there was one in Virginia—Chantilly. I remember this like yesterday. We agonized about "Should we invite Lou?" because nobody knew Lou then. "He's busy," we thought. Finally we said, "We should invite him." The invitation that went to his office was, "Lou, we want you to come and speak to our customers but it's only going to take an hour. You'll be back in your office by 10 o'clock in the morning." He asked a couple of questions. He said, "Who's there?" "About 300 CIOs in North America. Big banks, General Motors, that kind of thing." "Well," he said, "shouldn't I stay and have lunch with

them?" "No, no—execs don't stay," we said. He said, "I don't under-stand. These are your best customers." So he said, and I remember this: "I'm going to the whole conference. I'll be there the first night. I'll have dinner with them. I'll have breakfast with them. I'll have lunch with them. And any IBM executive who wants to attend must stay for the whole two days." We were all erasing our calendars, say-ing, "I was always going to be there two days."

He'd only been in the company for a short time and he gets up and speaks. And it was a speech like we'd never heard from an IBM executive. He opened into dialogue with them and he started to single IBM executives out. "This executive will fix that and get back to you this afternoon." It was unheard of—"The CEO's siding with the customers!"

When we originally framed it as only an hour and then you're back on the plane, we were thinking that's going to get him there more likely. Lou turned the thing way upside down—the most im-portant thing a CEO does, or any executive in this company does, is meet with customers. That was like a rocket through the company.

Gerstner's no-nonsense focus on bottom-line business issues also made an impression, as evidenced by Etherington's account of their first one-on-one meeting.

I rehearsed my time with him. I'd tell him the history of IBM Canada, my career history, how anxious I was to do well. Lou gets in the car, says to the driver: "Too hot." The driver turned up the air conditioner and Lou turned to me and said, "What the hell hap-pened in the 2Q?" Because I've just missed my forecast. Way down in my briefing I was planning to casually mention that we were a lit-tle short of profit. He went right to that. For the whole hour in the car, which couldn't go fast enough, he quizzed me on business—didn't want to know about the economy, didn't want to know about the geography in Canada—just wanted to know about the business.

Incentivize and Lead the People

When he arrived, Gerstner knew IBM competitors were drawing up lists of key employees to hire away from the company. Having experienced a costly flight of personnel when he took over RJR Nabisco, he very quickly went to the board for approval of changes to the company's stock plan. The changes allowed senior employees whose options were "under water" (the current market value of the IBM stock was less than what the stock options could be exercised for) to exchange them for a smaller number that were not. The new options included vesting and other conditions designed to keep people from leaving. Omitted from the repricing scheme were the 23 most senior executives. The repricing action was widely interpreted as a signal that the new CEO was willing to pay for performance, but that the collegiality that had protected the seniormost executives under the old regime would not continue. As one executive put it, "Lou is plenty collegial, but it's clear that has nothing to do with the business."

Gerstner engaged in a variety of activities to get himself up to speed on IBM's business as quickly as possible. He asked each of the senior executives to write two papers, one on the executive's business and another on what the executive thought ought to be done to turn around the company. After receiving and reviewing the papers, Gerstner spent a day with each executive talking about the business, using the papers as a starting point. At the same time, he was visiting industry leaders and customers. Through these activities, Gerstner quickly achieved internal, industry, and customer views on how the company was doing.

Some of the things he was learning on his visits alarmed him. He saw disconnection between research and the market. He was distressed by a lack of sophisticated marketing techniques, and lack of a public relations (PR) policy. He resolved to make IBM think more like a marketing company. Most disturbing, he saw slippage in what had been traditionally a great strength and differentiating factor in the very sales-oriented company: managing relationships with customers. Customers appreciated the investment IBM was willing to make in relationships and recognized this as a contrast with most other technically oriented companies; but in recent years customers had been too often frustrated by how the relationship with IBM was actually going.

As Gerstner traveled to different company sites, he met with employees to explain his approach, saying, "I hope you understand what I'm trying to do with this company." He wrote frequent notes to be distributed to all employees. One executive noted the direct nature of communication from CEO to employees: "We had no idea when he was going to send them; we got them when everybody else got them."

Respond to the Customer

Gerstner's visits outside IBM were leading him to second thoughts about the plans already in motion to break IBM into pieces. Gerstner summarized the message he was hearing from customers:

> They said repeatedly, "We don't need one more disk drive company, we don't need one more database company, we don't need one more UNIX server company. The one thing that you guys do that no one else can do is help us integrate and create solutions." They also saw the global nature of the company. It wasn't just product integration and solutions. It was as much "I use you guys all over the world."

This message was consistent with Gerstner's own experiences as an IBM customer, as Etherington explained:

> He [Gerstner] tells a story about being at RJR and trying to automate his manufacturing. He called McKinsey in and they said he was going to save $40 million. He said, "Great, let's implement." The CIO said, "Can't do that yet. We've got to get Andersen in to do the deployment strategy." So Andersen [now known as Accenture] came in and he paid them a couple million more bucks. "Can I implement it?" "No. Now we've got to bring IBM in to figure out what technology we need to do the deployment." He said, "This is bizarre. Why can't I just talk to one company?"

Gerstner concluded that the ability to integrate and deliver global solutions was a special quality of IBM; it was a big reason companies turned to IBM, and it was something that customers wanted more of, not less. In the summer of 1993, he called his team together to announce that he had decided against the breakup.

"Going to market as one IBM" became a centerpiece of the turnaround program. Gerstner, writing from his kitchen table, set out the following eight principles derived from the idea of doing business as one company.

- The marketplace is the driving force behind everything that we do.
- At our core, we are a technology company with an overriding commitment to quality.
- Our primary measures of success are customer satisfaction and shareholder value.
- We operate as an entrepreneurial organization with a minimum of bureaucracy and never-ending focus on productivity.
- We never lose sight of our strategic vision.
- We think and act with a sense of urgency.
- Outstanding, dedicated people make it all happen, particularly when they work together as a team.
- We are sensitive to the needs of all employees and to the communities in which we operate.

The simply worded principles emphasized integration, cost reduction, a return to the customer, and a faster moving organization. They made no attempt to incorporate the historical "basic beliefs" of the company; this omission, along with stylistic differences from pre-Gerstner corporate statements, created a minor sensation among employees. Etherington explained why the statements seemed like such a break from the past:

> Normally, when this sort of thing would come out in IBM, it'd be very structured. We'd have goals, then beliefs, and from those we'd derive a statement—but these were just principles. It wasn't systematized, it was just a statement.

From that point in time the idea of going to market as one IBM would be the driving impetus behind all programmatic action. It would be the basis for organizational alignments and a more global, process-centric perspective on the company's operations and management systems.

Streamline the Back Office

IBM had a back-office applications portfolio of legacy systems that seriously encumbered its ability to implement different ways of doing business. Gerstner initiated a streamlining program consisting of reengineering IBM business processes, reducing reliance on staff analyses, cutting costs, and simplifying the organization.

Reengineering

In the fall of 1993, Gerstner gathered seven of his most senior managers and assigned to them eight reengineering projects. Their priorities were first to get cost out as quickly as possible, and second to "clean sheet" the process and redesign it for global use so that cost reductions could be sustained. These projects would achieve their cost savings at a rate that surprised even insiders, but the effort to redesign processes for sustainability was a long-term one (some redesign would continue over several years). It was made clear to these line executives that they were charged with making sizable and sustainable improvements in their assigned processes. Resulting processes were to be globally common and were to span the boundaries of the historical organization, in keeping with the notion of integrating the company's divisions into one IBM.

Less Reliance on Staff

Gerstner's instructions to executives also signaled changes in the company's style of management. No longer would unwieldy committees in Armonk hold important decisions hostage. Line executives were to make the important decisions themselves and they would be held unambiguously accountable for the results. Executives were to write their own papers and give their own presentations in meetings, and not rely on staff members. The practice of always using overhead projectors would end (projectors were physically removed from office furniture).

Cost Reduction

At the end of April, Jerry York, a former Chrysler CFO, was hired to lead the cost-cutting charge. York made an acerbic splash amid the civilized culture of IBM's financial staff. In a company where navy suits and starched white shirts had been the norm, he was not above coming to Saturday morning meetings in a Harley-Davidson T-shirt with a cigarette pack rolled up in the sleeve. One senior manager described him as "the pit bull who came to sell everything and not approve anything."

York launched a benchmarking study; consultants where hired to determine how IBM's costs in each of its businesses compared with costs of other companies in those businesses. The results of the study portrayed a daunting challenge. The ratio of expense to revenue, currently 42 percent, needed to be reduced by 9 percent. The combination of SG&A and R&D needed to be reduced from $26.8 billion to $20 billion. Overall, the company was too expensive by at least $7 billion. York's staff presented him with scenarios for achieving the reductions; he rejected all of these, advocating instead "taking the whole pill at once."

Layoffs numbering 40,000 to 50,000 had been approved early in 1993. Now the management team decided that another 35,000 would be asked to leave. Unlike earlier cuts, these would not be in any sense voluntary, and severance packages were not as generous as they had been in the past. Gerstner encouraged his team to accept that permanent employment had ended in 1991 and move on. The new approach to layoffs held that one swing of the scythe was preferable to the slow and traumatic reductions of the past. In total numbers of jobs, the post-Gerstner reductions were smaller than those that had come before—but they came in bigger slices. To pay for the reductions, there would be another charge against income, this one nearly $9 billion.

York pushed relentlessly for cost reduction. He all but killed a Byzantine transfer pricing system that led IBM divisions to expend effort on internal negotiations and accounting games, and that made it difficult to ascertain divisional performance. He sold off some noncore businesses, including the Federal Systems Company, for $1.58 billion. York's cost-cutting vehemence gave other senior executives hope that enough cost could be removed without breaking up the company.

Organizational Simplification

Gerstner reorganized the company into one global organization. He pulled divisions together into groups and formed the Corporate Executive

Committee (CEC), about a dozen senior executives who would meet every two weeks to focus on strategy. Another group, called the Worldwide Management Council (WMC), would be composed of the top 35 people including geographic leaders and also division presidents, and would meet quarterly. At this time, also, a new performance evaluation system was introduced that emphasized execution and relied on a forced curve.

In the winter of 1994 attention turned to the sales organization. One of the complaints Gerstner had heard on his customer visits was that salespeople lacked product knowledge. Because the sales organization was based entirely on geography, salespeople were generalists focused around accounts rather than products. This meant that a salesperson selling a product that was not in the individual's area of expertise needed to rely on a support organization for help in preparing bids. The entire process was cumbersome. Consequently, bid preparation at IBM took much longer than at competitor companies.

To address these problems, senior IBM managers took dramatic action. They globalized the sales organization that had been based on geographic segments. No longer were country sales organizations near-sovereign entities operating in a decentralized manner. In addition, IBM split the sales organization into two kinds of workforces: customer relationship managers and product specialists. The product specialists actually reported in to product groups but were integrated into the sales and distribution organization. Where the old IBM organizational matrix was aligned to products, industries, and geographies, the new matrix was aligned to products, industries, and global processes.

Even the board of directors did not escape restructuring. Around this time the board was reduced in size by a third as some members departed, and there were several new additions: Charles F. Knight of Emerson Electric; Alex Trotman, Ford CEO; and Cathleen Black, head of Hearst Magazines. Figure 7.1 reflects IBM's organizational structure in February 1993 at Gerstner's arrival, and Figure 7.2 indicates the simplified organizational structure that took hold in November 1994.

As a result of all of this activity, for the fourth quarter of 1993 IBM posted a small gain of $382 million. A similarly sized gain followed in the first quarter of 1994 ($392 million). IBM's stock continued to move up

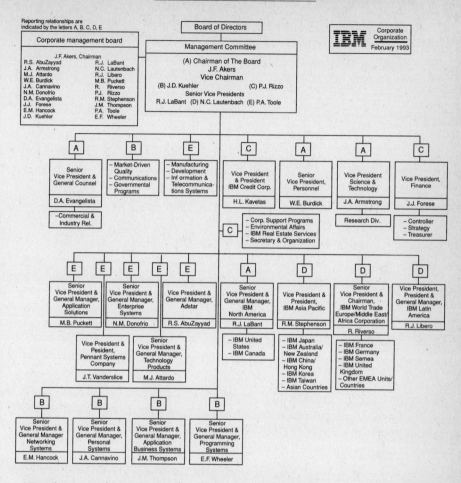

Figure 7.1 IBM's Organization Chart, February 1993
Source: Reprinted with permission from IBM.

from its low of $10 per share when Lou Gerstner took over as CEO to as high as $140 in 1999.

Managing Resistance to Change

The reorganizations were not welcomed by all at IBM. In particular, the managers who had once run IBM's country organizations perceived both a loss of control and a loss of ability to meet the supposedly idiosyncratic

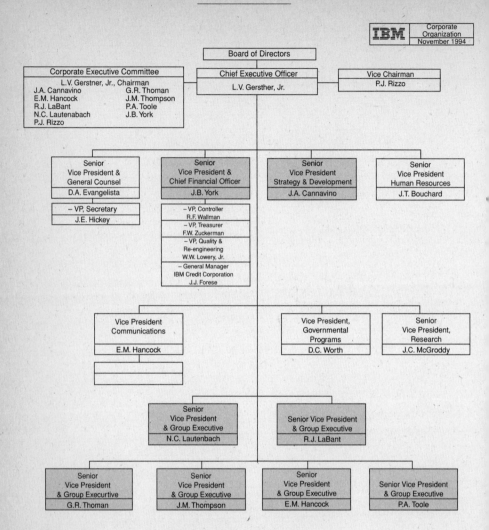

Figure 7.2 IBM's Organization Chart, November 1994
Source: Reprinted with permission from IBM.

needs of particular national markets. These managers believed that global managers could not be relied upon to make the right choices for local markets, that initiatives and instructions from IBM corporate needed to be customized for particular countries. The differences came to a head when Gerstner found that his notes to employees were being rewritten in Europe to better fit the European environment. The senior executive who had been running European operations was fired. Country managers left rapidly thereafter.

The problem of managers resisting changes was a general one. Bruce Harreld (senior vice president–strategy) described how resistance manifested itself:

At the top of the organization was a leadership team that really wanted to speed things up. The customer-facing parts of the organization felt that the changes were the right thing to do. But there was a group of people in the middle that didn't want to have anything to do with it. They just wanted it to go away. They wanted it to be the way it used to always be.

Some silent resisters lingered within the company, hoping for another coup. But over time most adjusted or departed. For Gerstner, some resistance was to be expected given the magnitude of what IBM was attempting. Overall, he was impressed by employees' capacity to absorb change. Lou Gerstner:

We changed almost everything in this company, literally, in three months, eight months, a couple of years. To me it's a credit to the inherent strength of the people who were in IBM that so many of them were able to make the transition. It's one of the most remarkable things that happened.

Gerstner's "Biggest Dot.Com" Strategy

Historically, IBM had played and dominated in virtually all segments of the information technology market. Questions remained about whether the company could adjust to a technological landscape in which it did not control standards and did not enjoy across-the-board market dominance.

New Product Strategy

Despite occasional appearances of recovery, the PC company continued to be a problem. IBM had changed a lot, but the PC business, with its thin margins and ferocious rate of new product introduction, was almost the opposite of the high-margin mainframe business that was IBM's historical forte. The company struggled to get its institutional responses in sync with the market. But criticisms of IBM during this time almost always began with the travails of the PC company.

A potential remedy that was seriously considered in 1994 was a purchase of Apple Computer. The combination of the companies seemed to make sense; Apple would contribute its renegade culture, small company agility, and the innovative Mac operating system; IBM would get Apple back into the business computing game. Discussions became very serious but the deal fell through when executives from the two companies failed to agree on a purchase price.

Without the Mac operating system, IBM was left with OS/2, a strong technical offering that was rapidly losing in the marketplace to Microsoft's Windows operating system. The PC company and operating system difficulties, together with the emergence in 1994 and 1995 of the Internet, led to rethinking of product strategy. Gerstner asked his senior team in early 1995 to begin focusing on a new vision. Etherington described how discussions went:

Client/server was coming to an end; there was something else happening. For a long time, we studied it. Lou kept saying, "Go to the market and talk to the customers." Somewhere in September of 1995, in a matter of 30 days, I can't even think of how it happened, but somehow we started to look at the Internet and say, "There's something here."

At about this same time, executives were deciding what to do with OS/2, which was losing substantial amounts of money for the company. The two agendas coalesced into a conclusion, reported here by Etherington:

We came out with this strategy that says, "Face it. The desktop war is over." We made a decision that our party was at the server level. We had a browser product to compete with Netscape, but we stopped that too.

At the computer industry's biggest trade show (COMDEX) in October 1995, Gerstner presented a new server- and network-based vision,

calling it "network-centric computing." The phrase was somewhat am-
biguous in meaning at this stage and it tested badly in focus groups, but
it met its intended purpose, becoming the battle cry for a new, more focused product strategy.

Also about this time, IBM decided not to give up on the mainframe as a
source of revenues and growth. Gerstner explained:

> We recommitted ourselves to the mainframe and reaffirmed the
> value of the mainframe. The company was on its way to believing
> the press and saying "mainframes are dead." We rescued the main-
> frame. That was a very important strategic decision. We decided
> not to rescue OS/2. We decided not to reinvest in competing with
> Intel in chips [manufacturing].

In mid-1994, IBM's services business hit its $10 billion revenue target
for 1995, a full 18 months ahead of schedule. But services were the only
segment of the company's business that was growing aggressively. The
hardware business was relatively stagnant, although the mainframe business had recovered somewhat from its early 1990s weakness. Consistent
with the company's new network-centric orientation, server software
emerged as another potential high-growth business. Gerstner asked John
Thompson (senior vice president and group executive—software) to look
into how to make this happen.

Thompson agreed that the company could grow the businesses in distributed computing software and in middleware, which provides the infrastructure for major functionality that resides between desktops and
enterprise computing platforms (such as mainframes or large servers). But
he identified two areas in which current offerings available within IBM
were not likely to be competitive anytime soon: collaborative messaging
and software management. The strategy for filling these two holes turned
quickly to talk of acquisitions.

Lotus Development Corporation was an obvious potential target in the
collaborative messaging space. The company had two major product categories, desktop applications software (e.g., word processing, spread-
sheets, etc.) that competed with offerings from Microsoft and Novell,
and, most importantly, Lotus Notes, an advanced technology for com-
puter-supported work collaboration. Because it was faring badly in the

desktop battle against Microsoft, Lotus's stock price was down to less than half its historic high, making it a tempting target. After proposing a friendly acquisition and being rebuffed, Gerstner and his team rapidly translated the friendly takeover offer into a hostile one. In June, the deal was consummated for a price of $3.5 billion.[3] The uncharacteristic (for IBM) speed with which the company moved on its target was not lost on observers. Some people were beginning to concede that this really was a new IBM.

Financial results for 1995 established that IBM's recovery was real. Profits increased to $4.2 billion on revenues of about $72 billion. Gerstner believed he saw a new IBM with new strategies and improving prospects:

> There was a product strategy related to networks, a product strategy related to hardware, then we built a software product strategy [in part through the Lotus acquisition] to build a major software business. There was a strategy to build a gigantic services business. We were deciding what to keep of the old IBM and what to build in the new IBM. Most of the pieces were in place.

Network-Centric Strategy

Gerstner's network-centric strategy has matured into IBM's e-business strategy. It is clear that Gerstner recognizes the importance of the Internet in the information age, and he has realigned IBM to execute an Internet-based product strategy with the same strong leadership and fervor characterizing his turnaround of IBM.

In Gerstner's May 1999 annual meeting with Wall Street analysts, he presented IBM as, in *Business Week*'s phrase, "the biggest dot.com."[4] IBM generated more revenue than the top 25 dot-com companies. The top 25 dot-com companies combined generated about $5 billion in revenue while incurring $1 billion in losses, compared to IBM's generation of more than $20 billion in profitable e-business revenue. Further, IBM's more than 100,000 Global Services consultants generate more than $20 billion in revenue, which is more than three times Accenture's revenue.

While most companies offering dot-com consulting services have been focusing on getting companies onto the Web, Gerstner saw the lucrative opportunities to assist companies in executing transactions on the Internet.[5] Accordingly, Gerstner allocated 25 percent of IBM's R&D budget for Internet projects.

Gerstner's realignment to the e-business strategy involves both adding the "e" to its product strategy and adding the "e" to its internal operations.

IBM's e-business product strategy:

- E-Services—consulting services.
- E-Engineering—reengineering business processes services.
- E-Outsourcing—outsourcing of operations, applications development, and ASP (application service provider) services.

e-IBM:

- e-Care—self-service for customers using IBM's I-Net.
- e-Commerce—selling and delivering IBM products and services using IBM's I-Net.
- e-Learning—delivering both internal and customer training using IBM's I-Net.
- e-Procurement—buying goods and services using IBM's I-Net.

IBM's traditional customer base is made up of large traditional companies on the brink of making major investments in building I-Nets. These investments are running in the hundreds of millions of dollars for each of the companies. IBM's transformation has made IBM a viable player to win this business. Gerstner's e-business strategy is projecting IBM as a major contender in the area.

Going Forward

The IBM transformation has been remarkable. At the start, most people felt there were impossible odds against pulling it off. Gerstner and his management team defied the odds. A close examination of the turnaround reveals focus and an extremely effective execution. The IBM turnaround process provides not only hope for traditional companies but also a rough map of how to do it. It is unfortunate that IBM had to begin to go down a road of bankruptcy before Gerstner was brought in to mobilize the company for the turnaround. Impending bankruptcy tends to get the company motivated for change. Hopefully the hundreds of traditional companies will be able to learn from IBM and begin transformation without having to face the threat of impending bankruptcy.

While the IBM turnaround was extremely impressive, it is not the most important story. The most important story is the way Gerstner has built on the foundation of a viable IBM and created a business strategy to restore IBM to industry leadership in the information age. IBM's stock (and market value) hit its high in mid-1999 when the turnaround had been assured. Since then IBM has been going beyond the turnaround to execute its new e-business strategy. Uncertainty can be seen in the behavior of its stock price since then, and as Lou Gerstner says, it is now all in the execution of the strategy.

In Lou Gerstner's words:

Okay, so we're going to keep this company together. The customers wanted that, they told us that. And it made a lot of strategic sense. There were thousands of companies that could do little pieces. But there was only one IBM. There was no other company that could put it all together. That's all fine.

But how do you manage that kind of company? How do you lead that kind of company? We know what our strategy is. But how do you execute that strategy in an $80 billion company going through explosive growth? So it is the execution of this "we are a single company" idea that has been the challenge, from a strategic point of view, from a process point of view, from a culture point of view, and from a systems point of view. That's the real issue.

IBM's 2000 annual report is organized into chapters, and discusses Gerstner's turnaround approach almost in the form of a novel:

Chapter 1: Reports of Our Demise: Feisty Comebacks in Servers, Storage, and Databases
Chapter 2: The Leader's Dilemma: Managing Success, Growth, and Expansion in Services, Software, and Semiconductors
Chapter 3: The Plot Thickens: Changing the Game through Linux and e-Sourcing

IBM's annual report is refreshing in capturing the challenges and the richness of innovation required to manage a complex company into the information age.

Key Concepts

- It takes an outsider to see the forest, not just the trees, and to mobilize the organization to see the same thing.
- High costs challenge viability, and must be halved in short order.
- Customer sensing and responding is key, and it is a long haul for the transformation of the industrial age company.

8

What Keeps Drugstore.com in the Game

Part of the dot vertigo experienced by incumbent managers is due to the fact that the dot-com business model is so different from traditional business models. While the most obvious difference between the two is the role of the Internet, there are other differentiating factors that lie deep within the company's infrastructure and culture. Our in-depth case analysis of Redmond, Washington–based drugstore.com highlights the differences by analyzing the anatomy of a dot-com business model and its pattern of execution.[1]

We tracked drugstore.com from its conception to its emergence as a serious industry challenger as the leading online drugstore. Typical of most industries being restructured in the information age, the retail drug industry is not very high-tech, nor is it an industry based solely on providing one service, as physical products have to be manufactured, ordered, and shipped to customers.

Creating a Dot-Com Business Model

The stories of venture capitalists throwing money at dot-com entrepreneurs are, in fact, urban legends. Stories of these venture capitalists, characterized as "venture vultures" or "vulture capitalists," supposedly intent on making a killing, might hold an inkling of truth. However, my experience has been exactly the opposite in most situations.

Indeed, most dot-com entrepreneurs are young. However, I find them much more savvy as information age entrepreneurs than most experienced executives. Unlike many experienced managers, these entrepreneurs have grown up in the information age where the Internet is as familiar as TV is to baby boomers.

Drugstore.com's founder, Jed Smith, is a typical dot-com entrepreneur. After college he worked in Silicon Valley with Oracle Corporation and then with Tribe Computer Works. While a student at the Harvard Business School, Smith conceived CyberSmith, a store devoted to providing an affordable computer experience.[2] He founded the business with his father during his second year at HBS, and opened the first store upon graduating in the spring of 1995. Smith formally left CyberSmith in January 1998. During the fall of 1997, he began thinking about more mainstream opportunities in e-commerce, and developed a list of products that he believed to be uniquely marketable over the Internet. This list was similar to the now famous list of 20 products marketable over the Internet developed by Jeffrey Bezos, founder and CEO of Amazon.com. Smith continued to explore business concepts with Dave Whorton, whom he had met while working in Silicon Valley and who was now an associate at the venture capital firm Kleiner, Perkins, Caufield & Byers (KPCB). Whorton, who was as enthused as Smith about the idea of a drugstore, became his advocate at KPCB. In November 1997, Whorton introduced Smith to John Doerr, who directed him to Russ Siegleman. After listening to Smith's presentation, Siegleman, a partner at KPCB, steered Smith toward a "personal bathroom valet"[3] business concept. Siegleman suggested that the Internet could keep track of the personal drugstore items that a customer uses and develop an automatic facility to remind him or her when an item was running low and needed reordering. Will Hearst, another Kleiner partner, reinforced the importance of health content and information services. The idea of an Internet drugstore took form.

Smith completed the first draft of a business plan in December 1997 and presented it to John Doerr in January 1998. The KPCB partnership expressed interest but did not immediately offer to fund the project.

More work was required to develop the customer value proposition and business model.

After Doerr talked with the president of a major drugstore retail chain who was concerned about a competitive Internet entrant, Doerr called Smith. Two days later Smith met with Doerr and Bezos, whose company Amazon.com was funded by KPCB and was interested in becoming an investor in a similarly funded Internet-based drugstore. There seemed to be synergy between the business models of Amazon.com and drugstore.com, and opportunities for a strategic alliance between the two.

Brook Byers, KPCB senior partner responsible for health-care ventures, introduced Smith to health-care industry leaders, with whom he further developed how prescription drugs could be sold over the Internet. KPCB asked Smith to continue developing his business plan and agreed to seed funding.

Finally, KPCB partners approved the drugstore.com plan on June 4, 1998, and first-round financing was completed. Further discussions with Bezos led to a significant partnership with Amazon.com, increased participation in drugstore.com's funding, and a seat on the board of directors for Bezos.

Smith's final business model was to build a virtual drugstore on the Internet that would provide both prescription and nonprescription health and beauty aid products. Compared to about 3,000 in a typical bricks-and-mortar drugstore, the number of drugstore.com's SKUs would be 17,000 initially and then later would be increased to 100,000. Fulfillment would be controlled by drugstore.com, but executed by distribution centers arranged through outsourcing agreements. United Parcel Service (UPS) and other overnight delivery companies would be used to ship products to customers.

Information would be exploited to track customer buying patterns and configure the virtual drugstore to individual customers. Also, information about drugs, prices, adverse side effects, and diseases would be heavily analyzed and made available to customers to empower them while purchasing drugs. Automatic alerts would be e-mailed to drugstore.com customers upon discovery of information about negative drug side effects or unintended interactions.

Once the online ordering of drugs was better understood through experience, a secondary stock issue would be used to finance specially designed in-house distribution centers to enable high-tech picking and fulfillment of individual customer orders. Most existing distribution centers had been designed to distribute consolidated orders for inventory to physical drugstores where break bulk and shelf stocking were done. (Bulky cases were received from the distribution centers by the individual drugstores, and then the individual products were unpacked from the boxes and put on the store shelves.)

Recruiting the Drugstore.com Team

Another misconception about the dot-com business models is that they are flawed by not including experienced industry management at the outset. There are good reasons why these teams do not include industry-experienced managers. First, they are entering a new industry as an information age company— for drugstore.com they were building a virtual drugstore. They wanted a team that knew how to build in the virtual space, not one that simply knew how to build a physical space. Second, they put a high value on innovation in creating the virtual store on the Internet. Nothing dampens innovation faster than someone who says, "That won't work; we tried that before." Third, the whole rapid development approach is foreign to traditional managers. The rapid development approach is to get something out in the marketplace expediently that will work, learn from your customers, and then continue building with real customers' needs in mind.

With the assistance of John Doerr, in June 1998 the hiring of top management went into high gear. The search for a world-class CEO led to Peter Neupert.[4] The 42-year-old Microsoft senior executive (who had built the Microsoft Windows operating system into a powerhouse in Japan and successfully managed the development of high-profile media projects such as MSNBC and *Slate* magazine) was named CEO of drugstore.com in the summer of 1998.

Neupert assembled a skeleton team for drugstore.com in his garage, which although not air-conditioned did have high-speed ISDN (Integrated Services Digital Network) lines and mail servers.[5] With a business vision, funding, and a CEO, drugstore.com further ramped up recruiting and mobilized to build a virtual drugstore.

Peter Neupert (CEO):

From day one, I knew my number one challenge was getting good people. My wife was director of recruiting at Microsoft for 10 years, so I have been well schooled on the importance of getting good people and how it is done.

John Doerr in his efforts to really get the company going had been recruiting a CIO. The one that they were recruiting decided not to come, but they introduced me to Kal Raman. Kal was familiar with my work at Microsoft, and the chemistry was right; Kal's raw talent was apparent to me.

On his first day of work at drugstore.com on August 24, 1998, Kal Raman, vice president and CIO, brought the company's total employment to 12. In addition to Neupert and three VPs (Jed Smith, VP Strategic Partnerships; Susan Fine DelBene, VP Marketing and Store Development; and David Rostov, VP and CFO), Sean Nolan had been hired as director of development. In turn, Sean hired three technical developers, plus a college student who installed the computer network in the garage.

Peter Neupert:

Susan [Fine DelBene] had joined my Interactive Media team at Microsoft. When she raised her hand, I said yes. Susan knows how to do Internet deals. She's very disciplined from a marketing perspective; and she understands and can relate to the pharmaceutical business.

Russ [Siegleman] helped me get key talent to build the web site. Sean [Nolan] was a fantastic hire. Russ had worked with Sean at Microsoft. Sean brought half of his old team. And that's the way it works. Good people like to work with other good people; and good people know who the good people are.

We've hired 40 pharmacists in a very competitive market. I think that they came here in part because we're willing to change the rules of the game. So it's not only the equity opportunities, but also the fact that we will push new standards.

Another important component of the team was the board of directors. Kleiner, the venture capitalist for drugstore.com, had two active board members. In addition, active investors on the board included the CEO of Amazon.com and CEO of Starbucks.

drugstore.com Board of Directors

Member Name	Title and Affiliation	Age
Peter Neupert	Chairman of the Board; president and CEO	43
Jeffrey Bezos	Director; founder and CEO of Amazon.com	35
Brook Byers	Director; partner of Kleiner, Perkins, Caufield & Byers	54
L. John Doerr	Director; partner of Kleiner, Perkins, Caufield & Byers	48
Melinda Gates	Director	35
Mary Sammons	Director; president and COO of Rite Aid	53
William Savoy	Director; president of Vulcan Northwest, Inc.	35
Howard Schultz	Director; founder and CEO of Starbucks	46

By the end of the summer of 1998, the team was in place that had the capabilities to build a major information age industry challenger.

Building the Virtual Drugstore

After recruiting the key talent, the next order of business was to build the virtual drugstore.

Sean Nolan (director of development):

The data model and data structure began to be the unifying piece that brought things together. One of our big key decisions was to have two complete representations of our data: one for the front end and one for the back end. The front-end web site needed to be extremely fast and flexible. The back-end technology needed to be extremely efficient in purchasing, inventory tracking, and order processing. The back-end system needed to be tuned to a point where we could run like Wal-Mart or Kmart in an environment with very thin margins.

We built pipelines to connect the front end and the back end. We worked hard to tightly integrate the two systems so that we did not end up with two independent systems that happen to share the same floor space.

Kal Raman (CIO):

By mid-November, we defined the dichotomy of the front office and the back office. People that I hired for the back office came from retailing systems backgrounds. The back office staff numbered 18. The front office dev team numbered 7. By November 15, we had the technical systems so that the buyers could now determine the items that they wanted to stock in the store. There are about 17,000 SKUs in our store, and it could go as high as 100,000. In the pharmacy, prescriptions come from about 3,500 units of medicine called NDCs (after the National Dispensing Committee), which is a numbering system like the Universal Product Code (UPC). However, 90 percent of the prescriptions are made up from about 200 NDCs.

On November 15, we prototyped how we wanted the store to look on the Web. Then on December 15 we stocked the shelves, and began operating the drugstore.

Sean Nolan:

We take 24-hour out-of-stock data from our back-office systems and pass it through the pipelines to the web site where we can show live out-of-stock conditions to the customers. We probably couldn't have done this if we were entirely on the front-end technology. The synchronization and the transaction load would paralyze the cycles we need to take orders and serve customers.

Our architecture investments have given us a great deal of important flexibility. For example, we recently put up a whole new beauty store boutique in our store to become more brand oriented than product oriented. My team was able to respond to this major change in a week using HTML [Hypertext Markup Language] resources as opposed to having to develop from scratch. It's really cool.

Kal Raman:

On January 28, we begin to pilot the pharmacy part of the drugstore. On February 24, 1999, we are up and running live selling both over-the-counter drugstore items and prescriptions.

Built Fast and Highly Focused

Dot companies like drugstore.com can be up and running faster than anything that we have previously seen in business. Like Peter Neupert of drugstore.com, their CEOs are Internet savvy and very focused.

Peter Neupert (March 17, 1999):

> I want to win in this $150 billion category of retail drugs. My business model is to be an online drugstore. Focus has never been a problem for me.

By the time of its IPO fewer than 12 months later, drugstore.com had grown from 12 to over 300 employees—including more than 40 licensed pharmacists.

In short, the team had built a virtual drugstore on the Web. During the first six months of its existence more than 160,000 customers shopped for more than 17,000 different drugstore products and prescription drugs. Customer orders were electronically sent to distribution centers run by Walsh Distribution and RxAmerica, both located in Texas. Drugstore.com had entered into outsourcing agreements/partnerships for fulfilling the orders with these two firms.

Walsh Distribution received and packaged for shipment all drugstore.com's customer orders, including inventory purchased directly by drugstore.com from other vendors, which was held at the Walsh facility. Drugstore.com staffed its own customer care specialists at the Walsh facility to monitor quality control and order fulfillment. A clinical staff of pharmacists worked out of Redmond providing drugstore.com's "Ask Your Pharmacist" services.

Drugstore.com purchased all of its pharmaceutical products from Rx-America, a joint venture owned by American Stores Company (which was subsequently acquired by Albertson's, Inc.) and Longs Drug Stores Corp. In a July 1999 prospectus, drugstore.com management disclosed that they were planning to establish the firm's own distribution center over the next 12 months "to achieve greater control over the distribution process and to ensure adequate supplies of products to our customers."[6] In 2000, the first drugstore.com distribution center was built specifically to fulfill individual customer orders.

Drugstore.com pharmacists performed all aspects of the prescription fulfillment process and customer service. Drugstore.com shipped anywhere in the United States that was served by United Parcel Service or the U.S. Postal Service. Nonprescription product orders received before 9:00 P.M. central time Monday through Friday or before 5:00 P.M. central time on Saturday were shipped the same day. For prescription orders, the product was shipped as soon as the prescription had been verified and drugstore.com pharmacists had completed the drug utilization review.

Agile and Quick-Reacting Management

Dot-com management teams stand in contrast to more traditional management teams by their fundamental approach to the management tasks. The ethic is to keep forward momentum; don't worry about getting it perfect the first time. Take action, and then make it work. This approach can be seen in how the drugstore.com management team incurred a serious problem in drug purchase payments.

Pharmaceutical benefits managers (PBMs) covered 80 percent of the U.S. population that had insurance coverage. Initially, the online drugstores slipped into the PBM networks by simply filling out the paperwork required for the contracts. Soon, however, the PBMs began canceling the contracts with the online drugstores. This meant that insured individuals (i.e., almost everyone purchasing drugs) were required to pay prescription costs in full if they were to buy from an online drugstore like drugstore.com, and then submit the paperwork themselves to their insurers for reimbursement. This was a huge deterrent for customers wanting to do business with drugstore.com.

Neupert and his management team quickly reacted to the reimbursement problem. Informal discussions with Rite Aid, an incumbent and competitor, turned into serious negotiations. On June 22, 1999, drugstore.com sold Rite Aid 25.3 percent of its stock for $7.6 million (and other consideration valued at $200 million), and sold another 8 percent for $2.4 million to GNC (General Nutritional Corporation), a Rite Aid partner that sold vitamins and nutritional supplements. The CEO of Rite Aid was also given a seat on drugstore.com's board.

Rite Aid made drugstore.com the online drugstore of choice for PCS, its pharmaceutical benefits manager division that served 50 million people whose prescription drugs were covered by corporate health plans. As Jed Smith (vice president—strategic partnerships) explained, this solved drugstore.com's reimbursement problem.

The Rite Aid deal got us access to not only the more than 50 million covered lives of PCS, but also almost all the covered lives of other PBMs in the country. Rite Aid has contracts with most of the insurance plans in the country to fill prescriptions, as do the other major chains. If Merck-Medco, for example, decided to cancel PCS's contract, Rite Aid could retaliate by canceling Medco's contract. Canceling the reciprocal contract is rather unlikely in that overall customer service would be severely impacted in a negative way.

Peter Neupert (CEO):

Rite Aid knew they wanted to have an Internet play. They were on a path to do it themselves and I think they figured out that doing it themselves was just going to kill their P&L, and challenge their organization. I think they came to the conclusion that they were just better off partnering. Then the question became: partnering with whom?

Rite Aid had lots of assets to contribute, so they needed to get a big enough stake to get value for those assets. Rite Aid is an incredibly positive partner for us; we're an important part of their future and they're doing a lot to help our joint partnership be successful. While it was a difficult negotiation, I think that both parties very quickly got to what was a fair exchange.

From a brand point of view, Rite Aid was the best partner because they were uniquely positioned with both their PBM and their 3,800 retail stores. They recognized that the game was taking advantage of their PBM to get universal coverage so that their retail stores could fill prescriptions unencumbered. Rite Aid was willing to contribute the assets that they had in both the insurance relationships with all the PBM companies and preferred relationship with their PBM—PCS. So that positions us from an online store favorably against our competition. This was attractive to me, along with the Rite Aid management insight that they knew they were better off having a totally dedicated partner as opposed to a controlling interest in a partner.

So the key things from my point of view were: (1) I get access to the PCS network; and (2) I get access to a big revenue stream because I get to allow customers that have a refill at Rite Aid to order online and pick it up at a Rite Aid.

So without having to go do deals one-by-one myself, I get broad relationships with PBMs: anybody that Rite Aid has a relationship with, drugstore.com has a relationship with. It gets me into the business faster.

Now, over time I think I'll end up with my own direct relationships with the PBMs, but in the meantime, I've got the leverage of their 3,800 stores to move forward. So the Rite Aid deal accelerated my pharmacy revenue growth—that's one thing. The second thing is—I get access to Rite Aid's buying power. Building those merchandizing relationships with core suppliers after partnering with Rite Aid goes much faster than I could do it alone.

And the third thing I get is tons of marketing impressions—virtually every prescription vial and cash register receipt will say drugstore.com on it. Twenty-five percent of Rite Aid's advertising will mention drugstore.com in some way, and Rite Aid spends more than $200 million a year on advertising.

Thus, drugstore.com offered online shoppers the option of ordering prescription drugs on the Web and then picking them up at a local Rite Aid. Rite Aid also promoted drugstore.com in its 3,800 stores nationwide and linked to drugstore.com on its web site.[7]

Business Results

Net sales for the fourth quarter ending on January 2, 2000, were about $18.5 million. For the year, drugstore.com's sales were $34.8 million with a loss of about $97 million. By early 2000, drugstore.com sold products to approximately a million customers. A survey by Media Metrix, Inc., rated the drugstore.com web site within the top five most visited health-related Internet sites, with monthly visits of 1.2 million; in addition, it ranked 41st on the list of most visited web sites overall.

Drugstore.com was successful in its secondary stock option of raising over $100 million in March 2000. While the stock slipped badly with the dot-com crash of April 2000, later in August drugstore.com raised another $63 million, which was expected to get the company through to profitability in 2002. Analysts were impressed with the success of drugstore.com raising this amount of cash in a severely depressed stock market, and attribute the success to its strong business model and management team.[8]

The New Industry Landscape

By 2000, the retail drug industry landscape had changed. Three established incumbents, Walgreens, CVS, and Rite Aid, had similar histories of internal store growth and acquisitions. The Walgreen Company was founded in June 1901, when Charles R. Walgreen Sr. purchased the small neighborhood drugstore where he worked in Chicago. In 1916, Walgreen merged the seven drugstores he had acquired into one organization—Walgreen Co. Walgreens stores introduced the milkshake and the soda fountain in the 1920s. The 1,000th store was opened in 1984, and the 2,000th in 1994. By the late 1990s there was a total of 2,819 Walgreens stores. About 450 new stores were opened in 2000. In addition, Walgreens operated two mail service facilities and an Internet site. The Walgreen family was still active in the company, as Charles Walgreen III had served as chairman of the board of directors since 1963.

In 2000, the Walgreens web site permitted online prescription ordering and fulfillment through either mail delivery or pickup at a local Walgreens store. In addition, the online pharmacy provided a refill service, a refill status check, and drug information. However, nonprescription items and beauty aid products could not be ordered from the Walgreens site.

Walgreens had expanded its internal growth strategy to undertake an initiative with Peapod, a service that allowed a customer to order groceries over the Internet and have them delivered to the home. Under this strategic alliance, Walgreens supplied Peapod's distribution centers with over-the-counter health and beauty products for inclusion in Peapod's Internet offering. Walgreens assisted Peapod in the merchandising and inventory management of products. In addition, the parties cooperated in comarketing programs.

At about the time that drugstore.com was started, there were two other major Internet start-ups: Soma and PlanetRx. Soma, meaning "of the body" in Greek, was privately funded and founded by Thomas Pigott, president and CEO. Thomas was the son of Charles Pigott, the former chairman of Paccar, a $6.5 billion manufacturer of trucks in the Seattle area. Soma had licensed pharmacists available 24 hours a day, 7 days a week to fill new prescriptions sent in by doctors. Customers could order refills themselves after the initial prescription was filled. Delivery fees were charged, and options included U.S. mail, and overnight delivery by UPS or FedEx. Advertising was done using mass media such as radio ads. In May 1999 CVS, a major industry incumbent, bought Soma for $30 million.

PlanetRx was cofounded by Mike Bruner, who developed his idea for an online drugstore while a medical student at the University of Pennsylvania, and Stephanie Schear, who was previously managing health-care and e-commerce investments for Intel's venture capital group (coincidentally, Stephanie Schear graduated from the Harvard Business School in 1996, a year after Jed Smith). After receiving first-round financing from Benchmark Capital and Sequoia Capital, PlanetRx recruited a top management team headed by Bill Razzouk as CEO. Previously Razzouk was an executive vice president at Federal Express, and immediately before coming to PlanetRx he served a short time as president of America Online. Investors included Johnson & Johnson, and E*Trade.

The largest pharmaceutical benefits manager (PBM), Express Scripts, went online in July 1999 with its yourPharmacy.com. One month later, Express abandoned yourPharmacy.com and developed a strategic alliance with PlanetRx, including taking a 20 percent equity position in PlanetRx. By 2001, PlanetRx had burned through all of its cash, and closed its doors; drugstore.com assumed most of its customers.

Many Internet companies entered the retail drug industry during this time, in addition to many broader health-care industry players who launched various Internet initiatives, making the Internet an integral part of industry competition. However, by the turn of the millenium, drugstore.com had established itself as the major threat to the established incumbents.

The key advantages that online drugstores have over the established industry incumbents originate from several sources: costs, information resource management, and development from a greenfield site, among others.

Cost Advantage

While virtually all the transactions involved in the business can be impacted by the effective use of IT, the substitution of the virtual drugstore for the bricks-and-mortar drugstores dramatically illustrates the nature of the differences. Figure 8.1 contrast the bricks-and-mortar drugstores with the virtual drugstore. (This comparison is often referred to as "clicks versus bricks.")

The most dramatic difference is that it takes 2,800 physical drugstores to achieve national distribution for Walgreens and only one drugstore for drugstore.com. The difference between the costs of building, staffing, filling the shelves, and serving customers in 2,800 physical stores compared to running one cyber drugstore is dramatic. As a direct result of instant national distribution through one virtual drugstore, a number of the pharmaceutical companies decided to use drugstore.com to launch their new products rather than delay launchings three months while the incumbents moved the new drugs through their logistic systems and onto the shelves of their bricks-and-mortar retail drugstores.

Also quite dramatic is the difference in flexibility when changing the layout of the drugstores to either promote existing product lines or add new ones. In the bricks-and-mortar drugstores, physical layouts must be altered, shelves filled, and store employees trained in each of the 2,800 stores. In the drugstore.com model, software engineers make the changes

Figure 8.1   Key Differences between the
Business Models of Walgreens and drugstore.com

Walgreens	*drugstore.com*
• Stores	• Web site
• Store staff	• "Dev team"
• Store staff training	• Customer training
• Physical locations	• Virtual locations
• Drive to store	• Navigate to web site
• Wait in line	• Click
• Years to build	• Six months to build
• Bookstore brand	• Internet brand
• "Touch and feel"	• Virtual pictures and text

to the one cyber drugstore, and the changes are made with minimum physical hassles.

On the order fulfillment side of the business, the new products must be warehoused and picked for both Walgreens and drugstore.com. But even here drugstore.com is developing an important advantage. The Walgreens distribution centers were designed and built to pick case quantities to stock the 2,800 Walgreens drugstores. Drugstore.com designed and built its distribution center using technology to pick individual customer orders and ship directly to customers.

Information Resource Management Advantage

The economics of managing information resources are extremely favorable compared to managing the more familiar resources of people, capital, and materials. Further, effective information resource management can enable higher levels of service than are possible through conventional in-store personal service.

The most basic trade-off is to substitute information resources for physical resources; this is similar to the earlier substitution of the cyber drugstore for the bricks-and-mortar drugstore. Higher levels of service could be achieved through services such as tracking order histories of customers and providing customers with reminders when a prescription may be close to running out. More sophisticated information resource management might involve online testing of customer receptivity to new beauty products, enabling the drugstore to be more responsive and provide products that customers are likely to want.

Another example of customer convenience from effective information resource management is "one-click" checkout. Amazon.com has pioneered one-click buying by keeping the customer information in a secured database. When the customer signs on to the Amazon.com web site, the computer accesses the customer information, including credit card, preferred method of shipment, and shipping address. Upon checkout of the cyber store, one click of the mouse automatically processes the entire order without any further input from the customer.

The information resource threat is more a matter of aggressive exploitation of the information resource through IT rather than the dot-com company having a unique advantage. For example, there is theoretically nothing to prevent an established drugstore chain from also establishing a virtual drugstore to match the services of the pure cyber drugstore competitor. There are, however, culture differences between the dot companies and the established incumbents that tend to inhibit the incumbents from expediently matching the dot company's information resource exploitation.

Greenfield Site Advantage

Computers have vastly improved in costs and capabilities from the time they began appearing in companies in the early 1960s. The underlying technologies of computers have changed so fast that new companies like drugstore.com have distinct advantages over older ones like Walgreens, because they have incorporated cutting-edge technologies from inception.

Incumbents must unlearn old business processes before adopting new ones. Older, less capable technologies have to be cast off to make way for newer technologies. All the new entrants need to learn is the new business processes. The advantage of the greenfield site is similar to the advantages of building a new house on a vacant lot versus remodeling an existing house to incorporate central air-conditioning, an alarm system, and in-floor heating.

The relative IT emphasis is also critically important to understand. The incumbents have been almost totally focused on back-office IT: accounting, logistics, and purchasing. The dot com first focuses on the front-office IT—that is, building IT out to the customer for electronic connection and interaction. Here newer technologies are involved, as well as different development methodologies such as rapid prototyping.

Equity Advantage

Banks and internally generated cash flow have provided major sources of capital for industrial age companies. These traditional sources of capital have found the new dot companies too risky to provide the amount of capital they require to grow. Venture capitalists and equity markets have developed to the point that they now provide the major sources of capital for the new dot companies.

Lucrative stock options have been used to attract the very best people to these new companies. And if the dot companies appear to have winning management teams and business models, investors continue to buy these companies' stock. The stock options align key employees' interests with the companies' interests to grow and remain attractive to investors. Typically, a dot company obtains initial venture funding and guidance from active venture capitalists, who work with the company to get it to the point where an IPO (initial public offering) can be made. The IPO provides significant funding, allowing the new company to undertake major strategic initiatives such as building customer numbers and constructing new facilities (e.g., the new distribution center of drugstore.com).

Investors often see the dot companies as more capable competitors than the traditional incumbents and reward the newer companies with higher stock prices and valuations. If they do, the dot company can provide lucrative stock options to attract and keep key technical and management talent.

Internet Impact in the Industry

Jed Smith, founder of drugstore.com, commented on the entry of drugstore.com and its impact on the industry.

When I was working the business plan, there was a leak about drugstore.com, and the first article was written about us in July 1998. The article described this new hot Internet company funded by Kleiner Perkins. The article woke up the industry. All these folks from the medical provider community and the benefit manager community started knocking on our door asking questions: "What are you doing? What's going on? Are you a threat? Are you a competitor? Are you complementary?" The industry has never been the same since.

The more normal e-commerce value chain is a manufacturer who sells to a wholesaler, who in turn sells to the end consumer. The health care value chain is much more complicated. As shown in my exhibit [Figure 8.2], there are five main players: Drugs Suppliers, Benefit Managers, Medical Providers, Retail Distributors, and the Customer. Also as shown in my exhibit, there are already Internet players everywhere. Many places in the value chain influence who takes what drug.

What's interesting is that the lines between the circles representing the various transactions are being impacted by the Internet companies, making the boundaries of the circles fuzzy. With the Internet, transactions can take place across many of the players instantaneously.

Manufacturers and retail chains are deciding to do their own Internet pharmacy. Internet companies are trying to own the doctors' desktops. Yet only about 5 percent of the doctors currently have Internet connections. Better health content and disease information is available to patients over the Internet. Communities of patients with a common disease have formed, and information is traded on treatment approaches. Electronic patient records can speed up the whole system and make it more reliable. But electronic patient records raise a host of privacy concerns, and issues about who owns the information.

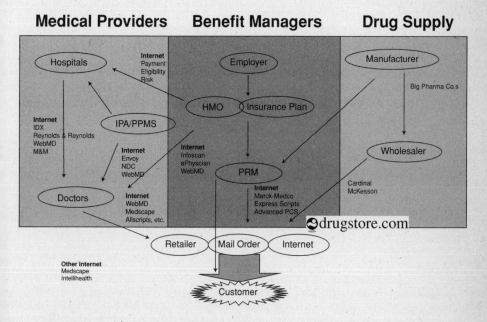

Figure 8.2   Once an Internet Player Enters the Industry, the Industry Is Never the Same

Source: Reproduced with permission of drugstore.com.

Also, big players such as Jim Clark—the founder of Silicon Graphics, Netscape, and now Healtheon—have entered the industry. Clark has stated that he felt that the health care industry was in a mess, and that it could be made better by hooking up the players with the Web. Obviously some people think that he is on the right track; Healtheon has a market value of over $4 billion.[9]

WebMD, which seems to have an approach similar to that of Healtheon, entered a $220 million Internet health-care alliance with DuPont in early April 1999. Then in late May 1999 WebMD and Healtheon announced that they had signed a definitive agreement to merge. The new entity is the first end-to-end Internet health-care and e-commerce company. What it means to be a drugstore and how one is operated are both changing within this new health-care industry restructuring.

Summary

Incumbents in the retail drug distribution industry spent decades building their businesses; it took their three major Internet-based challengers just a few short years to establish "drugstores" that do virtually everything the incumbents' thousands of physical drugstores do. These Internet drugstores are staffed with disparate people, differently motivated and trained than staff in incumbent organizations. Already innovation in the industry has skyrocketed and the pace of competition is accelerating to Internet time.

The dot-com business model is one that exploits the Internet by building out front-office IT to connect electronically with customers, and then engage them in ways that leverage the electronic interaction for convenience and with useful information. The front-office IT is built by small, highly qualified software engineer teams. These cadres of software engineers have mastered the rapid prototyping approach of building complex software systems in partnership with customers. The approach is all about interactive learning in the marketplace with customers, and then leveraging the learning through the software of the strategic I-Net. The differences between the IT teams of the dot coms and the IT departments of incumbents are dramatic. Further, the differences provide a difficult challenge for the incumbents, and a daunting challenge for those incumbents that don't even perceive that there are real differences.

It is hard to tell whether the existing Internet drugstores will be the ones that establish and execute sustainable business models, but it is clear that the retail drug industry, and even more broadly the health-care industry, will never be the same. And this pattern is being played out in one way or another in every industry between the dot coms and the incumbents.

Key Concepts
- IT strategic advantage has shifted from the back office to the front of-fice—that is, electronic connection with customers.
- Building from greenfield sites has huge cultural advantages.
- Once a dot company enters an industry, the industry is never the same.

9

Building the I-Net

The Case of Cisco Systems

In 1997, the Harvard Business School established a Research Center in Silicon Valley, from which I spearheaded a case research program with a number of companies in the Valley. Cisco was one of the companies I began studying, and continue to study to this day. Since this time I have developed three HBS cases on Cisco which tell an important story for managers on the building of a strategic I-Net.[1]

The Cisco story is different from the dot-com story told earlier in this book. Unlike drugstore.com, Cisco did not start by building out its front-office IT, but instead replaced its back-office legacy systems with up-to-date technology. The estimated cost was $15 million. Using its up-to-date back office systems as a foundation, Cisco then built front office systems at an estimated $100 million. By the year 2000, Cisco's investment of $115 million to build its strategic I-Net was returning annual benefits estimated at over $1.3 billion.

Renaissance CIO

The initiation of the Cisco case coincided with the 1993 arrival of the company's new CIO: Pete Solvik. Fresh from Apple Computer and approaching 40 years of age, Solvik had worked with two of Apple's inspirational leaders. Steve Jobs, the cofounder of Apple, who remains a legend in Silicon Valley for demonstrating that computers can indeed "change the world," and John Sculley, who after being recruited from PepsiCo to help Jobs realize the vision of building the "new enterprise" imparted a traditional corporate management discipline.[2] Yet things did not come together for Apple, and both Jobs and Sculley left, as did Solvik.

Solvik came to Cisco with a sense of what needed to be done to realize the strategic potential of IT. As important, he did not carry the excess baggage that burdened veterans of the data processing (DP) era, when computers were managed as "machines," with the associated command-and-control mentality and industrial age stereotyping that limited thinking about computers' role in business.

Solvik wasted no time addressing what he perceived to be Cisco's two key challenges. First he addressed the information systems (IS) department's status as a cost center reporting through the finance department, an internal orientation that he believed seriously constrained IT's contribution to the business. Solvik's second challenge was that the company's insufficiently flexible and robust systems were unable to support Cisco's projected growth.

To address the first challenge, Solvik changed the IS reporting relationship from accounting to customer advocacy. Second, he returned to each business function the part of the IT budget that pertained to it. As a result, just a small amount in general and administrative (G&A) expense remained dedicated to IT spending. From a technical perspective, Solvik centrally manages all of IT. He has solid line authority over Cisco's approximately 1,000 (circa 2000) IS staff and contractors. The roughly $300 million operating budget that he manages includes local and wide area network expenses, desktop software (i.e., Microsoft Office), and desktop support, but not telephone usage or PC acquisition cost. The engineering department's network expenses are included, but its IT expenses are not because they often require sophisticated and expensive equipment that is beyond the standard operating budget. Third, Solvik disbanded the central IS steering committee and substituted a structure that pushed investment decisions for IT applications projects out to the line organization. The projects continue to be executed by central IS.

To address the second challenge, Solvik proposed to president and CEO John Morgridge that all order/entry, manufacturing, and financial systems worldwide be replaced. In one big bang effort, his aggressive proposal implemented a $15 million Enterprise Resource Planning (ERP) system in nine months' time.

Generating Momentum by Making Business Strategy "Happen"

The most important difference between a renaissance and traditional CIO is that the latter manages IT so as to support, and the former seeks to make it integral to business strategy. Many of Cisco's core business principles stress the importance of customer satisfaction, short product life cycles, and lean management, and were articulated by Morgridge between 1988 and 1995. Successor John Chambers became CEO in 1995, while Morgridge and chief technology officer Ed Kozel crafted a four-component strategy that is still being executed in 2001 (see Figure 9.1).

Information age companies tend to be characterized by carefully thought out business strategies that are sustained for long periods of time. It is clear from the case study that all of Cisco's IT initiatives have related directly to its business strategy. Also worthy of note in this era of networking is how effectively Cisco's IT initiatives mutually reinforce the components of its strategy, as illustrated in Figure 9.1 by the arrows that connect each component to every other component.

Picking Up the Pace from Annual Budgets to "Internet Years"

We noted earlier that information age companies and the people who work in them are set apart by pace, specifically that a faster pace of business has become such a fact of life in high-tech industries that companies routinely plan their business activities in "Internet years." The pace of business is being quickened by (1) the ever-increasing IT content of product and service offerings and the concomitant rapid evolution of that content, and (2) the extensive exploitation of IT, primarily in the form of strategic I-Nets, to speed up product and service cycles and to sense and respond to customer needs in real time.

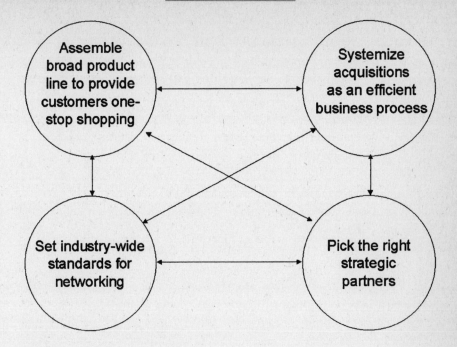

Figure 9.1   Cisco's Strategy
Source: Cisco Systems (as reproduced in "Cisco Systems Inc. Teaching Note," 399-074, November 16, 1998).

My earlier Harvard Business School research project explored the shift from traditional "make and sell" strategies of industrial age companies to the emerging "sense and respond" strategies of information age companies.[3] "Make and sell" strategies are mature management principles and techniques that support the manufacture of quite remarkable products. My first full-time position after completing my Ph.D. was as a financial systems manager for the Boeing Company's 737 branch; to this day I marvel at the feat of 60,000 people rolling out a Boeing 737 commercial jet every three days that without fail successfully completed its maiden flight. This and similar feats performed by industrial age companies around the world were made possible by a number of critical management principles.

First, complexity was accommodated by operating in time units of one year; only incremental change, on the order of 10 percent to 15 percent, was permitted from one year to the next. Second, technology was constrained by (1) building within current tested technologies and (2) maintaining high levels of vertical integration from procurement of raw materials to control of component manufacturing. Third, change was also constrained within production processes; engineering change orders were kept at a minimum, and almost all improvement was deferred to the next release in the product life cycle. Fourth, relatively lengthy product life cycles accommodated both the debugging of the manufacturing processes and subsequent long, consistent runs. Although customers might be consulted about needs in advance of product design, they were rarely involved in the design process, manufacturing, or postmanufacturing service delivery.[4]

Effective use of IT challenges almost every assumption of the industrial age management model. When customer needs can be sensed in real time, a company that allocates resources on an annual basis unnecessarily limits its ability to respond to these cues in real time. Information age companies meet customers' needs quickly by coordinating resources efficiently through integrated supply chains and involving customers directly throughout the product life cycle.

The magnitude of technological change and its revolutionary impact on management was brought home to me during a conversation with my then 29-year-old son, Sean. A veteran of Microsoft, where he was a lead software engineer for the company's network product, he subsequently cofounded a start-up software company. Within the year the founders sold their company for millions and Sean moved on to develop the Web-based software for drugstore.com, a sister start-up to Amazon.com, which is hoping to challenge Walgreens much as the latter challenged Barnes & Noble. As I was losing a debate with Sean about how to design the logistic systems for drugstore.com, I did what so many senior managers do: I appealed to the authority of experience. After all, I had worked at one of the best companies in the world, founded and built a successful consulting company, and was currently on the faculty of Harvard Business School. Altogether, this represented more than 30 years in business. Sean, multiplying his seven calendar years of experience by Internet years, announced that he had me beat by 19 years.

This made me think. Most of my experience had been paced by the annual budget cycles of the companies for which I had worked. Sean's experience had been paced by the frenetic speed of Internet years. More-over, his experience was more relevant than mine to the problem at hand. He was focused on front-office IT; my experience had been mostly build-ing out back-office IT. Our conversation was a wake-up call. Clearly, I needed to understand that information age companies differed from in-dustrial age companies not only in pace, but also in the management principles. One suspects that many senior managers stand to learn valu-able lessons from their younger, network era counterparts.

Two-Step Process

Step One: Replacing the Obsolete Legacy Systems of the Back Office

Cisco came to implement its strategic I-Net architecture for much the same reason that many other companies enact drastic measures: its legacy systems were crumbling and failing. In 1993, the $500 million company was supporting core transaction processing for financial, manufacturing, and order entry with a UNIX-based software package. Moreover, Cisco was far and away the biggest customer of the software vendor that sup-ported the application.[5] Solvik's experience and Cisco's significant growth prospects convinced him that a change was needed.

Pete Solvik:

We wanted to grow to $5 billion-plus. The application didn't pro-vide the degree of redundancy, reliability, and maintainability we needed. We weren't able to make changes to the application to meet our business needs anymore. It had become too much spaghetti, too customized. The software vendor did offer [an upgraded version], but when we looked at it we thought by the time we're done our systems will be more reliable and have higher redundancy, but it will still be a package for $300 million companies and we're a $1 bil-lion company.

Believing strongly that IT budgetary decisions should be made by the functional areas, albeit with solid line reporting of the IT organization to a central authority, namely him, and concerned by the tendency of ERP implementations to become "mega-projects," Solvik was initially inclined to avoid an ERP solution.[6] Instead, he planned to let functional areas steer their own course while using common architecture and databases in keeping with Cisco's strong tradition of standardization. This approach was consistent with the organizational and budgetary structures he had installed.

Systems replacement difficulties in the functional areas perpetuated the deterioration of Cisco's legacy environment. Incremental modification continued while the company sustained an 80 percent annual growth rate. Systems outages became routine, and the product's shortcomings exacerbated the difficulties of recovering from outages.

Finally, in January 1994, Cisco's legacy environment failed so dramatically that the shortcomings of the existing systems could be ignored no longer. An unauthorized access method—a workaround motivated by the inability of the system to perform—malfunctioned, corrupting Cisco's core application database and effectively shutting down the company for two days.

Cisco's struggle to recover from this disaster brought home the fact that its systems were on the brink of total failure, and convinced Solvik and other Cisco managers that the company needed an alternative to its autonomous approach to systems replacement.

Solvik requested and received sponsorship from the senior vice president of manufacturing, Carl Redfield, who, like Solvik, realized that implementing a system to meet business needs would require heavy involvement from the best people in the business community. "If it was easy," Solvik quipped, "then we were picking the wrong people. We pulled out people that the business absolutely did not want to give up."

Solvik and Redfield believed that equal partners were a necessary complement to a strong Cisco team. One of these had to be an integration partner with more than sufficient technical skills and business knowledge to assist in both the selection and the implementation of a solution. Solvik explained the choice of KPMG:

KPMG came in and saw an opportunity to really build a business around putting in these applications. They also saw this as kind of a defining opportunity, to work with us on this project. As opposed to some other firms that wanted to bring in a lot of "greenies," KPMG was building a practice of people that were very experienced in the industry.

With KPMG on board, the team of about 20 set about identifying the best software packages. A multipronged approach leveraged the experience of others, as large corporations and the Big Six accounting firms were asked what they knew and research sources such as Gartner were tapped.[7] Orienting the selection process to what people were actually using while continuing to emphasize speed allowed Cisco to narrow the field to five packages within two days. After a week of high-level evaluation the team decided on two candidates, Oracle and another major ERP vendor.

Ten days were spent writing a request for proposal (RFP) to which the vendors were given two weeks to respond. While it awaited the responses, the Cisco team, continuing its due diligence, visited a series of vendor-provided reference clients. After analyzing the RFP responses, Cisco invited the vendors to make three-day software presentations to demonstrate, using sample data provided by Cisco, how key information processing requirements were met (or otherwise accommodated) by their packages. In the end the team selected the Oracle ERP suite.

Aware that Cisco executives were worried that such an enormous project might spin out of control and deliver substandard results, the team nevertheless took a pragmatic approach to estimating project requirements. Solvik described the process:

> Our quarters go August to October, November to January, February to April, and May to July.[8] So right here on May 1, beginning of the fourth quarter, we are asking, "How long should it take to do a project to replace all of our core systems?" This is truly how it went. We said, "You know we can't implement in the fourth quarter; the auditors will have a complete cow. If it takes a year we will be implementing [in the] fourth quarter and that won't work." We thought it really should take 15 months, July or August a year later. Tom Herbert, the program manager, said, "There's no way we are going to take 15 months to get this done. That's ridiculous." So we started going in the opposite direction and said, "Well, can we do it in five months?" That just didn't seem right. Understand, we did not have a

scope yet. In the end we basically settled that we wanted to go live at the beginning of Q3 so we would be completely stable for Q4.

Next came the task of estimating a project budget. Once again the team was aggressive. Instead of developing a formal business case (i.e., a financial analysis) to estimate the project's impact on the company, the team chose to focus on the issues that had sparked the analysis in the first place. "We just looked at how much it touched," explained Solvik, who believed that Cisco had little choice but to move.

> The reliability, the scalability, and the modifiability of our current applications would not support our anticipated future growth. We needed either upgrades to the new version of the current application or we needed to replace it. If we replaced it, we could either do it in parts or do it as a whole. We evaluated those three alternatives, talked about the pros and cons of each, and recommended that we replace our systems, big bang, with one ERP solution. We committed to do it in nine months for $15 million for the whole thing.

Figure 9.2 provides an estimated breakdown of the cost of the ERP initiative.

At $15 million, the ERP implementation would be the single largest capital project ever approved by the company. Although Cisco was to some extent compelled to implement ERP, proceeding without a formal economic justification was also a matter of management philosophy. As Redfield put it, "You don't approach this kind of thing from a justification perspective. Cost avoidance is not an appropriate way to look at it. You really need to look at it like 'Hey, we are going to do business this way.' You are institutionalizing a business model for your organization."

Once it had board approval, the ERP team promptly established a structure for the implementation. To proceed with implementation the team would need to be expanded from its 20 core members to about 100, representing a cross section of Cisco's business community.[9] Again, only the very best were sought. One rule of engagement for those who worked on the implementation was that it was to be short-term in duration and was not to represent a career change. The effort was framed to those who

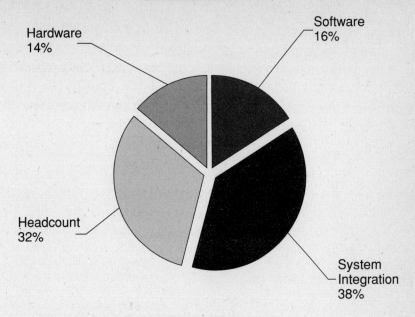

Figure 9.2   ERP Implementation Cost Breakdown

Source: Cisco ERP Steering Committee Report, October 20, 1994 (as reproduced in "Cisco Systems Inc. Implementing ERP," 9-688-020).

would work on it as a challenge, a "throw down the gauntlet sort of thing." Recruitment was by this time no longer a problem.

Team members were distributed among five process area teams—order entry, manufacturing, finance, sales/reporting, and technology—managed by a project management office that included both a Cisco business project manager and a KPMG project manager. Each team was assigned a Cisco information systems leader, a Cisco business leader, business and IT consultants from either KPMG or Oracle, and additional personnel as deemed appropriate.

Sitting atop the entire project management structure was an executive steering committee that was comprised of Cisco's corporate controller, the VPs of manufacturing and customer advocacy, Solvik, Oracle's senior VP of applications, and KPMG's partner-in-charge of West Coast consulting. The presence on the steering committee of such high-level Oracle and KPMG executives signaled the importance these organizations attached to the project's success.

Cutover to the new ERP system was on schedule. Tough performance problems were resolved during the following three months, and the system stabilized.

Step Two: Building Out the Web-Enabled Front Office Systems on the Back Office Systems' ERP Foundation

The ERP system was the centerpiece of the $100 million initiatives that saw all of Cisco's IS applications and platforms replaced by network era technologies. "In a two-year period," Solvik elaborated, "we literally replaced every piece of technology in the company. We have a very low-cost/high-value technology architecture. We have no mainframes, no minicomputers, and no legacy technology. Everything is current."

Cisco standardized its IT platform architecture throughout: 100 percent UNIX at the server level; 100 percent Windows NT at the LAN (local area network) level; 100 percent Windows-based Toshiba and Hewlett-Packard PCs at the client level; 100 percent Oracle at the database level; and 100 percent TCP/IP (Transmission Control Protocol/Internet Protocol) for the worldwide network. Voice mail, e-mail, meeting scheduling software, desktop and server operating systems, and office productivity suites are standardized, and virtually all business functions utilize single application packages worldwide. Cisco's platform architecture is detailed in Figure 9.3.

Capitalizing on the workings of Moore's Law, Cisco's network era technologies are dramatically more cost efficient and effective than its older legacy systems. Moreover, Cisco's ERP foundation not only runs on the latest computers, but it is deployed in a manner that was not economical even a few years ago. Specifics of the deployment included:

- Client computer-equipped workers connected to the network.
- One central, companywide database.
- An event-driven messaging network architecture that supports real-time transactions processing database updating.
- A common browser interface for all applications.
- A web site interface as a portal to the entire company.

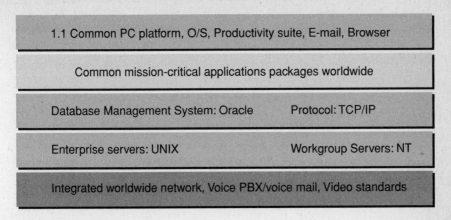

- No legacy systems
- Data warehouse
- ERP system
- Centrally administered and maintained PC software to manage total cost of ownership (TCO)

Figure 9.3   Cisco's IT Architecture: Technology Standardization
Source: Cisco Systems (as reproduced in "Cisco Systems Inc.," 9-398-127)

Capturing the Benefits of the Strategic I-Net

Building its business processes on its own fully integrated global I-Net enabled Cisco to deploy people around the world and enabled those people to interact in a coherent way to address business issues and customer needs. Linking its intranet to the Internet in order to access strategic vendors and customers directly opened up new possibilities for using the power of computers to innovate in new product development service delivery.

Employee Self-Service: Internal Applications

Today, virtually all of Cisco's internal applications are Web enabled: sales applications, executive information systems (EIS), decision support systems (DSS), training (including distance learning), and self-service human resources (HR). Touted in Cisco's annual report:

Cisco Employee Connection (CEC) supports instant global communications among the thousands of Cisco employees worldwide. Whether an employee wants information about a company event, requires access to health benefits registration, or needs recent expense-tracking reports, CEC streamlines business processes and lowers costs throughout the company. For example, one application called METRO—accessed over the intranet using a standard Web browser—automates the processes of making travel arrangements and submitting expenses. In excess of 1.7 million pages of information are available to employees, who access CEC thousands of times each day. Because of internal applications such as CEC, the need for written memos and printed documents has been sharply reduced.[10]

By 2000, with the replacement of internally designed, and conversion of vendor-supplied, applications, virtually every Cisco application employs a Web browser as its only user interface.

Communication and Distance Learning

Cisco has exploited its I-Net to enhance communications with its employees at multiple levels and in meaningful ways. In 1997, for example, employees began viewing from their desktops Chambers' address at the company's quarterly meetings. Approximately one thousand employees tune in to view the address in real time and another thousand watch it in a delayed broadcast over the I-Net, using their PCs to bring up a video window. Cisco has effectively utilized the streaming of live video to strengthen its culture by making employees feel closer to the company. Solvik estimates that the two thousand employees who view the address remotely equal those who were present at it. Hence, Chambers effectively doubles the audience for his quarterly address.

Solvik negotiated with the search engine company Yahoo! the development of a Cisco-tailored version of My Yahoo!, a type of "push" technology application whereby agents search the Internet for the information specified by users and "push" it out to their desktops. When users sign onto the Internet, the requested information—be it breaking news reports about competitors or up-to-the-minute information about worldwide financial markets—is waiting for them. My Yahoo!, particularly as used in conjunction with e-mail, has become a powerful tool used at Cisco.

Its I-Net has also enabled Cisco to add a new dimension to employee training. The company has devised a feedback loop whereby the use of distance learning modules accessible to employees at their desktops is tracked, and the tracking information is used to gauge the effectiveness of the modules, and thereby improve their quality. This ensures higher levels of effectiveness as organizational needs change.

Customer Self-Service: Electronic Connections for Service and Supply with Customers

Cisco Connection Online (CCO), a comprehensive, Web-based, online information resource and set of networked applications, is the centerpiece of the customer focus component of Cisco's strategy. It identifies problems through its "Bug Navigator," notifies employees of the problem ("Bug Alerts"), and resolves them through Cisco's "Open Forum" and "Troubleshooting Engine." The CCO is accessed approximately 1.5 million times per month by approximately 150,000 active registered users worldwide, making it the primary vehicle for delivering responsive, around-the-clock customer support. Customers rely on CCO to answer questions, diagnose network problems, and provide solutions and expert assistance. In fact, more than 80 percent of technical support is delivered to customers and resellers electronically, saving Cisco in excess of $150 million annually and improving customer satisfaction. To serve international customers, Cisco has had portions of CCO translated; at present it has approximately 50 different country pages.[11]

Solvik reflected on the importance of the customer to Cisco.

I have 150,000 registered customers hooked up—those are customers with a big "C"—compared to 30,000 Cisco employees. In contrast to the internally focused IT organizations in many other companies, my mission does not primarily focus on providing services and systems to meet the needs of the employees of the business. In fact, I refer to my employee users as clients and not as customers.

Customers that are using our systems directly express higher satisfaction with us and enjoy a lower cost of doing business with us than those who do not use our systems. And, of course, we also lower our cost of doing business.

Seventy percent of the employees in Cisco have a very significant bonus multiplier tied to our annual customer satisfaction survey. The first thing we review at every senior staff meeting is the status of critical accounts. Every night John Chambers gets a personal update on the status of every critical account.

e-Commerce: Shipping Product over the Internet

Cisco was an early pioneer in using the Internet for full electronic commerce—that is, full-service Internet commerce priced, configured, placed, checked, and serviced customer orders and invoices. It inaugurated support for simple transactions more than three years ago and for nearly two years has had online support for configuration and order placement for its entire product line. Solvik recounted the company's experience.

> We've learned an incredible amount in the 24 months of live e-commerce. We have racked up Internet shipments of product from zero percent in July of 1996, to 2 percent of our revenue in August of 1996, to $800 million in calendar 1997, and now to $1.5 billion each quarter today in 1998—a current run rate of 65 percent of our total revenue [in 2001, about 75 percent of total revenue]. Software shipped over the Internet does not have to be transferred to CDs, physically packaged, and physically sent, and the product arrives in minutes rather than days. Cisco operates the biggest electronic commerce site in the world.

As of June 2000, Cisco had 1,826 registered companies, an order per day run rate of $50 million, and a yearly run rate of $18.2 billion. Customers anywhere in the world can place orders on the World Wide Web and use vendor-supplied applications to check instantly the status of pending orders. Moreover, fully 90 percent of Cisco's software upgrades are now delivered through the Internet at a much lower cost and in less time than when traditional distribution methods were used. For example:

At Sprint it used to take 60 days from the signing of a contract to complete a networking project. Now, thanks partly to the efficiency of ordering Cisco equipment online, it takes 35 to 45 days. Sprint has also been able to cut its order-processing staff from 21 to 6, allowing the other 15 employees to work instead on installing networks.[12]

Productivity gains of 60 percent for Cisco and 20 percent for customers and resellers are being realized through online commerce.[13]

Information Transparency in the Supply Chain

In the course of developing and implementing applications that extended its enterprise to suppliers and customers, Cisco made the determination that its core competencies lay in design and fulfillment rather than in physical transformation. Hence, as early as 1992 Cisco began to outsource much of its manufacturing, retaining final assembly and testing inhouse. Supply chain functions are performed jointly by Cisco and its contract manufacturers, necessitating interaction and information exchange throughout labor-intensive processes. Central to Cisco's philosophy was removing barriers that impeded the flow of information within the company and between the company and its business partners, thereby tightening integration with its constituents and increasing the overall power of the supply chain. By June 2000, 55 percent of Cisco's orders went straight through the company's supply chain.

Cisco embarked upon five initiatives in connection with the automation of its supply chain.

1. *Single enterprise.* Cisco used networked applications to integrate suppliers into its production systems, creating, in effect, a "single enterprise." Electronic links across this single enterprise enabled key suppliers to manage and operate major portions of its supply chain, which, in turn, enabled Cisco to respond to customer demands in real time. A change in any node is propagated almost instantaneously throughout the entire supply chain. Other improvements include the elimination of purchase orders and invoice processing.

2. *New product introduction (NPI).* A Cisco study revealed as many as four to five iterations of prototype building are required for each new product introduction, with each iteration taking, on average, one to two weeks. One of the biggest drivers of cost and time delays in the prototype phase was the labor-intensive process of gathering and disseminating information. Automating the gathering of product data information reduced the time requirement from as much as one day to less than 15 minutes. Cisco's use of networked applications in NPI has reduced time to volume—that is, from the time the new product is introduced to the time of high-volume sales—by three months and reduced total cost by $21.5 million for 1997.

3. *Autotest.* Cisco builds cells that performed standardized product tests automatically with minimal labor. Testing processes were made routine and embodied in software test programs that ran the test cells. Automated and standardized testing was outsourced entirely to suppliers, enabling quality problems to be detected at the source. However, although it has outsourced testing, Cisco continues to supply the intelligence (i.e., the software code of the tests to determine if the product worked) that supports it.

4. *Direct fulfillment.* When shipping was performed exclusively by Cisco, products configured by partners had to be shipped first to Cisco and then to the customer. Shipping time between each of these parties was approximately three days. In 1997 Cisco took its first step toward global direct fulfillment, when it electronically sent its software to the manufacturer and the manufacturer installed the software and shipped the finished product directly to the customer. (The several manufacturing partners who have completely made a transition to this system represent about 45 percent of Cisco's unit volume.)

5. *Dynamic replenishment.* Before it automated its supply chain, Cisco's manufacturers and suppliers lacked real-time demand and supply information, resulting in delays and errors. To compensate, inventory levels and overhead were maintained at higher than acceptable levels. Cisco's dynamic replenishment model flows directly through market demand signals to contract manufacturers without distortion or delay and enables the contract manufacturers to track Cisco's inventory levels in real time.

EIS (Executive Information Systems) and DSS (Decision Support Systems)

Executive and decision support information maintained by Cisco is universally accessible from the Web browser. The company's Web-based EIS system—used by sales managers and executives worldwide, including the CEO—provides summary and drill down bookings, billings, and backlog for all products, customers, channels, geographies, and markets.

Sales tracking and reporting are also done on the I-Net. A Cisco salesperson who wants to track, for example, sales for a particular product in a given region on a weekly basis merely calls up the browser template and requests the information. Several mouse clicks later, assuming that the salesperson has authority to access the information, the report is automatically delivered to the desktop at the level of detail and for the period of time requested.

Integrating Acquisitions into Cisco's Strategic I-Net

Acquisitions have been—and will for the foreseeable future continue to be—an important part of Cisco's strategy of creating an extended and virtual enterprise. One analyst estimates that Cisco derived approximately 40 percent of its 1997 revenues from acquired businesses,[14] which has continued to increase. Moreover, about a third of Cisco's senior executives have come from acquired companies.

Cisco seems to have mastered the acquisition process. It avoids hostile takeovers and targets only companies with "market congruent" visions. Just 1 in 10 targeted acquisitions is formally executed.

Cisco follows a documented and repeatable process for integrating acquired companies. Generally, companies are acquired for their R&D or because they have developed products that contribute to providing end-to-end solutions for network customers. R&D and product organizations of acquired companies are grafted onto Cisco's product side, which includes branding and product family integration. Manufacturing, sales, and distribution are integrated into Cisco's respective functional organizations. A designated group within Cisco's IS organization immediately eliminates nonstandard technology and integrates the acquisition's information systems into Cisco's infrastructures and core applications. Its IP- and standards-based IT architecture enables Cisco quickly and efficiently to add whatever capacity is required to handle acquired businesses' administrative processes. Most acquisitions are fully integrated within 60 to 100 days—a short period rarely seen in other companies.

Assessing I-Net Benefits

A study conducted in 1997 by Cisco to assess the benefits of its global I-Net initiatives concluded that its marketing, employee, manufacturing, customer support, and commerce applications collectively would save in excess of $550 million annually in operating costs (see Figure 9.4)[15] after full implementation. By 2000, the identifiable benefits exceeded $1.3 billion a year.

Summary

As Cisco demonstrates, building a strategic I-Net is not only a high-return activity; it is absolutely one of the most strategic investments that a

Figure 9.4   Financial Impact of Internet Business Solutions (FY 2000)

Internet Business Solutions	Financial Impact
Supply Chain Management	$695 million
Cost benefits—$307 million	
Income: Faster time to market—$388 million	
Customer care	$506 million
Workforce optimization	$86 million
Internet commerce	$65 million
Total financial impact	$1,352 million

Source: From updated Cisco Systems Web-enablement case, 301-056.

company can make. However, building a strategic I-Net is a long-term proposition—a foundation must be laid and built upon. And, as Cisco demonstrates, if strategic value is to continue to be captured, the building can never stop.

Cisco discovered that its web site had "brand" characteristics—that is, that those who accessed its I-Net through this portal needed to believe that they would receive individualized treatment and that Cisco would not abuse information they conveyed to it. Because those who access Cisco's web site do so for different reasons, it is necessary to quickly identify them, display the appropriate page content, and enable them to navigate the I-Net in ways that meet their needs. Cisco continues to work on and improve its web site, employing focus groups, for example, to evaluate its functioning.[16]

Key Concepts

- The renaissance CIO makes the difference.
- Don't even think about it unless your CEO is Internet-savvy and Internet-ready.
- Internet benefits are managed; they don't just happen.

10

Act Like a Venture Capitalist

Creating an Action Agenda

As with most business methods and techniques, the I-Net initiative must be tailored to the unique situation of each particular company. The chapters you have read so far have given you the language, context, and tools for thinking about how your company can best develop and use an I-Net. Hopefully, the preceding four chapters in particular offered ideas, models, and benchmarks for successful I-Net initiatives emerging from a broad array of organizations. Based on what you now know, the goal of this chapter is to help you to formulate a mind-set and agenda centered on executing an I-Net initiative in your own particular firm based on your company's unique set of needs, goals, and resources.

This chapter has two objectives: The first is to approach the I-Net initiative with the mind-set of a venture capitalist, who combines a penchant for risk taking with a focus on measurable results. From my experiences in companies that span industrial organizations to Internet pure plays, it is clear to me that I-Net initiatives are best implemented when viewed as business ventures. The second goal is to guide you in creating an action plan for spearheading an I-Net initiative in your company based on an understanding of where your firm stands in the evolutionary chain of becoming a permeable organization. To achieve both goals, it is imperative that you be familiar with the characteristics of those companies entering the dot space. These companies fall into four categories based on a number of criteria, and the examination of these criteria yields an assessment of the resources needed to execute an I-Net.

Managing I-Net Initiatives as New Ventures

It is clear to me from my work with such companies as IBM, Cisco, and drugstore.com that I-Nets are best implemented when the management team overseeing the initiative places itself in the venture investor's role.[1] In this capacity, the task at hand is to deploy a finite amount of resources across a portfolio of investments and manage those investments to produce the highest possible return. Figure 10.1 draws from a schematic developed by Professor Bill Sahlman of Harvard Business School, an expert on the venture capital industry, and provides a frame of reference[2] for understanding the risk/return potential of new ventures.

In any new venture, there is some probability that the investment will have to be written off completely. In an I-Net implementation this would happen if the initiative were abandoned without producing any tangible

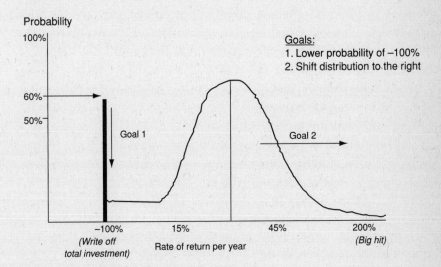

Figure 10.1   Goals in Managing an Investment to a Successful Outcome
Source: From HBS working paper 9-897-101 and class notes created by Professor William Sahlman.

benefit. This possibility is shown by the spike above the -100 percent return in the diagram. The probability of various rates of return greater
than -100 percent are spread out in a distribution represented by the
curve in the figure. The VC managing such an initiative has two goals:
(1) reducing the height of the -100 percent spike (that is, lessening the
probability of a total write-off); and (2) moving the distribution of returns
to the right, so that higher returns will occur with greater probabilities.
There are numerous ways the experienced VC manages investments to
achieve these goals, but we will focus on three factors that are of primary
importance: staging, risk sharing, and people.

Staging

Because of the integrated systems making up an I-Net initiative, it is easy
to get into the mind-set of contracting for the total estimated cost at the
outset. The paradox is that, say, a mere $20 million investment in an I-
Net won't achieve a net benefit, but a $100 million investment (if exe-
cuted correctly) will. VCs have another name for this sort of cash flow
profile: "a lousy business opportunity."

Different business opportunities have different cash flow profiles.
Starting an airline, for example, requires a very large up-front investment
followed by unknown future returns. Starting a magazine, on the other
hand, requires relatively little up-front investment, and subscribers pay in
advance, locking in returns early. VCs want to invest in businesses with
cash flow profiles like those of magazines, not airlines.[3] I-Net as portrayed in the paradox resembles an airline more than a magazine as an investment opportunity. In part this really is because of the inherent nature
of the I-Net. But what is helpful about the venture capital frame of mind
is that it forces us to think about whether there are ways of managing the
initiative that make it more like a magazine.

In a recent experience in the field, we encountered a company strug-
gling to implement an I-Net. Interviews with senior managers revealed,
however, that the biggest problem they were having was the size of
the up-front commitment. No matter how you considered this investment, its size and need for commensurate resources made it nearly impossible for them to support. The I-Net team had "hit a wall" with
senior management.

A breakthrough for this company came when they realized that they were not locked into the initiative as framed by the IT way of thinking but that they were empowered to invest in more manageable chunks. So what if it was harder to do technically or the initiative benefit/cost stream did not look immediately positive. Senior management knew intuitively that the initiative did not make business sense in its all-or-nothing form. Their concerns about the size of the investment and its risk/reward profile were completely reasonable.

Bill Sahlman, writing about venture capital initiatives, has pointed out the prevalence and importance of staging high-risk VC investments:

> If a company believes it ultimately will need $10 million to develop and introduce a software product, they are likely to find that no investor will invest the full $10 million. Rather, the investor will stage the commitment of capital over time, preserving the right to invest more money and preserving the right to abandon the project. . . . the issue of how much money to invest . . . is exceedingly difficult and the perspectives of the players often differ. Entrepreneurs want all the money up front, while investors want to stage the capital over time in order to "buy" information.[4]

The right approach for a management committee to take is a similarly tough-minded view to staging the I-Net investment somewhere between the extremes.

When Tektronix, Inc. implemented the ERP component of its I-Net, the overall initiative was subdivided into roughly 20 "waves." Waves were managed independently, but interdependencies were constantly monitored. Each wave delivered a specific set of functionality for a division or geographic region. For example, the first wave delivered integrated financials (minus accounts receivable) for all three of the company's divisions, but only in the United States. When the company began implementing supply chain functionality outside the United States, the waves were scaled back in size to reflect greater risk of unanticipated problems. First the team installed the system at a single distribution center, and then they expanded the implementation to pilot sites. Only after the pilot installations were successful and they had incorporated learning from earlier waves did they commence a general rollout in Europe. As one implementation team member noted, their intention to buy information was explicit: "We decided to plan incrementally, and roll out future waves as we learned more about the process."

Staging something as large and complex as an I-Net initiative can be extremely difficult. It is the sort of work that IT staff, system integrators, and I-Net product vendors dread, mostly because it involves examining the generations-old legacy systems being used by the client before deciding how best to divide the investment into stages. As I-Net product vendors will be quick to point out, you may also end up spending more money in the long run for your total implementation and realizing less total return on your investment. What you will get in exchange, however, is a lower probability of a write-off. Most people are willing, even overjoyed, to trade some return for risk reduction in this already very high cost range.

I-Net product vendors and system integrators are getting better and better at staging, because they must. The plain fact is that senior management's legitimate concerns about earnings per share (EPS) and other financial performance measures stand in the way of implementation of the I-Net in large chunks. But a staged I-Net implementation is not easy work, and it does not fit into the reflex, planning-intensive IT frames of mind that many working on the initiative will find natural.

The staging mind-set is not always easy for a management team, either. There is a tendency to think of the I-Net initiative as a standard capital investment, even though the risk profile of an I-Net implementation is very different from most (e.g., a capital equipment acquisition). Unlike more certain investments, staging an I-Net initiative involves setting tough goals and commitments for the short term only. The large degree of uncertainty means that expenditures on stages must be regarded as buying information about the right combination of people, strategy, and

---

Carrier Uses Web to Cut Costs by $100 Million[5]

Carrier is the world's largest manufacturer of air conditioners, with revenues of nearly $10 billion. Carrier buys more than 50 percent of its components and services through a Web-based procurement system. Last year cost savings from use of the Web was $100 million.

tactics to succeed, rather than buying guaranteed execution. The I-Net end product may not look much like the original plan. And when events reach a crisis point, as they will repeatedly, the reflex behavior must be cooperative problem solving, not panic or cutting and running by immediately shutting down the venture.

One barrier to staging is a misalignment concerning the incentives of the I-Net implementation team, especially system integrators. Once awarded a large commitment, integrators see a stream of billable hours. They are reluctant to admit unanticipated problems that subsequently arise and that might call for scaling back or abandoning the commitment. Very few vendors are naturally inclined to say things like "We've discovered a problem with the plan, and it won't make sense for us to bill that $40 million you promised us." The management team needs to retain the right to decide whether to continue to back the implementation team and the initiative and how to stage it: Management should never cede those decision rights to the implementation team.

Incentive Alignment and Risk Sharing

It stands to reason that if all the parties lose when an I-Net initiative fails, then everyone has an incentivize to make the project work. VCs have evolved a sophisticated set of practices to produce this kind of incentive alignment among all of the parties involved in a new venture. Some of these incentive alignment practices can offer models for the incentive relationship between senior managers and the I-Net team.

Risk sharing arrangements should encourage the cooperative problem solving behaviors when crisis erupts during an I-Net initiative. One way VCs accomplish this is by influencing membership on a new venture's board of directors. For example, board members from other companies important to the success of a new venture can ensure appropriate attention to problems that might arise between the companies. The interests of involved parties in an I-Net venture initiative can be similarly interlocked by carefully composing oversight committees. Cisco included on the steering committee for its I-Net implementation both a vendor vice president and a senior partner from the systems integration firm. Because all implementation team members knew their senior executives were so closely involved, relatively few problems became serious enough to demand steering committee attention. The mere fact of senior management involvement from all team partners gave the team incentive to work effectively together.

Another way VCs make sure incentives are aligned is by writing formal contracts that reward the venture team only when investors realize concrete rewards. In the I-Net context, this means linking payments to systems integrators and vendors and bonuses for client company managers with the accomplishment of real objectives of the implementing organization. Everyone might get paid, for example, when the company implementing I-Net achieves a targeted inventory reduction.

Ideally, senior managers' compensation will also be linked to the success of the initiative. Because I-Net implementation requires not only changes in technology but also, and most importantly, changes in the way business is done all over the company, all members of the management team need to have "skin in the game." Because of the size and uncertainty of the I-Net investment, the reflex reaction of senior managers can be to line up behind the initiative conditionally or to approve of the initiative enthusiastically so long as it is in someone else's area of responsibility. This sort of conditional endorsement is a death knell for an I-Net initiative. Without all senior managers clearly communicating to their own troops that "this shall be done," an I-Net initiative will repeatedly run aground as different parts of the company feel empowered and take a stand against changes the I-Net initiative requires.

Enthusiasm for sophisticated incentive schemes should be tempered, however, by common sense. It is possible to get "too cute," to produce incentives that have complex dysfunctional effects. The I-Net team will

---

Bellagio Resort: Hire 9,600 Workers in 24 Weeks[6]

In 1998, Mirage Resorts completed Bellagio, a lavish 3,000-room resort in Las Vegas that cost $1.6 billion to build, and hired 9,600 workers in 24 weeks. They screened 84,000 applicants in 12 weeks, interviewed 27,000 finalists in 10 weeks, and processed 9,600 hires in 11 days—all of which was done completely online—without using one sheet of paper.

need to establish a level of trust and open communication that rises above contractual obligations. And, like everything else in such a high-risk initiative, incentives might need adjusting. At one point in the Tektronix implementation, managers decided to shift away from results-oriented payments to systems integrators toward a time-and-materials basis. Their justification was that the two parties had by then established a strong trust-based relationship and were spending too much time deciding on reasonable linkages between payments and milestones.

The other factor that worked strongly to align incentives in both the Cisco and Tektronix[7] cases might be called the "hungry vendor" effect. Cisco was a high-profile prestige client for systems integrators, who wanted to expand their I-Net practice, and also for the product vendor, who wanted to demonstrate the manufacturing capabilities of a new release of its software. Tektronix used a relatively small systems integrator that was also eager to leverage success into more I-Net clients. Not every company can be a prestige client. But how hungry your vendors are and how much public reputation they stand to lose if the initiative fails are important factors to consider right alongside vendor capabilities and experience.

"People, People, People!"

The first and foremost consideration of VCs as they evaluate a business proposal is people—specifically the makeup of the team that is involved. There is an old adage among VCs that goes "I'd rather back an 'A' team with a 'B' idea than a 'B' team with an 'A' idea."

In deciding whether the team is well composed, it is useful to ask questions like the following:

- Who are the team members?
- What have they accomplished in the past?
- What I-Net experience do they have?
- What skills do they have?
- What is their ability to draw on additional resources within their own company and beyond, should that become necessary?
- What is their reputation?
- Can they adapt when things change?

- Is the team complete? Who else needs to be on the team?
- How will the team respond to adversity?
- What are the possible consequences if one or more team members leaves?

A successful I-Net team will include committed leadership at various levels. Senior managers will act as venture investors who are actively involved in management of the venture. Line management who will carry out or enable I-Net implementation must be invested also, perhaps through risk-sharing arrangements. For example, the stock option program used at Cisco Systems, making all the employees holders of Cisco stock, works to ensure that all the workers at Cisco look beyond their immediate paychecks to act in a way that is beneficial for the longer term of the company.

At least one senior manager should take on the task of becoming process literate—that is, he or she should acquire the ability to tell when team members who have greater technical expertise are communicating too optimistic a message. This requires doing some homework and paying close attention to the initiative but it does not require becoming an expert in I-Net technologies.

The team will also need to include some sources of specific expertise. The implementing company will need to supply a strong project manager, excellent technical resources, and a good financial analyst. It is important that the client company retain strong people in project management and technical roles, or else the project expertise will gravitate toward the vendor members of the team. This is a recipe for letting the initiative get out of control. Arrangements in which vendors do the bulk of the project management and technical work can be effective, but only if the client company keeps strong people close to shadow the work being done. We refer to this as the unsnowable requirement. Someone on the client side must have the expertise and organizational stature to say "hold on" when proposals are overly optimistic or fail in some other way to sufficiently protect the interests of the client company. The vendor representation on the project team would ordinarily include systems integrators as well as people from the I-Net product company.

Even if you know who the right people are, it is not always easy to get them on *your* team. It is extremely important to obtain assurances from vendors that appropriate resources are available for your I-Net initiative. A systems integrator might have the best I-Net experts in the world, but if they never work on your implementation that fact is of little use to you. Make sure your vendors not only have the expertise needed to solve hard problems, but also that they are willing to make it available to you in a timely manner.

Getting the right people on the team can be a challenge even inside your own organization. Cisco used a high standard in staffing its internal I-Net team: "We pulled out people that the business absolutely did not want to give up." Selected individuals were willing to participate because Cisco had framed the initiative as a career opportunity, one that was not career-diverting. By working to raise the profile of the initiative, the I-Net implementation became *the* opportunity within the company.

Both companies adjusted their team composition in an ongoing manner. Cisco changed its hardware vendor. Tektronix replaced a large systems integrator with a small one. At one point in the Tektronix implementation, integrators and consultants were provided by the product vendor. In originally choosing partners, both companies underwent a thorough, though not necessarily lengthy, process. Cisco, for example, tapped all of the information sources it could find in a short period of time, calling on large corporations, big accounting firms, and research sources for information on experiences with products and service providers.

Final Thoughts on Thinking like a VC

The exceptionally high levels of cost, risk, and benefit associated with I-Net initiatives make them more closely resemble the creation of a new venture rather than a capital acquisition. They should be managed in a way that fits with this fact. Making this happen will require casting off some of the conventional knowledge about how initiatives should be justified, how contracts should be written, and how teams should be rewarded and managed. Two basic ideas are at the center of this way of managing, and anyone who wishes to manage this way must take these two ideas to heart.

First, in an environment of great uncertainty, money often buys information and not much else. Knowing something that you did not know before—that an approach you are taking does not work, for example—is very valuable when you are managing a new venture, even if it is not accompanied by concrete progress toward a planned milestone. Managing I-Net as a new venture requires that we redefine how we think about progress.

Second, nothing must be done that interferes with the lines of communication between the various members of the I-Net team. This rules out many traditional mechanisms aimed at control of a project. If you insist that systems integrators provide you with sophisticated metrics to prove their progress, they no doubt will—but that won't be nearly as successful as a candid conversation about a recently discovered problem. It should be clearly established up front that there is a significant exploration component in so uncertain a project as an I-Net implementation. Unanticipated problems must not be interpreted or punished as failures.

Emphasis should be on maintaining effective problem solving—by structuring the initiative correctly and getting the right people on it—rather than on monitoring compliance with plans. Create detailed plans, but recognize that they are obsolete from the moment they are finished. Appreciate plans primarily for the understanding that is generated in the process of creating them.

The peculiar characteristics of an I-Net initiative bring to mind something once written by the philosopher Friedrich Nietzsche: "That which does not kill me makes me stronger." With your new mind-set in place, let's move on to creating an executable plan of action.

Establishing an Action Agenda

Critical to mapping out an agenda for creating an I-Net is pinpointing where your company is in its evolution to becoming a network organization. Your agenda will be determined by your company's current level of permeability. For instance, building a strategic I-Net from a greenfield site founded in the late 1990s is very different from transforming a large hierarchical or multidivisional organization into a streamlined business while simultaneously building an I-Net. The hybrid bricks-and-clicks company positioned between pure Internet plays and the type of traditional incumbent we've discussed in this book so far as being a victim of dot vertigo requires a different approach as well.

We can characterize the main differences among the three scenarios by mapping companies in the IT industry onto the stages S-curves as shown in Figure 10.2.

Figure 10.2 highlights two key dimensional starting points for building an I-Net and becoming a permeable company: complexity (starting with a greenfield site or an existing organization), and the existing state of IT (legacy systems or post-1995 Internet IT environment).

The two dimensions provide four quadrants, which can be thought of as defining the key starting points for creating network organizations. Large, complex industrial age organizations and deep penetration and dependence of legacy systems characterize Zone 1 companies. IBM is an

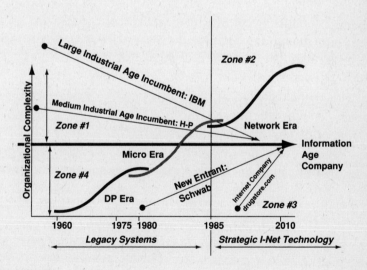

Figure 10.2   Different Starting Points for Transformation and Building Strategic I-Nets

example of a company that started in Zone 1 at the time that Lou Gerstner became CEO.

Zone 1 companies have a level of complexity that is associated with becoming large without the benefit of modern technologies. Thus, the incumbents integrated new technologies incrementally during the time that IT was evolving from playing a relatively minor role in companies as a support resource to having a major role as an enabler. The speed of this technological evolution and the rate of assimilation into large organizations was not in sync, and we have seen large companies continuing to fall behind in incorporating the latest technologies into their businesses.

Zone 2 companies can be bricks, bricks-and-clicks, or Internet pure plays. Their primary attribute is that they were conceived of and founded with a high level of scalability. Zone 2 companies include firms that have spun off from larger parent firms and adopted business approaches that emulate the dot-com competitor. The Ford supply chain initiative in which a new company is established to supply Ford and the rest of the auto industry offers an example of a company in Zone 2—organizational complexity is high, but the new organization starts out from a greenfield site.

Low organizational complexity and an environment of no legacy systems characterize Zone 3 companies. In addition, the IT environments of both Zone 2 and Zone 3 provide the availability and affordability of network technologies including the Internet. Drugstore.com is an example of a Zone 3 company.

Zone 4 companies are characterized as businesses that establish or enter new markets before they become part of the mainstream. Schwab and Microsoft are examples of companies that started in Zone 4.

Figure 10.3 examines the four overriding factors in more detail, highlighting the comparative strengths, weaknesses, and exposure of companies represented by the four zones.

A quick look at the asset/liability assessment in this figure indicates that the management of the Zone 1 incumbent is facing a daunting challenge and therefore must leverage its asset positions to counterbalance dealing with its liabilities.

While Zone 3 companies have important assets that allow them to challenge the incumbent's position, scaling the company and building the back-office IT and operations are critical challenges. One of the most im-

Figure 10.3   Relative Strengths and Weaknesses of Companies in the Information Age

Factors	Zone 1: Incumbent Companies (Complex/ Legacy)	Zone 2: Incumbent Start-ups (Complex/ Non-legacy)	Zone 3: Dot-com Companies (Simpler/ Non-legacy)	Zone 4 "Bricks-and-clicks" Companies (Simpler/ Legacy)
Human Resources				
Management	Asset	Liability	Liability	Asset
Employees	Liability	Asset	Asset	Asset
Culture	Liability	Asset	Asset	Asset
Financials				
Balance sheet	Asset	Liability	Liability	Asset
Cash flow	Asset	Liability	Liability	Asset
Cost structure	Liability	Asset	Asset	Asset
Revenue per employee	Liability	Asset	Asset	Asset
Internal Organization				
Control	Asset	Liability	Liability	Liability
Scale	Asset	Liability	Liability	Asset
Flexibility	Liability	Asset	Asset	Asset
Innovation	Liability	Asset	Asset	Asset
Speed	Liability	Asset	Asset	Asset
Extended Organization	Liability	Asset	Asset	Asset
Customer Relationships	Asset	Asset	Liability	Asset
Information Technology				
Back-office IT	Liability	Asset	Liability	Asset
Front-office IT	Liability	Asset	Asset	Liability

portant advantages is that these companies are coming of age during the same time that the Internet and its associated technologies are becoming well established.

The bricks-and-clicks companies in Zone 4 hold the strongest position. These companies were generally started in the 1980s and have competed against incumbents by building technology-enabled organizations.

They have also generally moved aggressively to build out their front of-fice systems.

Zone 1: Transforming a Large Industrial Age Company—IBM

IBM is characteristic of the Zone 1 multidivisional incumbent, and in-volves the highest level of sheer complexity of all the four zones. IBM had not only reached a large-scale, global operation before the wide-spread proliferation of personal computers, but built many of its back-of-fice administrative systems during the data processing era when computers cost in the millions of dollars versus the thousands that they cost today. Further, the body of knowledge about how to develop infor-mation systems and the tools for software development were much less sophisticated than they are today.

Information systems that integrate supply chain management systems, which in turn incorporate data warehouses and online communication technologies, enable simplification of operations that was not feasible earlier. Without one database and online updating, information on sales, payments, and shipments must be continuously reconciled by armies of clerical and accounting personnel. These activities become institutional-ized into the organization, and the suborganizations involved in the ac-tivities take on lives of their own.

Ways of operating in the pre- or partial computer environments be-came institutionalized as standard operating procedures. For example, many decisions were made on the basis of estimates rather then on up-to-date information, which further complicated analysis and coordination.

As indicated in Figure 10.2 with the horizontal line delineating relative organizational complexity to which the lines for the types of companies converge, a less complex organization is possible today while holding revenue constant. The middle line of the y-axis represents complexity of an organization. Highly complex companies are attempting to simplify, and less complex companies (building from greenfield sites) are attempt-ing to cope with higher levels of complexity involved in scaling up oper-ations. Operating with one logical database for the company coupled with real-time updates from transactions and events reduces the complex-ity in organizations by many orders of magnitude. The less complex information age organization can process similar revenue volumes and complicated customer orders, but much more efficiently with the computer keeping track of things in real time.

Action Agenda for Managers of Zone 1 Companies

Scanning down the column in Figure 10.1 for Zone 1 companies shows many more liabilities than assets. Thus, management must aggressively leverage key assets. Lou Gerstner has provided a pretty effective action agenda for Zone 1 companies that can be translated into a four-point action program. The key action items for managers who need to make a similar transformation involve the cost structure of the company, the ability to manage a large transition, rethinking the company's goals and priorities in light of customer service, and redesigning the company's business processes and operations.

Action Point #1: Cost Structure
The main exposure for Zone 1 companies is a noncompetitive cost structure—and the risk can be huge. Since most Zone 1 companies have been around for a long time, their products and services take on commodity-like characteristics, exposing the company to price competition and loss of market share. New entrants are drawn into the industry and put pressure on margins.

Business processes in general are poorly leveraged with IT. As a result, there are too many people doing the work of the company. An outdated culture and attitude toward use of IT plagues the Zone 1 company.

Drastic and quick measures are required to deal with the cost structure problem. Benchmarking business process costs against best practices, including number of employees required to do the work of the company, is a first step. This step then must be followed by downsizing to the right number of people and ensuring that IT is available for the employees left to carry out their business processes in new ways.

Action Point #2: Change Management
The large scale of the incumbent is an asset, but can turn into a liability unless effective management is carried out during the transition from legacy systems to IT-leveraged business processes. Massive

numbers of people must be retrained for new jobs and business processes. Also, job skills in general reach higher levels as all workers are expected to use computers. Some separations of workers either uninterested in developing higher levels of skills or incapable of developing them is inevitable.

Action Point #3: Focus Management on Customer Relationships
Another asset that is at risk to change to a liability is the established customer relationships of the incumbent. IBM, for example, had its technology installed in the majority of Fortune 1,000 companies. It had established a reputation with CIOs that "You never get fired for buying IBM." IBM earned this reputation by providing IT that worked and service levels that were extremely responsive when customers incurred inevitable breakdowns in their complex system environments.

When Lou Gerstner took over IBM, he quickly realized that this full-service reputation and customer penetration were unique to IBM; no other company had achieved this position with customers. These were valuable and unique assets to build upon.

To prevent the squandering of IBM's unique assets, among Gerstner's first actions was to curtail a move to break up IBM into smaller companies. Then, we also observe his personal leadership in emphasizing the importance of the customer relationship during the upheavals associated with the company's transformation.

Action Point #4: Redesign Business Processes and Install Up-to-Date Technologies
Dealing with the liabilities of legacy systems and a culture that views technology as more tactical than strategic is a problem that requires some time to be effectively dealt with. IBM is still in the midst of executing an action plan here.

To get a general perspective on the magnitude of the resources required and the time needed to address the problem of obsolete business processes and legacy systems, the initiative of A&P, a $10 billion supermarket chain, is representative. A&P's initiative includes over 100 A&P key employees devoted full time, 80 IBM full-time consultants, and a rollout program that will take two years to complete and touch all of its 81,000 employees.

Operating on a scale like A&P involves processing volumes of transactions that are staggering in numbers and overall complexity. The company cultures that have grown up in these companies have tended to buffer and resist change. Thus, the critical management challenge is to make transformational change while simultaneously running the business in a manner that does not result in a total breakdown.

Simultaneous with restructuring the company, the executive management team must figure out how to make the transition from its cumbersome vertically integrated structure to a virtually integrated network structure. Integral to successfully making this transition is leveraging IT to ensure coordination among partners in place of controls used in a vertically integrated organization.

Zone 2: Incumbent Spin-Offs—Ford's Subsidiary, Visteon

Zone 2 companies start out with scale. Ford, for example, set up Visteon Corporation in 1997 as an independent company to supply parts and components to Ford and other automobile and truck manufacturers. In 1999, Visteon had revenues of about $20 billion and 81,000 employees. A primary objective of these spin-offs is to untangle inefficient vertical integration. In addition, it is hoped that the new spin-off will be able to capitalize on a near-greenfield site in building an organization and I-Net. General Motors established a similar spin-off called Delphi Corporation. Delphi is similarly large with revenue of $29 billion and over 200,000 employees.

A different kind of example of a Zone 2 company is OptiMark and Island—both ECNs. Here an ECN like Island links into an established shared infrastructure for stock trading and clearing. As a result, Island can virtually integrate with the existing infrastructure to trade millions of shares of stock efficiently and can build its greenfield organization and technology while focusing on its core value proposition.

Action Agenda for Zone 2 Companies

Zone 2 companies are relatively new, and few, so it is hard to get a good fix on their detailed strengths and weaknesses. Indeed, they do have some advantages of being near-greenfield sites. However, they inherit a number of legacy systems and business processes that must be replaced in their creation of a new organization and I-Net.

Zone 3: Dot Companies—Drugstore.com

Drugstore.com is characteristic of Zone 3 companies. Zone 3 companies need to gain momentum and maintain it to survive. Since dot coms are all about speed, agility, and flexibility, they need to use their assets to maintain momentum in driving revenue, building relationships with customers, and showing a path to profitability. Anything less than perfect execution will jeopardize momentum, which in turn will risk causing investors to lose interest in their stock.

Action Agenda for Zone 3 Companies

Peter Neupert of drugstore.com has laid out an effective action agenda for Zone 3 dot companies. First, get together the most savvy Internet team possible. Second, build out the front office to connect with customers and interface with back-office outsourcers to quickly get a product offering out. Third, grow the company in partnership with your customers, and as soon as possible build out the back office designed in a way to be driven by real-time information from customers. All the while, maintain momentum to retain the interest and favor of investors required to fund the company.

Zone 4: Bricks-and-Clicks Companies—Schwab

Charles Schwab Corporation is characteristic of Zone 4 companies. Visionaries, who have been the first movers into the network age, generally conceive of and found Zone 4 companies. Charles Schwab understood the concept of empowering customers before most, and he understood the potential of IT to empower customers with information before most as well.

Schwab experienced some hard times during the proving of the business model. He ran short of cash, which necessitated selling his company to Bank of America. The management of Bank of America never seemed to understand the power of the Schwab business model. As a result, Schwab then bought his company back from Bank of America, and the rest is history. The company proved its business model and is now an industry leader.

Action Agenda for Zone 4 Companies

Zone 4 companies like Schwab, Microsoft, and Wal-Mart have been the industry's first movers into the information age. All of these companies have been led by visionaries, who also realized the need to build capable management teams who could, in turn, craft management strategies and execute the strategies to build major companies. Both vision and execution have been key to the success of Zone 4 companies.

Charles Schwab partnered with David Pottruck to build a company that was true to Schwab's vision, but built and scaled with an operational discipline. David Pottruck had the operational capabilities, as well as the intelligence to see the value of Schwab's vision and the rare skill of partnering with Schwab, the visionary, to realize the vision. Charles Schwab had the rare additional skill of a visionary that enabled him to appreciate Pottruck's skills and develop an equal partnership with him.

In a similar manner, the Bill Gates and Steve Ballmer partnership has led to a like outcome.

Zone 4 companies are different from most Zone 3 dot companies in two ways. First, Zone 4 companies have scaled up to become large and complex companies. Consequently, Zone 4 companies have to continue to focus on speed and flexibility within a more complex environment.

Second, based on when they were founded, Zone 4 companies still have to grapple with legacy systems. Once real-time front-office IT is built out to customers, the legacy systems problem is amplified. For example, when Schwab strategically decided to drop its commissions to $29.95, a legacy system constrained the firm from capturing revenue from other sources in the commission structures. Since then, Schwab has fixed this problem as it continues to migrate off its legacy systems.

One of the key issues that we discuss when teaching our Schwab cases is the positioning of the Zone 4 company. David Pottruck, Schwab's co-CEO, describes Schwab's strategic positioning as "a category of one." Rather than thinking of Schwab as stuck in the middle between the Zone 1 incumbent Merrill Lynch and the Zone 3 dot com, E*Trade, the idea of "a category of one" is that all three companies are competing for different investor segments. However, the strategic moves by all three companies seem to indicate they are all competing for investors in general.

Indeed, IT has expanded the strategic options and the way that companies can compete by discovering unique customer needs and creatively serving those needs. Thus, the practice of thinking about customers in broad segments seems to be much less relevant than it was.

The key challenge for the Zone 4 company is to maintain a lean cost structure while being willing to stay on the leading edge by cannibalizing its own products and services before competitors do. Schwab has been an exemplar here.

What If You Need Help Getting Off the Runway?

There are a variety of service providers who can help fledgling I-Net initiatives get up and running. This section examines six types of companies that provide I-Net consulting services.

Systems Integrators

Systems integrators specialize in large system implementation and integration projects. These large firms tend to conduct higher-priced projects, where they can leverage their scale. While the category as a whole provides offerings in the entire range of needs, individual firms tend to specialize in either technology or strategy. Examples include Accenture (formerly Andersen Consulting), Pricewaterhouse-Coopers, Cambridge Technology Partners (now a part of Novell), Sapient, and IBM. These firms are working to reinvent themselves by spinning off separate e-business consulting divisions, acquiring smaller firms that have e-business experience, and using aggressive hiring programs to acquire Internet capabilities.

Web Design Firms

Web design firms tend to be smaller undifferentiated firms that emphasize technical delivery with little focus on business strategy. Most of the estimated 4,500 firms in this category were launched specifically for the delivery of Web-enabled applications.

Interactive Agencies

Interactive agencies entered the industry from advertising. They tout their creative design, branding, and marketing expertise. To these firms, web site design and development is a natural extension of the services they already offer to their clients. Notable firms in this category included Agency.com, Razorfish, and Poppe.Tyson.

Management Consultants

Management consultants view Web strategy as an extension of their traditional business strategy roles. They use their powerful brands and traditional high-level relationships to move into the e-business space, but rarely go beyond strategy into actual application development. Examples include McKinsey and Boston Consulting Group.

Pure Internet Players

Pure Internet players comprise a new segment that crosses boundaries. Firms in this segment, including USWeb/CKS, Viant, Scient, and ZEFER, use a combination of creative and strategic talent to develop e-business strategy and messages. They also deliver applications, either by playing a general contractor role or by using their own development staff. The firms have different strategic positioning and messages. For example, Viant and ZEFER have a more strategic orientation than USWeb/CKS, which emphasizes creative and technical design over strategy.

ASPs (Application Service Providers)

The shortage of software engineers and the rapidly expanding capacity along with dropping bandwidth cost of the telecommunications infrastructure have led to the ASP model. In general, the ASP model is for a company to host a firm's applications on servers housed in a data center. Servers access customer applications and files from storage devices. ASP end users access the remote applications through their desktop computers equipped with a Web browser. From a market under $100 million in 1998, the ASP market has reached about $6 billion by 2001.

The growth potential of the ASP market has brought more than 100 companies into this nascent industry. These ASP service companies have come from different origins. Both IT outsourcing providers (e.g., EDS) and consulting firms have entered the ASP industry.

Enterprise Resource Planning companies such as SAP and Oracle have entered the industry. Oracle introduced a new business unit, Oracle Business Online, to sell and host its own ERP suite. SAP has chosen to enter the industry by outsourcing its ERP software through partnerships with established ASP companies.

The ASP market has also fueled growth in large hosting data centers such as Exodus. These professionally run network data centers can bring a level of sophistication in maintaining, backing up, and running large, up-to-date operations that are increasingly hard to staff with in-house personnel.

Key Concepts

Thinking about the future:

- Making I-Nets happen and realizing the potential benefits require a renaissance CIO working with a renaissance CEO.
- People make the difference.

11

Five Myths of the Internet

Dot companies have given us quite a ride, bringing us to dizzying heights and then plunging us toward the earth faster than a turbocharged roller coaster. The Internet is the fastest technology ever to reach 50 million users; the Internet took only 4 years to reach 50 million users.[1] It took 13 years for television, and 38 years for radio.

Almost overnight, Internet penetration raced to more than 100 million users with more than half of U.S. homes having an Internet connection. The Internet provided access to more than a critical mass of customers. Entrepreneurs rushed to provide virtual stores to sell books, prescription drugs, pet supplies, automobiles, securities, and auctioned plane tickets over the Internet. But the stratospheric heights of the stock prices and flood of dot companies were not sustainable; most tumbled beginning in April 2000 when the bellwether Amazon.com had not become profitable after five years, and its prospects for profits in the foreseeable future were a bit cloudy. By 2001, more than 90 percent of dot companies had fallen from their IPO highs; many crashed and burned, and closed their virtual doors.

MBAs that flocked to Silicon Valley to hang their stars on a fledgling B2C or B2B dot com have now reinterpreted B2C to "back to consulting" and B2B to "back to banking"—the two industries that were favored

185

among MBAs before dot companies. So it would seem that the Internet was not such a big deal as was being made of it. A common refrain heard today is "dot nothings."

Like some of the other sleeping giants, IBM, which earlier was proclaimed "the biggest dot.com" and even brought out its 1999 annual report with only ".com" on the cover, in its 2000 annual report seems to have backpedaled a bit on its earlier enthusiasm for dot companies.

This rather dramatic backlash reaction is typically American: What is so quickly embraced as the "new new thing" can be abandoned just as quickly as its meteoric ascension. However, such a hastily drawn conclusion about the Internet and dot companies is more the result of dot vertigo from the wild dot-com ride than careful reasoning. And such a conclusion is strategically hazardous for senior executives. It is associated with five Internet myths, the first one being the most dangerous.

1. Dot companies are "dot nothings."
2. Legacy systems can be built upon.
3. The United States is the Internet leader.
4. PCs provide the Internet access.
5. English is the language of the Internet.

Myth 1: Dot Companies Are "Dot Nothings"

Dot companies exploded on the business scene and were built with the advantage of a full-featured Internet. Rather than having to build out expensive bricks-and-mortar physical distribution stores, dot companies were able to reach customers through virtual stores over the Internet. Rather than having to buy shopping carts for accumulating customer purchases and cash registers for taking customers' money, dot companies built virtual shopping carts and used the electronic banking system to take customers' money over the Internet. Rather than the customer having to drive to the store, shop, and pick up purchases, dot companies used the highly automated and efficient overnight shippers of UPS, Federal Express, and the U.S. Postal Service. The economics of these businesses are extremely favorable for three reasons: (1) The Internet is a shared infrastructure, (2) the transaction is carried out using the customer's own computer, and (3) the existing economic infrastructure of established companies can be virtually integrated to access services (like credit verification) to complete the transaction. These elements are the essence of the dot-com business model and provide important efficiencies and unique services not before available to customers. And, of course, the desirability of these efficiencies and unique services was pretty obvious to all and fueled the 1998-2000 dot frenzy.

What caused the frenzy to stall and nose-dive had to do with all the other aspects of scaling and building a business in a manner that provides a foundation for long-term growth and profitability. Long-term growth and profitability involve the complex processes of accounting and finance, operations, marketing, personnel, and planning—in short, good management. However, it was and isn't obvious how traditional management practice applies and needs to be adapted to the speed and flexibility made possible by the new Internet-based dot companies. It is clear that the industrial age management principles cannot be simply applied "as is" to the dot companies.

At the Harvard Business School, we have been studying the process of managing dot companies and transforming successful incumbents of the industrial age to become successful in the information age. The two processes are fundamentally different. The dot com builds from the greenfield site; the incumbent must transform from one form to another form. The process for the incumbent is one of creative destruction.[2] The most important challenge for the incumbent is to appropriately incorporate IT and master the process of information resource management. The most important challenge for the dot company is to master management; dot companies typically expect too much from IT, and don't pay enough attention to building a solid management infrastructure. Often heard from the dot company management team is that the key is to hire the brightest people available, equip them with the most sophisticated IT possible, and fight bureaucracy; the rest will sort itself out. Upon hearing such arrogance, it is easy not to take the dot company seriously.

The large established industry incumbent and the dot company represent two ends of a continuum. The established incumbent starts with a level of complexity required to support a scale of operations that was not originally designed with incorporation of IT. These companies, like IBM, have continued to incorporate IT in their operations, enabling major downsizing while growing revenues. IBM has reduced its employment from a high of 400,000 to around 300,000 while continuing to increase revenues. The role of IT continued to be a key factor in leveraging employees; IBM moved from less than $150,000 of revenue per employee in 1991 to more than $280,000.

IBM scaled up to become a large company before computer technology was available. Its early use of computers in the data processing era led to an applications portfolio supporting the company with systems that have now aged; these are known as legacy systems. IBM's challenge is to transform both the organization and legacy IT portfolio to simpler and speedier systems supporting an IT-enabled organization structure.[3]

In contrast, the dot company drugstore.com started from a greenfield site in 1998 and built its IT applications portfolio with the benefit of network era technologies and Internet standards. Its challenge is to scale up its IT-enabled network organization to become a more efficient, larger organization.[4]

In between IBM and drugstore.com are near-dot companies like Microsoft and Cisco that were founded in the mid-1980s; they were able to take advantage of the Internet before they became too complex and labored under institutionalized legacy systems built during the DP and micro eras. Since dot companies are still relatively new, we can learn more about building organizations and IT infrastructures from greenfield sites by examining the near-dot companies. It appears that these companies have benefited from their longer experiences in constructing their organizations and management structures. Cisco in particular embraced the Internet technologies early; it proceeded to replace all its back-office legacy systems in 1996 at a cost of $15 million, and then went on to Web-enable its back office systems and build out its front office systems for product/service delivery to its customers for a cost of about $100 million. By 2000, Cisco's annual benefits for the $115 million investment were more than $1.3 billion. A large proportion of these benefits came from shipping software products over the Internet to customers, as well as providing more than 85 percent of customer service electronically over the Internet.[5] Further, Cisco has used IT to implement what it calls an extended organization, which includes its suppliers and customers. Cisco's returns from investing in an IT-enabled organization structure and use of the Internet have been compelling.

A number of luminaries of the information age such as Geoffrey Moore[6] have concluded that the market value of a company is an important indicator of the viability and quality of the company's business model for generating income in the future. Using market value as a benchmark for company performance in the IT industry, within a short 10-year period, the industry market value leader role shifted from IBM to Microsoft to Cisco. IBM started with a complex vertically integrated organization and still today is the most vertically integrated company in the industry. Cisco has maximized the Internet in building a virtually integrated organization with suppliers and customers, which it calls its extended enterprise.

Myth 2: Legacy Systems Can Be Built Upon

It is extremely hard for senior managers to face up to the hard fact that their investments in IT prior to 1995 (before the Internet) are now completely obsolete and must be discarded. For the uninformed, it is so tempting to conclude that these IT systems can be built upon in providing the new IT infrastructure. Yet the evidence suggests otherwise.

From the Cisco case it is clear that there are huge benefits from integrating back office systems with front office systems. To do so, the back office systems must be up-to-date, and most importantly, integrate Internet standards and protocols. Another not-so-obvious lesson, however, is that the IT strategic focus shifts from back office systems to front office systems. The implication of this shift in focus is for management to be much more open than they were to installing standard ERP systems for updating the back office.

There are two underlying technical problems with legacy systems. First, Moore's Law has continued to work to provide more powerful and cheaper computers to the point that the way that systems were developed in the past was quite archaic compared to today—computers that cost millions of dollars only a few years ago cost just thousands of dollars today. Databases and real-time processing, which were prohibitively expensive during the DP era, are now standard for all systems. Further, many of the features available today and commonly incorporated in software and hardware simply were not invented when many legacy systems of companies were developed (e.g., graphic user interfaces, data compression, and data mining).

But even more serious than the technical problems is the organizational architecture problem. The organizational architecture of industrial age companies is the functional hierarchical organization paced by the annual budget cycle. The annual budget cycle is the heartbeat of the organization when major resource decisions are made. In contrast, the dot company or information age organization architecture is the IT-enabled network; the resource decisions are paced by real-time messaging computers enabling dynamic resource allocation. Consequently, the information age company can move from a "make and sell" strategy to a "sense and respond" strategy.[7] The slower pace of the industrial age organization is like watching and waiting for water to boil on a stove.

As is often said, dot companies are all about speed and flexibility. Network organization structures enabled by post-1995 IT provide the speed and flexibility missing in older organizations. The legacy systems of the older incumbents have set in concrete the older way of operating on annual budget time versus real time.

Myth 3: The United States Is the Internet Leader

Many business managers maintain that the United States leads the development of e-business models and solutions, and will do so indefinitely. Several factors indicate otherwise.

Industry forecasts show the United States being dwarfed by China's Internet penetration rates. U.S. companies are no longer the gold standard of what works and doesn't work involving the Internet. For example, many B2B and B2C ventures have failed in the United States, whereas non-U.S. companies have launched successful B2B projects. Managers are simply blinding themselves when they measure technological success exclusively through domestic ventures.

In the case of Japan, even though thousands of miles of wire had not been laid, millions of consumers had easy access to the Internet. Japan is not likely to be the only Asian country showing tremendous leadership in developing Internet technologies and business models. In fact, several companies, including Li & Fung[8] and Alibaba.com,[9] have demonstrated

Japan Invades United States with Wireless Internet

DoCoMo, a subsidiary of Nippon Telegraph and Telephone (NTT), by investing in AT&T Wireless intends to duplicate its success with i-mode in the United States. DoCoMo has 33 million subscribers in Japan, holding a 60 percent market share. Since August 1999, DoCoMo i-Mode "always on" mobile Internet service has signed up more than 20 million subscribers in a little more than 18 months, and has built more than 25,000 content sites.[10]

how companies outside the United States are successfully executing global strategies and beating the United States in capturing emerging markets.

One obvious indicator that the United States is falling behind as a global technological leader is its workforce. For example, at the epicenter of America's high-tech community, Silicon Valley, there has been a dearth of tech-savvy individuals in the market. This has resulted in an enormous swell of immigrants in recent years. Approximately 200,000 people from India, arguably America's most successful immigrant group, live in Silicon Valley today. Combined, this population is worth $235 billion, and without these Indian immigrants, *Fortune* proclaims, "the Valley wouldn't be what it is today."[11] This is because U.S. schools do not produce enough qualified engineers to fill the thousands of jobs the New Economy has created. In 2000 alone, over 800,000 jobs were not filled due to an unqualified workforce.

The need for a more qualified workforce calls for better preparation of students from kindergarten through secondary school for the New Economy. According to the CEO Forum on Education & Technology, most schools "do not prepare students to prosper in tomorrow's workplace." Although the computer-to-student ratio is now one to five, *Business Week* writer William Symonds contends:

Most of America's 53 million children in kindergarten through 12th grade still attend schools designed for the industrial, if not the agrarian, era. Everything from the school calendar, which still reflects the rhythms of farm life, to chalk-and-textbook instruction are better suited to prepare kids for the past than the future.[12]

In order to have a competitive edge, America's schools must reform the same way many U.S. companies have—through computers, the Internet, and Internet-related technologies. For example, long-distance learning must be available for students without advanced placement courses taught at their schools (much like a senior executive video conference), school projects must be able to be conducted via the Internet (much like researchers), and Web creation assignments must be possible (like Web developers). By developing these skills in students in primary and secondary schools, IT worker deficits can be avoided in the future, and the need to import talented workers will not be as great.

A second trend dispelling the notion of U.S. high-tech leadership is the downfall of the United States as the standard for what constitutes technological success. For example, in the United States, B2B businesses that were once projected to thrive are failing one by one. Aviation, Inc., an airline-to-supplier B2B, never even went online because it didn't realize the magnitude of airplane parts and the diversity of different kinds. After four months, M-Xchange.com, Inc. went under because the minority supplier enterprise failed to bring in sufficient profits to survive.[13] Chemdex, an earlier touted B2B success, just closed its doors for business. As even bigger brand names stumble in the U.S. market, many managers have written off B2B and B2G (business to government) ventures as doomed. On a global scale, however, many B2Bs have been successful, especially in emerging markets like China that have impressive manufacturing abilities. Managers have to realize that just because something isn't successful in the United States doesn't mean it can't succeed in another part of the world.

With China and other global Internet markets just beginning to develop, companies with already extraordinary value will soon be among many like powerhouses. Take, for example, Li & Fung, a 95-year-old global export trading company that was worth $2 billion at the end of 2000. Headquartered in Hong Kong, almost 70 percent of Li & Fung's sales were in the United States and almost 30 percent were in Europe. With 3,600 employees in 48 offices in 32 countries, Li & Fung represents the future of business. According to one source:

The company provided value-added services across the entire supply chain in a so-called "borderless" manufacturing environment. A down jacket's filling, for example, might come from China, the outer shell fabric from Korea, the zippers from Japan, the inner lining from Taiwan, and the elastics, label, Velcro, and other trim from Hong Kong. The garment might be dyed in South Asia, stitched in China, then sent back to Hong Kong for quality control and finally packaged for delivery.[14]

In addition, Li & Fung produced customized goods for retailers via its web site. Using the newest IT capabilities, users can go to the site, pick specifications such as buttons, colors, and collars, and place their orders (see Figure 11.1). Available 24 hours a day, Li & Fung's company web site provides a cost-efficient and convenient tool reaching global large buyers as well as SMEs (small/medium enterprises).

Another dot company out of China, Alibaba.com, allows SMEs to promote themselves, find trading partners, and conduct business transactions online for no fee. Unlike most B2Bs, Alibaba.com brings together sellers

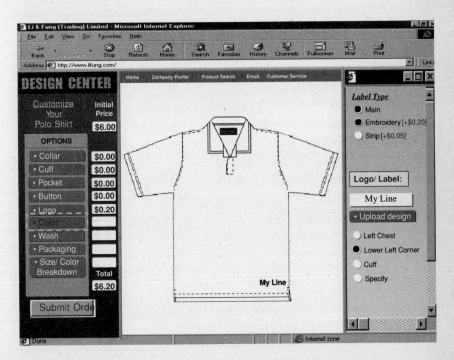

Figure 11.1   Limited Mass Customization (Web Page Sample)

Global Virtual Integration in High Tech

Guadalajara is a microcosm of the revolution in high-tech manufacturing. Cisco, Sun, Hewlett-Packard, and Intel in fact don't manufacture their own products anymore. Solectron ($14 billion in revenue) and Flextronics ($12 billion in revenue) actually build most of the routers, servers, printers, and PCs that the so-called OEMs (original equipment manufacturers) design and market.

Solectron employs 71,000 workers at 60 facilities around the world. In Guadalajara, about 175,000 people work in the electronics industry. Solectron is Guadalajara's largest employer, with more than 10,000 employees working at its 716,000-square-foot plant.[15]

and buyers from 27 different markets. Also unique to Alibaba.com is its target customer—small to medium firms that do not have the means to do business on a global scale. Alibaba.com matches these firms up with other global players using its "My Trade Activity" feature, which allows members to purchase and accept offers as well as negotiate online. Aside from being a Chinese company that is successful throughout Asia and especially India, Alibaba.com's global presence is illustrated through its widespread membership. Realizing that the Chinese market was "a unique strength that [was ours] to lose," Alibaba.com saw the future of the marketplace as being dependent on China and other parts of Asia, and that as a global enterprise it would find that developing these markets would be beneficial in the long run.[16]

Unlike U.S. managers, the Alibaba and Li & Fung management understood not only the importance of wearing a global "hat," but also the potential of Eastern markets enabled by the Internet. By not disqualifying Internet business models and strategies that were unsuccessful in the United States, they were able to import these ideas and subsequently find success.

Myth 4: PCs Provide the Internet Access

A myth held widely by U.S. managers is the relationship between the Internet and PCs. Many mistakenly think that without a PC a stay-at-home mom cannot buy plane tickets and a teenager cannot check out favorite teams. This assumption is based on the widespread dependence on PCs in the United States, and is not necessarily the case beyond our borders. In Japan, for instance, NTT DoCoMo has made the Internet available to over half its population through wireless handheld devices. The i-mode phone is just one example of how the Internet is made available outside of the PC and thrives in previously ignored population segments.

While in the United States the PC has remained the most popular way of accessing the Internet, on a global scale it is not considered absolutely necessary for Web access. Even though foreign use of the PC will continue to grow in the next five years, especially in Asian nations, countries like Japan have already earned the second spot for most Internet users without widespread use of PCs.[17] This phenomenon is made possible by the Japanese NTT DoCoMo i-mode phone. Since its debut in February 1999, the i-mode has grown to 12 million subscribers. With 20 million subscribers by February 2001, NTT DoCoMo has a user base that took AOL eight years to achieve.

What is particularly unique about the i-mode is that it has almost all of the functions of a PC; it can send pictures, trade stocks, check e-mail, and

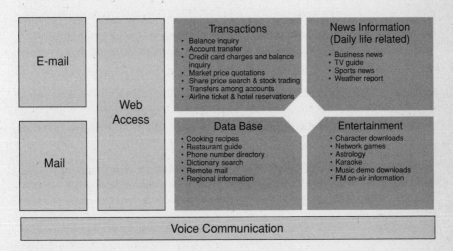

Figure 11.2   Summary of I-mode Services. Exhibit from "NTT DoCoMo: The Future of the Wireless Internet?" by Research Associate Matthew Sandoval and Supervised by Professor Stephen Bradley, Harvard Business School case N9-701-013, published September 22, 2000.

transfer accounts (see Figure 11.2). The i-mode's popularity in Japan can be attributed to several factors. First, because of its diverse array of services, the i-mode can reach varying age groups within the Japanese market. For example, i-mode services such as animation, games, and inexpensive e-mail successfully attract the teenage segment in Japan. As a matter of fact, just two months after the i-mode was launched, 88 percent of wireless subscribers were in their twenties. Secondly, the i-mode offers the DoPa Network that allows users to "pay-by-the-bit" of information transferred over their i-mode phones. Once the transfer has taken place, the user has a constant, "always on" connection to the information the user has downloaded. For example, once the transfer has taken place, a teenager can read e-mail hours after receiving it from his or her friend.

Another important reason why the i-mode took off was because the Japanese language characters are difficult to input on the traditional PC. In addition, consumers have high local calling costs. On average, Japan's dial-up users pay three times the U.S. rates for an hour of access. Japan also had a low penetration of PCs (approximately 14 percent) that allowed room for the new technology of the i-mode phones. The i-mode phone was the perfect solution to high dial-up prices and low PC penetration, and the Japanese have a well-known liking for small devices such as cellular phones. In the eyes of NTT DoCoMo, the Japanese market conditions and consumer preferences provided an excellent opportunity to bring the Internet to people via the i-mode phone. The company's strategy worked. Not even a year after its launch, NTT DoCoMo's stock soared to ¥3,640,000 in January 2000, showing a 269 percent return from just six months earlier.[18]

The recent and rapidly growing success of Japan's i-mode is the best example of how the Internet has managed to penetrate a market without widespread PC use. In order for U.S. companies to remain competitive, managers must realize Internet access can be obtained through various devices other than traditional mediums.

Myth 5: English Is the Language of the Internet

The Internet started as an American phenomenon. The United States has more Internet users than any other country; about 80 percent of the content on the Internet is in the English language. Thus, English is the unofficial language of the Internet.

Those facts may be true today, but in a matter of a few years there will be another set of facts. According to *Atlantic Monthly* writer Barbara Wallraff, author of a recent article entitled "What Global Language?," the increasing use of the Internet throughout the world will not necessarily lead to the globalization of English. As Eastern markets begin to embrace the Internet, countries like China with four times the number of native speakers to English speakers will begin to shape how information is communicated on the Internet.

Contrary to popular belief, the Internet will not necessarily spread English around the world. Author of "The Decline of the Native Speaker" David Graddol contends that the English-speaking population will shrink between the years 1950 and 2050 from 8 percent to less than 5 percent.[19] With countries like China growing user bases at rapid rates, the assumption of the English language growing because of the Internet is highly unlikely.[20] Already, China's number of wireless Internet users equals Japan's, the catch being that this figure represents only 1 percent of China's population and half of Japan's. Even with the absence of telecommunication standards and a controlling government, every six months China's user base has managed to double.[21] In a year or two, China will be replacing the United States for first place in Internet users, and will continue to overwhelm most countries in influencing the Internet as more and more of its 1,113 million native speakers gain Internet access.[22] As shown in Figure 11.3, China has 22 million Internet users, but the 22 million make up only 2 percent of China's population.

For a company to be considered a global leader, it must provide customers with web sites in languages other than English. According to Euro Marketing Associates, approximately 44 percent of the global online users do not speak English at home. This comes as no surprise; one study shows that 5.7 billion people have a native language other than English compared to 372 million who are native English speakers.[23] The myth of English, the language many fields such as science and finance have adopted, as the official language of the Internet is false.

Unfortunately, many American companies have failed to form a global strategy that takes into account different languages and cultures. By the beginning of 2000, only 17 percent of U.S. companies offered their com-

Figure 11.3   Number and Percent of
People Online Worldwide, July 1999

Country	People (millions)	Percent of Country's Total Population
United States	111	41%
China	22	2%
Japan	18	14%
United Kingdom	14	24%
Canada	13	43%
Germany	12	15%
Australia	7	36%
Brazil	7	4%
France	6	10%
South Korea	6	12%
Taiwan	5	22%
Italy	5	8%
Sweden	4	43%
Netherlands	3	18%
Spain	3	7%
Total	236	—

Source: *Industry Standard/Computer Industry Almanac,* "The
Net World in Numbers," February 14, 2000. China
figures are updated from *South China Morning Post,* January 29, 2001, "Cisco Systems Developing Full
Speed," by Mark O'Neill.

pany web sites in different languages and with culturally sensitive web
designs, as opposed to 63 percent of companies that offered no transla-
tion, period.[24] U.S. businesses are in great need of recognizing that vertical integration doesn't complete the formula for success; instead,
awareness of emerging markets and their effect on the New Economy is
needed to keep businesses viable in the new millennium.

Action Management

In the past decade, the United States has been responsible for introducing the world to many of the wonders of the Internet, I-Nets, and dot coms. It is clear why most managers, averaging around 35 to 45 years of age, would assume English to be the language of the Internet and PCs to dominate as the leading hardware to access the Internet.

The global reach of the Internet has extended far enough that we are only now beginning to see the possibilities it will create beyond U.S. borders. Thinking "outside of the box" must apply not only to the domestic front but also to how the world will function once absorbed by Internet technologies.

Senior managers need to stay on top of Internet developments and continue to incorporate the Internet into their strategies. Maintaining a balanced perspective and destroying popular myths is a start.

1. Dot companies and near-dot companies hold important lessons previewing the nature of the role of the Internet in an organization's strategy.
2. Legacy systems must be replaced with Internet-compatible technology. But legacy systems are generally not strategic; the focus for strategic IT has shifted to front office systems enabling real-time connections with customers.
3. The Internet has already been globalized, and leading innovations can originate in any country.
4. Internet access will quickly broaden beyond the PC to include many types of intelligent computer-based devices, including wireless, Global Positioning System (GPS)-enabled devices, and embedded computer chips in products.
5. English will not be the dominant language on the Internet. Companies will have to provide multiple translators for their web sites to accommodate carrying out business globally.

We are in a unique time in the management of business whereby the dominant technology for building business is shifting to information technologies. These emerging technologies provide opportunities to build more effective organizations, serve customers better, and enable a speed in global execution not before possible. With the huge changes in the technology landscape also come risks and disorientation—what we have called dot vertigo. By sharing the insights and experiences of those leading managers pioneering the new management described in this book, other managers can learn and move their companies ahead in a more effective manner while avoiding many of the perils of dot vertigo.

Appendix

Toward a Set of Network Age Management Principles

Management principles are the foundation for establishing the policies and procedures that govern an organization's operation. In an earlier book, we identified 13 internally consistent management principles as the foundation for industrial age companies characterized by functional hierarchical organizations.[1] The industrial age management principles were built around the ideas of scientific management first proposed by Frederick Winslow Taylor at the beginning of the last century. During the twentieth century, the principles of scientific management provided the foundation for organizing and conducting work. These principles were inculcated into the culture of business and the society as a whole.

Now in this new century of the information age, we see that these principles no longer hold as they once did to guide business organization and execution of work. As we observed throughout this book, new business models have emerged. In order to scale the new business models, a set of new information age management principles must emerge to provide the foundational underpinnings for the new business models. CEOs of the new organizations of the information age have continuously discarded the obsolete industrial age management principles and searched for a better set. Some CEOs (Bill Gates, for example) themselves served as models to communicate the management principles that they expected of their employees. Other CEOs such as John Chambers have codified new principles into a set of values focused on serving the customer. Lou Gerstner has written down eight simple principles and distributed them to every IBM employee (see Chapter 7).

Explicating and codifying the management principles are important to transforming and building companies in the information age. While information age management principles are still emerging, we can begin to see the new common set take form. This Appendix is intended to begin a definition of the new set of information age management principles and also to contrast the new set of information age management principles with the earlier set of industrial age management principles. Earlier, I applied the idea of creative destruction to the way industrial age companies transformed to information age companies and evolved from relying on industrial age management principles to finding new ones for the information age. "Creative destruction" is a useful way to describe the transformation process. As we continue to observe transformation of industrial age companies like IBM, it is clear that the creative destruction process is an extremely complex art form as exercised by information age CEOs and their management teams.

Some of the 23 management principles we identified as the foundation for the IT-enabled information age organization are salvaged from industrial era management principles; others are entirely new.[2] During transformation, the company is run with a hybrid set of management principles, which gives rise to inconsistencies that create conflict. Quality initiatives, for example, necessitate teamwork, which is in conflict with industrial age management principles of authority, performance measurement, and compensation.

The 23 emerging information age management principles are organized into three categories: obsolete principles that should be cast off, principles that are salvageable given appropriate parameter changes, and the requisite new principles. Each principle can be assessed and scored on a five-point continuum, and then the total scores summed to provide a rough indicator of information age transformation.

Obsolete Industrial Age Management Principles

Industrial age organizations were highly structured, and were somewhat ossified through the integration of the accounting system into the chart of organization as we discussed in Chapter 3. The integration of organization with accounting enabled a high level of control to be exercised through budgeting and division of labor. The division of labor of the departments is rolled up through the hierarchy into a set of activities that resulted in the production of a set of finished products or services. The financial results of each department rolled up through the hierarchy as well. Through vertical integration, the hierarchy could be extended to gain tight control of suppliers and distribution.

Modern computer systems have made all but obsolete the need to maintain an inflexible organization chart and integrated accounting systems. Modern computer systems and open standards have also eliminated the need for high levels of vertical integration. In fact, the inefficiencies of focus by having one company do everything has been curbed through allowing many companies to compete in narrow areas such as running computers, providing call center services, and the like.

The large, deep, vertically integrated hierarchies characteristic of the industrial age are all but obsolete, and are being replaced with organizations made up of parts drawn from a menu of organizational components. Major outsourcing of business activities began this trend, and the trend continues with the emergence of ASPs (application service providers), that provide outsourcing of individual business processes.

Hierarchy principle—The organization is structured in a multilevel three-tier hierarchy: top management over middle management and middle management over production workers.

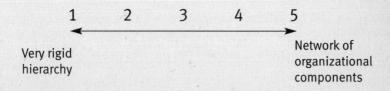

1   2   3   4   5

Very rigid
hierarchy

Network of
organizational
components

The traditional functional hierarchy with hard boundaries of what is in the organization and what is out based on control gives way to the organization being made up of a group of networked organizational components. The boundaries are not hard in the sense of a unit being either in or out of the organization, but boundaries are more like a continuum ranging from in the organization to out, but with a lot of variations in between, including outsourcing relationships, strategic partnerships, and global networks that can draw upon resources as needed.

Functional principle—Tasks are organized into fixed functions of line and staff based on type of functional expertise.

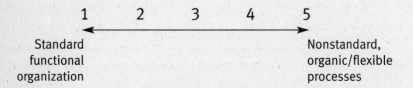

The functional principle was also exceptionally rigid. Functions were categorized into line and staff. Line functions were production and marketing, which were directly involved in producing and selling the product. Staff functions were in support of line functions. The functions were directly correlated with expertise, and universities and trade schools were organized to train people for the various functions.

Coordination with IT-based systems enable a much more tailored approach to organizing the company to the task at hand. Thus, strict adherence to a rigid functional organization is too inefficient to be viable in today's competitive environment.

Centralization/decentralization principle—Organizations are divided internally into corporate and divisions-the M-form.

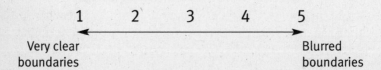

The main problem with the principle of centralization/decentralization is the way that the principle has been operationalized in the industrial age. The principle was used to define decision rights assigned to corporate and those assigned to divisions. You can think of the decision rights as existing on a continuum where at one end you have a highly centralized structure where corporate makes all the important business decisions; on the other end is where a decentralized division would make all the important business decisions. In the highly decentralized case, corporate would consist of a very small number of people and be primarily concerned with ensuring that the consolidated financial reports of the company were produced annually. The decentralized divisions would operate almost like independent business units, and be held accountable for end-of-the-year profit and loss. In the industrial age, as companies got larger and larger and operated in many lines of business, the decentralized model was extremely popular and powerful.

As modern computer systems became more and more integrated into business, other more efficient business models emerged. For example, the structure of Cisco exemplifies the trend toward highly centralized business processes that can be efficiently coordinated though information transparency. In addition, innovations such as the IT-enabled balanced scorecard can provide real-time information on the various business performance metrics required to efficiently manage highly complex, global businesses.

Salvageable Industrial Age Management Principles

Salvageable management principles are tricky to deal with. These principles are still valid, but their parameters are altered by IT in various ways or influenced by other management principles.

Leadership principle—Senior management formulates and coordinates the firm's vision and plays a central role in defining projects.

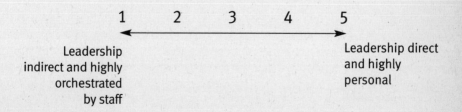

The CEO and senior management team played important roles in setting an example and leading the company in the industrial age and still do so in the information age. However, the top management leadership has become more personal and direct. There are fewer levels of staff between the CEO and the workers. This shift was dramatic at IBM when Lou Gerstner became CEO. Gerstner sent out e-mails directly to IBM employees. The direct leadership of the CEO provides employees with a closer feeling toward the leader, substituting for the industrial age's loyalty to the company.

Span-of-control principle—Span of control is variable and not limited by the need to directly observe workers.

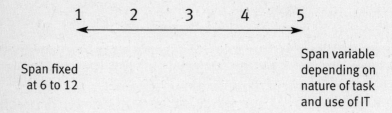

The limited span of control that is dependent on face-to-face supervision of workers is made obsolete by the use of information technology. IT and the notion of the shadow partner discussed in Chapter 1 make it possible to coordinate the work of many workers across the globe. Thus, the fixed limits of span of control can be variable and tailored to the task at hand. Larger spans of control can also enable organizations to be much flatter than typical industrial age organizations.

Worker-class principle—All employees are treated as a uniclass of knowledge workers versus the two-class system of white-/blue-collar workers.

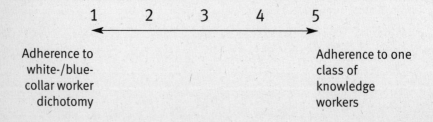

The white-/blue-collar worker dichotomy of the industrial age organization was strongly inculcated in organizations. It provided a simple and powerful way of structuring work and behavior in the industrial firm. It also was highly integrated into the reward systems and culture.

Dress signaled the class of the worker. As the worker crossed into the boundary of the company, blue-collar workers generally punched a time clock to begin recording their time worked. White-collar workers generally did not punch in. A culture arose that those higher in the hierarchy had authority to tell those below what to do. Orders flowed downward in the hierarchy; information also flowed downward.

The white-/blue-collar culture and way of operating are inappropriate in the information age. Much of the low-level and clerical work has been automated, and the nature of the work today requires two-way information flows, innovation, and creative problem solving.

Supervision principle—Supervision is indirect and based on results of assessment information as opposed to direct worker observation.

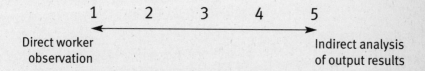

Modern computer systems take real-time readings from sensors throughout the product/service development and delivery process. Thus there is little need to resort to the industrial age practice of a supervisor directly observing the way employees are working. Yet the cultural overtones of direct supervision run deep. Observe, for example, what typically happens when a manager walks by an office of a worker who might be thinking and sitting back gazing out the window. The tendency is for the worker to immediately begin doing something physical such as typing on a computer keyboard. Nevertheless, it is now easy to measure the outputs of work to manage work more effectively than by the previous process of managing the actual process of doing the work.

Reward principle—Rewards are performance-based as opposed to position-based.

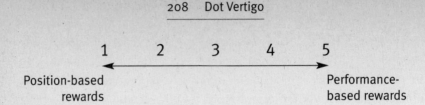

1   2   3   4   5

Position-based rewards   Performance-based rewards

In the industrial economy, rewards for work were highly integrated into the hierarchy and the class of worker dichotomy. Blue-collar workers were paid on an hourly basis—inputs if you will. White-collar workers were generally salaried, and pay was geared to seniority, loyalty, and position in the hierarchy. The widely used and somewhat notorious Hay point system[3] was used by a large number of companies to benchmark jobs in the hierarchy in such a way that the jobs could be rated. Since many of the large industrial age organizations used the Hay point system or something like it, there existed a high level of pay similarity among similar jobs across companies.

The movement away from the fixed hierarchy and the shift from white-/blue-collar workers to a uniclass of knowledge workers in the information age has led to new ways to reward people. There is a universal movement to use equity to reward people on the basis of the performance of the company's stock in the equity markets. Microsoft was one of the pioneers in the trend to pay modest salaries and rely heavily on stock options to reward employees. Now almost all dot companies use this approach. Slowly, transforming industrial age companies are moving toward greater use of equity for rewarding workers.

Task principle—Work is organized into projects and carried out by team members assigned to projects on the basis of the expertise needed to accomplish project goals.

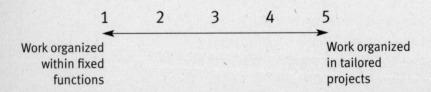

1   2   3   4   5

Work organized within fixed functions   Work organized in tailored projects

The task is the low-level unit for organizing work. In the industrial economy, tasks were defined at a very low level, and the idea was to make the tasks repetitive in order to execute them in the most efficient manner. As more and more low-level tasks have been automated as we move into the information age, the tasks carried out by workers have become higher-level and more complex. With the use of IT along the lines of the shadow partner, even higher-level and more complex tasks are assigned to workers in project form rather than within fixed functions.

Strategic-orientation principle—The strategic orientation of the firm is to serve customers' needs as opposed to manufacturing a product or service.

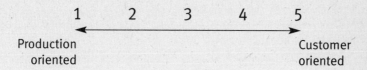

Information age companies seem obsessed by serving customers compared to industrial age companies. Industrial age companies are more oriented to production than customers. However, this is somewhat of an illusion.

The industrial age companies focused on building and running mass production facilities to produce standardized products. Over time, production processes have matured, and many of the manual processes have been automated. The IT capabilities have provided the ability to tailor products in ways that were previously uneconomical. Joe Pine coined the term "mass customization" to describe the ability to highly customize products for individual customers without forgoing the favorable economics of mass production.[4] As a result, the strategic focus of companies has shifted to serving customers. Mass customization and its associated economics are assumed.

Communication principle—Communication is swift, spontaneous, and point-to-point as opposed to formal paper memos and frequent committee meetings.

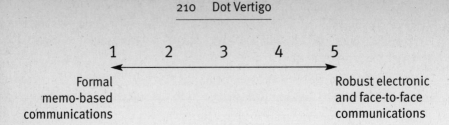

The nature of and frequency of communications is a major differentia-tor between industrial age companies and information age companies. The industrial age company relies on slower and more formal communi-cation technologies and processes that are geared for a slower pace of op-erations and a slower rate of change. In contrast, the information age company heavily relies on real-time communications to operate at a faster pace, which has become known as Internet time.

Also, the communications in an information age company are less for-mal and more direct—that is, going through channels is seen as an un-necessary slowing down of communications. Nevertheless, information is still associated with power, and trust becomes an important factor in ef-fective communication within the information age company.

Accordingly, face-to-face communication does not go away, nor is it reduced in frequency. Instead, face-to-face communication plays an important role in enabling effective electronic communications. Most information age companies have global dimensions, and pay par-ticular attention to ensure that face-to-face meetings take place among their workers.

Authority principle—Authority for resource allocation decisions changes continuously based on which worker's expertise allows him or her to make decisions most effectively.

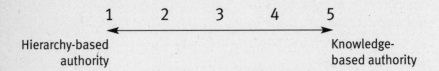

Industrial age companies were largely about consistent execution on the factory floor. Any deviation from standards either corrupted quality or negatively impacted cost and profits. The tasks were reduced to the most straightforward possible, and the pace of the assembly line dictated productivity and profitability. The manager and supervisor authority over the worker was paramount in making the system work.

In direct contrast to the industrial age role for authority stands the information age model for authority. In the information age model, the primary task at hand is innovative problem solving designed to maximize customer satisfaction with the company's products and services. Rather than mass-producing standard products, the objective has changed to mass customization of products, and enhancing the functionality of the products through superior customer service. Accordingly, the role of authority shifts from what is often called "command and control" to rendering expertise required to solve the problem at hand. Thus, expertise becomes critically important, and the exercise of authority defers to the one with the requisite expertise required to solve problems. Any other exercise of authority only gets in the way of serving the customer.

Cycle-time principle—Resource allocation decisions are made in real time as opposed to being made on the fiscal year cycle.

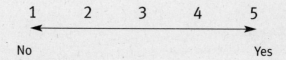

We have made the point a number of times that the heartbeat of the information organization is paced by real time in direct contrast to the heartbeat of the industrial organization, which is paced by the annual budgeting cycle. The frenetic pace of real time looks like chaos to the untrained eye. However, the result of effective application of IT to enable real-time resource allocation gives the information age company many more chances to respond to economic and customer changes than the industrial age company.

The industrial age company provided lots of time to do analysis and figure out the best course of action. The information age model provides a superior process allowing experiments to be tried, evaluated, and either discarded or leveraged to obtain a business advantage. This time advantage overwhelms many of the other disadvantages of information age companies compared to industrial age companies.

New Information Age Management Principles

While we can debate whether what I propose to be new information management principles are really new, the proposed principles are not traditionally accepted industrial age management principles, so we can consider them new for purposes of this discussion.

Value-creation principle—All activities of the firm are directly rationalized to maximize customer value.

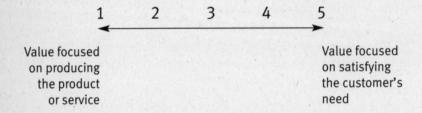

The fundamental difference between the industrial age company and the information age company is focus on serving the customer. In the industrial age company the big deal was efficiently producing products that amazed and delighted customers. In the information age company, the big deal is serving customers products and services that meet their needs, whatever those needs might be.

Coordination principle—Firm activities are purposeful and efficient through extensive information flows that enable workers to anticipate and expediently correct problems.

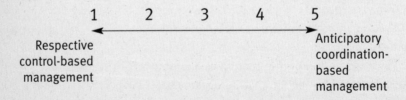

In the transformation of the industrial age organization, the strong command-and-control culture gives way to a looser but more powerful culture of IT-enabled coordination. Command-and-control business processes were based on assumptions that workers had to be strictly controlled to execute work at the standards and pace required to achieve organizational productivity.

Indeed, much of the lower-level work in the industrial age organization was boring, repetitive, and required a control discipline to ensure execution in the standard ways specified. However, now much of that same work has been automated. Also, the bar for acceptable products has been raised to not only provide cost-effective products to customers, but provide products that meet individual customer needs and delight customers. Control-based management is bankrupt in terms of clearing the new bar. Coordination of resources required to clear the new bar provides a much more promising alternative.

Information principle—All organization members have open access to all information as opposed to restricted flow based on "need to know."

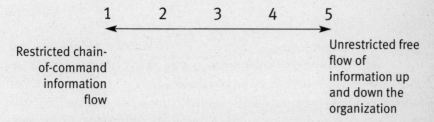

| 1 | 2 | 3 | 4 | 5 |

Restricted chain-of-command information flow

Unrestricted free flow of information up and down the organization

In the information age company, information is viewed as a unique and valuable asset. The information resource is enabled by IT; as a result IT and information resources are inextricably interrelated. Information transparency gives all people inside and outside of the company access to information through the company's I-Net. Of course appropriate security and privacy protections are implemented to ensure that the proprietary information of the company is not compromised and the privacy of the company's information about employees, customers, and partners is not compromised.

The recognition of information as a unique and valuable resource is in direct contrast to the view of information in an industrial age company.

The industrial age company did not view information as a unique re-source, but as potentially disruptive to the focus of the company. Thus, information flows were carefully monitored through formal memoran-dums, policies, and procedures. The information on results of operations flowed up the hierarchy, and corrective information to operations flowed down the hierarchy, which became known as the "command and control" attribute of functional hierarchies. The give and take necessary for learn-ing and interactive problem solving seen in information age companies today was all but absent.

Dynamic-balancing principle—The firm's surplus is monitored in real time and equitably distributed to stakeholders based on current information.

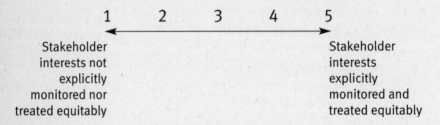

The key stakeholders of a company are the employees, the customers, and the investors. They each contribute to the success of the company, and need to be equitably rewarded based on their contributions. Over time much of the distribution of the profits, or what economists call the "rents," become incorporated into wage rates, market prices, and the like. However, there are times when imbalances occur.

For example, during the 1960s the big three manufacturers in the U.S. automotive industry operated with a very large market share in the United States. Unions were powerful and were able to keep wage rates rising. Management was also strong, and maintained high salaries and at-tractive perks. The automotive companies were able to pass higher prices on to the customer. Without much competition, the price rate increases did not keep pace with the value delivered. An imbalance occurred, and a gap began to widen.

Japanese competition entered the U.S. market offering higher-quality cars at lower prices than the U.S. cars. In a very short time, customers swarmed to buy the Japanese cars, resulting in a more equitable balance of value to the customer. Ultimately, the U.S. manufacturers increased product quality and stemmed top management perks and high rates of wage increases for union workers.

Information age companies are highly focused on providing value to the customer. A generally high degree of industry competition keeps the customer value proposition in balance. Equity is widely used in dot companies to reward workers and management for business results as interpreted by the equity markets. There is an incredible amount of information on companies today that is freely available over the Internet, which allows investors to invest in the companies that they think will effectively convert their investments into gains.

However, with the rapid pace of business today, it is important that the management of the company monitors each of the stakeholders and ensures that a dynamic, equitable balance is maintained for each.

Architect principle—Senior management acts as architect of the firm's structure through the design and redesign of infrastructures necessary for the operation of self-designed teams.

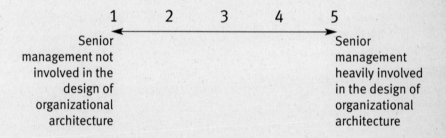

Industrial age companies treated labor as a ubiquitous commodity. When you needed more labor, you simply put an ad in the newspaper and specified the amount and type of labor that you needed: production workers, accountants, or engineers. Tasks were documented in job descriptions, and the new employee read the job description, received some on-the-job training, and began working.

The predominant knowledge work in information age companies is very different. Tasks change rapidly and are not subject to the same kind of rigorous definition and documentation as was typical of the industrial age organization. Outcomes are specified by senior management, and teams are formed to create specified outcomes using innovation and creativity resident in the team. Thus, senior management takes on the role of building designs for the teams to work within. The role becomes one of organizational architect rather than one of management control.

Team principle—Teams are formed by leaders offering compensation packages to attract knowledge workers with needed expertise to achieve project objectives.

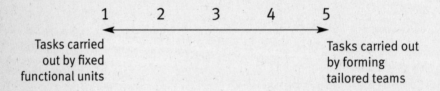

The industrial age company typically operated with a relatively fixed organization, a production goal that changed incrementally from year to year, and a relatively fixed labor force. The tasks required to meet the production goal changed little from year to year.

In direct contrast, the information age company continues to strive to learn and adopt the newest ways to leverage IT in the product development and delivery process. As products and services move from standard mass produced products and services to mass customized products and services, the skills and expertise required by the company continue to change rapidly. As a result, the rather mature use of standard functional units in a company gives way to the use of tailored teams made up of diverse skills required to create the outcome required. Thus, organization architectures are made up of tailored teams that change over time depending on the needs of the company at the time.

Control principle—Control is efficient through extensive feedback information and self-interest reward systems that motivate workers to maintain high levels of performance.

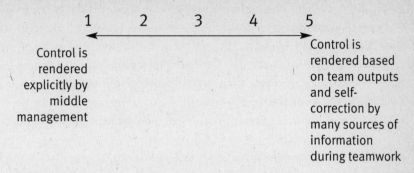

1   2   3   4   5

Control is
rendered
explicitly by
middle
management

Control is
rendered based
on team outputs
and self-
correction by
many sources of
information
during teamwork

Control changes from something that is measured and executed by middle management to something that is largely automatic, and inherent in the team process. IT provides the ability to obtain a great deal of information in real time. Thus, teams can monitor their progress toward achieving an outcome in many ways from the mundane such as achieving sales quotas to the sophisticated such as pilot testing new products or services with test groups of customers.

The traditional control process of having middle managers design control systems, obtain feedback, and then figure out the appropriate intervention to correct deviant results is too slow and too cumbersome to meet the needs of information age companies and survive in today's fast-paced competition. Self-control becomes an important part of a team's modus operandi, and IT provides an important means to implement effective self-control systems.

The use of equity to reward overall business performance also is an important ingredient in ensuring that teams are appropriately focused and efficient in their work.

Conflict-resolution principle—Conflict with customers, employees, shareholders, and suppliers is expediently mediated, the use of third-party mediation being the exception.

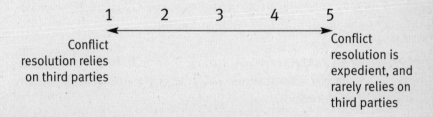

1   2   3   4   5

Conflict
resolution relies
on third parties

Conflict
resolution is
expedient, and
rarely relies on
third parties

Conflict is inevitable in business. The more that responsibilities are clearly specified and agreed to, the less conflict there is. Industrial age companies benefited from an overall maturity where conflict resolution means were well established, including grievance procedures, product guarantees, and defined responsibility and authority schemes.

In contrast, information age companies are relatively new and fast-paced, and simply do not have well-defined, established conflict resolution means. Yet information age companies generally have many relationships that are critically important to their success: outsourcers, strategic partners, suppliers, and the like. In all of these relationships, the possibility of disagreements and conflict is high. If the information age company cannot effectively deal with these conflicts, any potential success of the company can be brought to a grinding halt. Thus, a critical skill is for the senior management to anticipate areas of conflict and resolve them before they escalate into a crisis or before the cumbersome court system is accessed to resolve the conflict.

Information age companies have developed a number of expedient conflict resolution techniques. Of course, one of the most important is for the management team to make sure that it is continually informed about what is going on. IT is essential here.

Developing and maintaining a brand is an important way to communicate with customers about the company's products and services, and what they can expect. When a product is not representative of the company's brand, the company can take prompt action. For example, when IBM PCs incorporated an Intel microprocessor with known problems, IBM pulled the PCs with the defective chip off the market and announced that it would replace at its expense any of the IBM PCs with the defective chip.

Building trust among the partners and employees is another important factor in expedient conflict resolution. If customers and employees have been treated equitably in the past in relationships with a company, they will feel confident that they will be treated equitably in the future.

Opportunity principle—Activity is oriented toward fast-changing global market opportunities as opposed to overcoming organizational inertia.

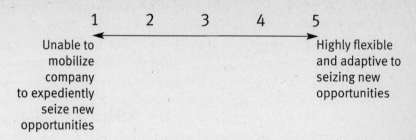

With the transition from the industrial age to the information age, new opportunities present themselves in serendipitous ways. Some of these opportunities can represent more lucrative and promising opportunities than the markets the company is currently pursuing. Dot companies like AOL and Amazon.com have demonstrated leadership and an organizational agility that enables their organizations to capitalize on opportunities as the opportunities present themselves. Microsoft stands as an example of a focused company that initially underestimated the importance of the Internet, but then was able to turn its organization on a dime to embrace the Internet fully in the company's strategy and execution, continuously expanding and contracting as various network relationships are added and subtracted from the firm.

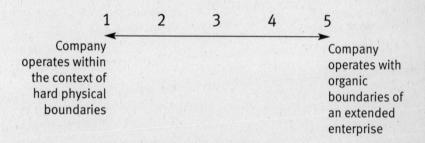

The industrial age company operated primarily within hard physical boundaries. Often guarded, chain-link fences around the buildings of a company defined the company's boundaries. Employees wore badges that allowed them to enter the company facilities. Work was done in fixed eight-hour shifts.

The information age company tends to operate in cyberspace similar to transacting business in drugstore.com's virtual drugstore. The physical

boundaries are less apparent. While information age companies still operate out of physical facilities and office buildings, work does not necessarily all take place in these company physical facilities. Work on the road,
in the home, or at customers' sites is just as likely as conducting work on
the company's premises. It is important that the concept of boundaries be
extended beyond the physical and include social, legal, and other demar-
cations. Also important is that the boundaries take on the reality of the
information age company having to change continuously. So the boundaries must accommodate the realities of an organic organization and recognize that there are many ways to use different types of boundaries to
delineate the extended organization.

Summary Analysis of Information Age Management Principles

To obtain your total company score for creative destruction/construction
of information age management principles adoption, add up each score
for the 23 management principles and mark it on the scale. (Maximum
score is 115, minimum score 23.)

→ → → →   → → → →   → → → →   → → → →   → → → →

23	40	65	90	115
Traditional organization		Shadow network		IT-enabled network

Over the past four years, various management groups at the Harvard
Business School have scored their companies using this continuum. Dot
companies tend to score 20 to 30 points higher than older, tradition-
bound companies; and the average for all companies continues to move
upward, the 2000 average being a total score of 70 out of a possible
115. During the process of transformation of the industrial age company to the information age company, the organization structure makes
a transition from a formal functional hierarchy to the hierarchy coexist-
ing with a rudimentary informal electronic-enabled network. E-mail is
one of the first technologies that begins the creative destruction
process. Somewhere in the middle of the transformation, the informal

shadow network floats over the formal hierarchy. This is a particularly confusing time for workers in the company, and it is important for senior management to emphasize the steady direction toward a formal network organization structure.

As more and more features such as data warehouses and ultimately a strategic I-Net are integrated, the formal hierarchy continues to fade into the background, and more reliance is placed on the IT-enabled network. During the later phases of transformation, the network becomes formalized as the company infrastructure, and the traditional functional hierarchy is integrated into the network structure.

The actual score is less important than accessing the principles that have very low scores. Low-score principles are often the sources of major problems for industrial age companies, slowing down effective transformation to information age companies. Dot companies, as a group, tend to embrace the new management principles in a more integrated manner, which is a main advantage gained from building a company from a greenfield site.

Chapter 1   Doing Business in a Permeable World

1. Figure 1.1, "GPO Growth in All IT-Producing Industries," *The Emerging Digital Economy II*, U.S. Department of Commerce (June 1999): 17.
2. From Amazon.com's 1998 annual report.
3. Ibid.
4. Richard L. Nolan, "Working with Your Shadow Partner in the IT Industry," Harvard Business School case 9-301-003 (August 25, 2000).
5. See Stephen P. Bradley and Richard L. Nolan (editors), *Sense and Respond* (Boston: Harvard Business School Press, 1998).
6. "Buzz" is used to refer to the talk/hype about a company. Bezos' marketing strategy helps to create a lot of buzz about the company.

Chapter 2   Keep an Eye on Your Instruments: The I-Net

1. The concept of zero time was introduced in the book *Zero Time* by Raymond Yeh, Keri Pearl, and George Kozmetsky (New York: John Wiley & Sons, 2000).
2. Mohanbir Sawhney and Deval Parikh, "Where Value Lives in a Networked World," *Harvard Business Review* (January 2001).
3. KPMG, Economist Intelligence Unit, "The E-Business Value Chain: Winning Strategies in Seven Global Industries," KPMG Study (June 2000).

4. George Metes, John Gundry, and Paul Bradish, *Agile Networking: Competing Through the Internet and Intranets* (Upper Saddle River, NJ: Prentice Hall PTR, 1998).

5. Ibid.

6. www.kpmg.com/industries/content.asp?l1id=70&l2id=350).

7. Bob Francis, "NetPCs Get a Boost—As Units Start to Ship, Gartner Study Lowers Estimated Cost of Ownership," *Information Week* (December 22, 1997).

8. *Source:* Patrick Barta, "Land Grab? Why Big Lenders Are So Frightened by Fannie and Freddie," *Wall Street Journal,* (April 5, 2001): A1, A10.

9. Stephan H. Haeckel and Richard L. Nolan, "Managing by Wire," *Harvard Business Review* (September–October 1993): 122–132.

10. As described earlier, the total cost of ownership (TCO) is the average cost of fully maintaining an employee's client computer. PCs integrated into a corporate network require a level of standards and management sufficient to keep their overall costs at appropriate levels and to ensure that diverse technologies do not interact in such a way as to make the overall network unstable. Some companies today employ thousands of computers, databases, and applications. Connecting all these components into an integrated network requires a new level of IT management.

11. Eric Schmidt, "Directory and Identity," Novell Brainshare99 Conference, Provo, Utah (March 27, 1999).

12. Haeckel and Nolan, "Managing by Wire," 131–132.

13. Chris Argyris, *On Organizational Learning* (2d Edition) (Malden, MA: Blackwell Publishers, Inc., 1999).

Chapter 3   How Did We Get Here?

1. Robert L. Glass, "COBOL—a Contradiction and an Enigma," *Communications of the ACM* 40 (September 1997): 11.

2. A "hurdle rate" is the minimum return on investment that a proposed investment must yield in order to be considered for funding by the corporation. For further information about hurdle rates see Clyde P. Stickney and Roman L. Weil, *Financial Accounting: An Introduction to Concepts, Methods, and Uses* (Philadelphia: Dryden Press, 1994): G-32, G-47. Stickney and Weil define hurdle rate as the required rate of return in a discounted cash flow (DCF) analysis. A DCF uses either the net present value or the internal rate of return in an analysis to measure the value of future expected cash expenditures and receipts at a common date.

3. By the 1990s, every electronic calculator costing $10 or more embedded

these complex present value calculations into their logic, enabling the calculations to be done by entering some basic data and pressing a button.

4. For example, see Paul A. Strassmann, *Information Payoff* (New York: The Free Press, 1985).

5. The Appendix includes an instrument employing Likert five-point scales that can be used to assess your company's transformation to an information age company based on management principles employed by the company.

6. Robert G. Eccles and Dwight B. Crane, *Doing Deals: Investment Banks at Work* (Boston: Harvard Business School Press, 1988).

7. Wayne E. Baker, "The Network Organization in Theory and Practice," in Nitin Nohria and Robert G. Eccles (editors), *Networks and Organizations* (Boston: Harvard Business School Press, 1992): 398.

8. For example, Hay Point systems were widely used by industrial age organizations that based compensation on the worker's position in the hierarchy and the budget responsibility that the individual was assigned.

9. Paul Firstenberg, "Downsizing: What's Your Game Plan?," *Management Review* (November 1993): 46.

10. David P. Norton, "Breaking Functional Gridlock: The Case for a Mission-Oriented Organization," *Stage-by-Stage* 8 (No. 2, 1988).

11. Thomas Moore, "Make-or-Break Time for General Motors," *Fortune* (February 15, 1988): 32.

12. K.A. Stephenson and S. Haeckel, "Making a Virtual Organization Work," *Focus* 21 (1997): 26-30.

13. Further information about the process of hierarchies and networks mutually reinforcing each other can be found by consulting Stephenson's web site: www.netform.no.

Chapter 4   The Value Economy: Following the Market Leaders

1. Gerald W. Brock, *The U.S. Computer Industry: A Study of Market Power* (Cambridge, MA: Ballinger Publishing Company, 1975): 21; Anonymous, "IBM Tightens Its Lock on Mainframes," *Fortune* (October 1, 1984): 7.

2. Statement is based on values from CompuStat. In 1981 IBM slipped to number two in market value, behind AT&T. In 1989 Exxon had the highest year-end market value; 1990 was the last year that IBM ranked first.

3. Statements based on an evaluation of the Global Fortune 500 rankings between 1975 and 1987.

4. Jim Carlton, *Apple: The Inside Story of Intrigue, Egomania, and Business Blunders* (New York: Times Business /Random House, 1997): 45.

5. Ibid., 38–61; 132.

6. David B. Yoffie and Andrall E. Pearson, "The Transformation of IBM," 9-391-073, Harvard Business School Case (Revised September 9, 1991).

7. AT&T's Bell Laboratories was held up as one of the most productive research organizations at the time. It was said that Bell Labs researchers produced a patent a day.

8. "Man's Best Friend? Bytes May Replace Barks," *News & Observer*, Raleigh, NC (January 24, 1999): E14.

9. Tarun Khanna, David Yoffie, and Israel Ganot, "Microsoft, 1995" 9-795-147, Harvard Business School Case (Revised July 23, 1996).

10. Mary Kwak and David Yoffie, "The Browser Wars, 1994–1998," 9-798-094, Harvard Business School Case (Revised December 3, 1998).

11. Paul Carroll, *Big Blues: The Unmaking of IBM* (New York: Crown, 1993): 75.

12. *Source: Fortune* (March 19, 2001): 72.

13. Carroll, *Big Blues*, 3.

14. See HBS Schwab case "Charles Schwab: A Category of One," N9-700-043, Revised October 11, 2000. Also see David S. Pottruck and Terry Pearce, *Clicks and Mortar* (San Francisco: Jossey-Bass, 2000).

15. America Online (AOL) was the first company to strategically mount an initiative to acquire customers through an expensive marketing program. AOL argued that its customer acquisition program was a strategic investment and qualified for capitalization on its financial statements over the estimated duration of the customer as an active AOL customer.

16. *Source:* Jason Dedrick, Kenneth L. Kraemer, and Bryan MacQuarrie, "Gateway Computer: Using E-Commerce to Move 'Beyond the Box' and to Move More Boxes," Center for Research on Information Technology and Organizations, University of California, Irvine (February 2001): 15.

Chapter 5   You Gotta Believe: Instilling the Critical Nature of Technology into Management

1. Robert Metcalfe invented the Ethernet at Xerox PARC (Palo Alto Research Center) in 1973. It is used today to network more than 100 million computers. Metcalfe went on to found 3Com Corporation in 1979.

2. See George Gilder, "Metcalfe's Law and Legacy," *Forbes ASAP* (September 13, 1983).

3. Loel McPhee and Rich Coyle, "Number of Internet Users and Shoppers Surges in United States and Canada," Nielsen Media Research Press Release (August 24, 1998).

4. *Source:* Morgan Stanley Dean Witter and eStats: www.emarketer.com/estat-store/skus/sku5/sku5a.html.

5. TechWeb Technology Encyclopedia (www.techweb.com/encyclopedia/defineterm?term=bandwidth) defines bandwidth as the transmission capacity of an electronic line such as a communications network, computer bus, or computer channel. It is expressed in bits per second, bytes per second, or hertz (cycles per second).

6. George Gilder, "Fiber Keeps Its Promise," *Forbes ASAP* (April 7, 1997): 2

7. For a discussion of the emergence of dominant designs in technology see William J. Abernathy and James M. Utterback, "Patterns of Industrial Innovation," *Research Policy*, vol. 14, no. 1 (January 1985); and Chapter 2, "Dominant Designs and the Survival of Firms," in James M. Utterback, *Mastering the Dynamics of Innovation* (Boston: Harvard Business School Press, 1994).

8. Market value is calculated by multiplying a company's current stock price by the number of shares outstanding in the marketplace. The market value roughly represents what shareholders think will be their return from the long-term earning value of the company.

9. Henry M. Boettinger, *The Telephone Book: Bell, Watson, Vail and American Life 1876–1976* (New York: Riverwood Publishers, 1977).

10. Richard L. Nolan and Kelley A. Porter, "Sun Microsystems and the N-tier Architecture," Harvard Business School Case 399-037 (November 30, 1998): 5.

11. Ibid.

12. Ibid.

13. B. Tribble, "Java Computing in the Enterprise: What It Means for the General Manager and CIO," Sun Microsystems Whitepaper (1996): 1-2.

14. See Louis A. Girifalco, "The Dynamics of Technological Change," *Wharton Magazine* 7 (Fall 1982): 31-37. Also, Edwin Mansfield, *Economics of Technological Change* (New York: W.W. Norton, 1968); Richard N. Foster, *Innovation: The Attacker's Advantage* (New York: Summit Books, 1986); and Clayton M. Christenson, *The Innovator's Dilemma: When New Technologies Cause Great Firms to Fail* (Management of Innovation and Change Series) (Boston: Harvard Business School Press, 1997).

15. "Institutionalizing Change," *Crossborder Monitor* (April 1, 1998): 1.

Chapter 6   Air Strikes: Merrill Lynch Takes Aim at Charles Schwab

1. Much of the material in this chapter is drawn from HBS cases on Merrill Lynch and Charles Schwab: "Merrill Lynch: Integrated Choice," 9-500-090, by Professor V. Kasturi Rangan and Research Associate Marie Bell (February 29, 2000; Revised March 14, 2001), and "Charles Schwab Corporation (A)," 9-300-024, by Nicole Tempest, Associate Director of the HBS California Research Center, under the supervision of Professor F. Warren McFarlan (September 10, 1999).

2. "Internet Trades Put Merrill on Horns of Dilemma," *Wall Street Journal* (February 12, 1999): C1.

3. This background on Schwab is taken from HBS case "Charles Schwab Corporation (A)," 9-300-024 (September 10, 1999), prepared by Nicole Tempest, associate director of the HBS California Research Center, under the supervision of F. Warren McFarlan P, the Albert H. Gordon Professor of Business Administration.

4. Quote taken from HBS Schwab case 9-300-024.

5. Referring to online brokerages that did not have branch offices.

6. Quote taken from HBS Schwab case 9-300-024.

7. Ibid.

8. Ibid.

9. See Schwab HBS case, and accompanying videotape of David Pottruck's address at my PMD (Program for Management Development) executive education class in fall of 1999.

10. Enacted in the 1930s, the Securities Exchange Act and the Glass-Steagall Banking Act prohibited banks from acting as brokers or securities dealers. This act is still in effect, but has been modified whereby today there is almost a complete overlap of services provided by various financial institutions.

11. "OptiMistic," *Economist* (January 30, 1999).

12. Michael Carroll, Hal Lux, and Justin Schack, "Trading Meets the Millennium," *Institutional Investor* (January 2000).

13. Ellen Jovin, "Planning Online-Fair Trades: Enthusiasts Say ECNs Level the Playing Field for Traders, but Many Others Remain Skeptical," *Financial Planning* (June 1, 2000).

14. Eric Moskowitz, "Marc Andreessen vs. Wall Street," *Money*, (July 2000).

15. The seven U.S. exchanges are the NYSE, American Stock Exchange/Nasdaq, and five regional exchanges: Pacific, Cincinnati, Chicago, Philadelphia, and Boston.

16. "Nasdaq Taps OptiMark as Its Matching System of the Future," *Wall Street & Technology*, vol. 16, no. 3 (March 1998).

17. "Stock Exchanges: The Battle for Efficient Markets," *Economist* (June 17, 2000): 69-71.

18. Ibid.

Chapter 7   Overcoming Dot Vertigo: The Case of IBM

1. In 1989, Lou Gerstner contacted Kim Clark, the dean of the Harvard Business School, and invited a team of HBS professors to come into IBM and capture the IBM transformation story in a series of HBS cases. I was asked to coordinate the case research effort. While the research is still ongoing, several cases have been written: "Transformation of IBM," 9-391-073; "Managing IBM Research on Internet Time," 9-601-058; and "IBM's Implementation of SAP."

2. This part of the chapter on Gerstner's transformation is taken from HBS case N-600-098, March 1, 2000, prepared by Professors Robert D. Austin and Richard L. Nolan. Professor Austin wrote the majority of the case from which the text is taken. Also, some of the material was extracted from HBS case 9-391-073, "The Transformation of IBM," prepared by Professors David B. Yoffie and Andrall E. Pearson.

3. Another acquisition, Tivoli Systems, based in Austin, Texas, filled the systems management software void in a $700 million deal the following year.

4. "Inside IBM: Internet Business Machines," by Ira Sager, with Peter Burrows, David Rocks, and Diane Brady, *Business Week* (December 13, 1999): EB 20.

5. Ibid.

Chapter 8   Anatomy of a Dot Com: What Keeps Drugstore.com in the Game

1. Much of this chapter is taken from the HBS case: "Drugstore.com," Richard Nolan, N-300-036.

2. Thomas A. Gerace and John J. Sviokla, "CyberSmith," 9-396-314, Harvard Business School Case (Revised January 27, 1998).

3. A personal bathroom valet would anticipate needs for over-the-counter drugs and personal hygiene product replenishment in much the same way that a personal valet tends to one's clothes.

4. It is important to note that founder, Jed Smith, who served as the initial CEO, understood that he did not have the background and experience to be the CEO of the company. He agreed at the outset that a world-class CEO was required—in fact, this was integral to the business plan. Here again is evidence that the business plans are generally well thought out.

5. John Cook, "The Eastside's Rising Stars of 1999: A New Cybergiant," *Eastside Journal* (February 4, 1999): 1.

6. See drugstore.com prospectus issued July 8, 1999, p. 10.

7. For a comprehensive discussion of the drugstore.com/Rite Aid equity investment, see Melanie Warner, "Drug Test," *Fortune* (July 19, 1999): 88.

8. See H.B. Becker of Lehman Brothers, Inc., July 13, 2000; and James C. Robinson, "Financing the Health Care Internet," *Health Affairs* (November-December 2000, Vol. 19, Issue 6): 72–88.

9. Jed Smith, founder and vice president, strategy, drugstore.com, interview with author on March 17, 1999.

Chapter 9   Building the I-Net: The Case of Cisco Systems

1. The Cisco case as presented in this chapter heavily draws upon the author's Harvard Business School (HBS) field cases: "Cisco Systems, Inc.," 9-398-127, and "Cisco Systems, Inc.: Implementing ERP," 1-699-022. Some of the description of the Cisco acquisition process is drawn from the joint Stanford/HBS Case: "Cisco Systems, Inc.: Post-acquisition Manufacturing Integration."

2. John Sculley and John A. Byrne, *Odyssey: Pepsi to Apple, a Journey of Adventure, Ideas, and the Future* (New York: Harper & Row, 1987): 90.

3. See Stephan H. Haeckel and Richard L. Nolan, "Managing by Wire," *Harvard Business Review* (September-October 1993): 122; and Stephen P. Bradley and Richard L. Nolan, *Sense and Respond: Capturing Value in the Network Era* (Boston: Harvard Business School Press, 1998). The ideas of the shift from generic strategies of "make and sell" of industrial age companies to "sense and respond" strategies of information age companies were first published in the *HBR* article, "Managing by Wire." Parallel efforts of exploring the dimensions of "sense and respond" strategies continue at IBM under the sponsorship of Steve Haeckel, director of strategic studies at IBM's Advanced Business Institute, and Professors Richard L. Nolan and Stephen P. Bradley at the Harvard Business School.

4. Richard L. Nolan and David C. Croson, *Creative Destruction: A Six-Stage Process for Transforming the Organization* (Boston: Harvard Business School Press, 1995). Upon returning to Harvard in 1991, I undertook a research project with David Croson (now a professor at Wharton) on the process of transitioning from industrial age management principles to information age management principles.

5. Most of the software vendors' customers ranged from $50 million to $250 million in revenue.

6. ERP stands for Enterprise Resource Planning, a derivative of MRP, material requirements or manufacturing resource planning. MRP represents a class of systems that focus on planning the material requirements for production. Forecast or actual demand is fed into the MRP system either manually or from other types of systems, and the demand information is then used to determine timing for raw materials and components as determined by production schedules. MRP functionality is embedded in the offerings of all leading ERP vendors' software packages. For a further description of ERP, see Thomas H. Davenport, "Putting the Enterprise into the Enterprise System," *Harvard Business Review* (July–August 1998): 121–133.

7. The Gartner Group is a leading source of information on ERP and other information systems and manufacturing-related research.

8. Cisco's financial year-end is July 31.

9. Total employment at Cisco was estimated at the time to be 2,500 people.

10. Cisco 1997 annual report: 11.

11. Cisco 1997 Annual Report: 11.

12. Shawn Tully, "How Cisco Mastered the Net," *Fortune* (August 17, 1998): 210.

13. Cisco 1997 Annual Report: 11.

14. Noel Lindsay, network analyst, Deutsche Morgan Grenfell.

15. Cisco 1997 annual report: 11, reflects 1996 savings; 1998 savings are estimated at $550 million.

16. "Cisco Builds Site for More Eyes; Ongoing User Testing Is Critical to Success of World's Highest-Volume," *San Jose Mercury News* (October 19, 1998).

Chapter 10   Act Like a Venture Capitalist: Creating an Action Agenda

1. Many of the ideas for this section have been taken from an earlier Harvard Business School working paper by Professor Rob Austin and myself, "How to Manage ERP Initiatives." In turn, the ideas in the paper and this section benefited from the work of Professor Bill Sahlman and our discussions with Bill about the process of applying his ideas about venture capital to managing ERP and strategic I-Net initiatives.

2. William A. Sahlman, "How to Write a Great Business Plan," *Harvard Business Review*, July–August 1997.

3. William A. Sahlman, "Some Thoughts on Business Plans," Harvard Business School note, 9-897-101.

4. Ibid.

5. Source: Paul C. Judge, "How I Saved $100 Million on the Web," *Fast Company* (February 2001): 174–181.

6.   *Source:* Bill Breen, "Full House," *Fast Company* (January 2001): 111–120.

7.   HBS case: "Tektronix Inc,: Global ERP Implementation," 9-699-043, by Robert D. Austin, Richard L. Nolan, Mark Cotteleer, and George Westerman (February 2, 1999).

Chapter 11   Five Myths of the Internet

1.   It should be noted that the Internet started as a U.S. government project in 1969. It was opened up to commercial use in 1995 with the commercial suffix ".com."

2.   The transformation process of incumbents is the subject of my earlier research with David Croson: *Creative Destruction* by Richard L. Nolan and David C. Croson (Boston: Harvard Business School Press, 1995).

3.   See HBS IBM case N9-600-098.

4.   Richard L. Nolan, "Drugstore.com," HBS Case 9-300-036, September 15, 1999 (Boston: Harvard Business School Publishing, 1999); Richard L. Nolan, "Cisco Systems, Inc.: Implementing ERP," HBS Case 9-699-022, September 30, 1998, Rev. 9/24/99 (Boston: Harvard Business School Publishing, 1999).

5.   See my series of HBS cases on Cisco beginning with its replacement of back office systems with ERP, continuing on to document the robust benefits achieved from its front office IT investments integrated with its back office ERP systems, and concluding with its new strategy to be the "Internet leader." "Cisco Systems, Inc: Implementing ERP," 9-699-022 (Rev. October 10, 1998); "Cisco Systems: Web-Enablement," 301-056 (March 24, 2001) (replaced "Cisco Systems, Inc.," 9-398-127); "Cisco Systems Architecture: ERP and Web-Enabled IT," 301-099 (March 24, 2001); "Cisco Systems: Building Leading Internet Capabilities," N9-301-133.

6.   Geoffrey A. Moore, *Living on the Fault Line: Managing for Shareholder Value in the Age of the Internet* (New York: HarperCollins Publishers, 2000).

7.   Enablement of "sense and respond" strategies were explored at a 1996 HBS Symposium chaired by Steve Bradley and myself, the results of which were published in our book: *Sense and Respond* (Boston: Harvard Business School Press, 1998).

8.   F. Warren McFarlan and Fred Young, "Li & Fung," HBS Case 9-301-009, Revised November 29, 2000 (Boston: Harvard Business School Publishing, 2000): 3.

9.   F. Warren McFarlan, Carin-Isabel Knoop, and David Lane, "Alibaba.com," HBS Case 9-301-047, November 30, 2000 (Boston: Harvard Business School Publishing, 2000).

10.   *Source:* Darryl Carr, "The Next Big Catch," *Upside* (March 2001): 112–117.

11. Melanie Warner, "The Indians of Silicon Valley," *Fortune* (May 15, 2000): 356.
12. William C. Symonds, "Wired Schools: A Technology Revolution is about to Sweep America's Classrooms," *Business Week* (September 25, 2000): 116.
13. Jason Anders, "The Lessons We've Learned—B2B: Yesterday's Darling," *Wall Street Journal* (October 23, 2000): R8.
14. Fred Young, "Li & Fung," N9-301-009, Harvard Business School Case (Revised November 29, 2000): 3.
15. *Source:* Michael J. Ybarra, *Upside* (April 2001): 110–123.
16. David Lane, "Alibaba.com," N9-301-047, Harvard Business School Case (November 30, 2000): 10.
17. Ibid.
18. Matthew Sandoval, "NTT DoCoMo: The Future of the Wireless Internet?," N9-701-013, Harvard Business School Case (September 22, 2000): 4.
19. David Graddol, "The Decline of the Native Speaker," in David Graddol and Ulrike H. Meinhof (eds.), *English in a Changing World: AILA Review* (Oxford: Catchline/AILA, 1999): 57–68.
20. Over the five-year period from 1998 to 2003, China is forecasted to have an annual growth rate (AGR) of 122.1 percent. Goldman Sachs, "China's Tangled Web," *Business Week* (July 17, 2000): 57.
21. David Lane, HBS Global Research Group, 2001.
22. Barbara Wallraff, "What Global Language?," *Atlantic Monthly* (November 2000).
23. Ibid.
24. Joseph Laszlo, "Reaching Global Audiences: Focus on a Web-Centric Strategy, but Leverage Non-PC Platforms," *Jupiter Communications Web Track*, February 2000.

Appendix: Toward a Set of Network Age Management Principles

1. Richard L. Nolan and David C. Croson, *Creative Destruction* (Boston: Harvard Business School Press, 1995): 12.
2. In addition, the process of creative destruction of the 13 industrial age management principles and construction of the 20 information age management principles is described in an earlier book: Richard L. Nolan and David C. Croson, *Creative Destruction* (Boston: Harvard Business School Press, 1995): 12.
3. The Hay Point system was developed by a compensation consulting firm called Hay Associates, and named after the founder.
4. B. Joseph Pine II, *Mass Customization: The New Frontier in Business Competition* (Boston: Harvard Business School Press, 1999).

Selected Bibliography

The selected bibliography is designed for those who may wish to pursue more deeply the chapter subjects. For each chapter, I have listed some of the key reference books that I consulted. In addition, I have included the Harvard Business School cases that make up much of the field research for the book. All of these cases are available through the case clearing house of the Harvard Business School Press.

Chapter 1   Doing Business in a Permeable World

Bradley, Stephen P., Jerry A. Hausman, and Richard L. Nolan (editors), *Globalization, Technology and Competition* (Boston: Harvard Business School Press, 1993).

Davis, Stan, and Christopher Meyer, *Future Wealth* (Boston: Harvard Business School Press, 1998).

Galbraith, Jay R., and Edward E. Lawler III & Associates, *Organizing for the Future* (San Francisco: Jossey-Bass Publishers, 1993).

Shapiro, Carl, and Hal R. Varian, *Information Rules* (Boston: Harvard Business School Press, 1999).

Swisher, Kara, *aol.com* (New York: Times Business, 1998).

HBS Case: "AOL in the Summer of 1999," 700-044 (August 27, 1999), prepared by Professor Stephen Bradley and Research Associate Kelley Porter.

HBS Case: "AOL–Time Warner Merger," 701-136 (September 15, 2000), prepared by Professor Stephen Bradley and Research Associate Matthew Sandoval.

Chapter 2   Keep an Eye on Your Instruments: The I-Net

Bradley, Stephen P., and Richard L. Nolan (editors), *Sense and Respond* (Boston: Harvard Business School Press, 1998).

Davenport, Thomas H., and Laurence Prusak, *Working Knowledge* (Boston: Harvard Business School Press, 1998).

Kaplan, Robert S., and David P. Norton, *Balanced Scorecard* (Boston: Harvard Business School Press, 1996).

Nohria, Nitin, and Robert G. Eccles (editors), *Networks and Organization* (Boston: Harvard Business School Press, 1992).

Stewart, Thomas A., *Intellectual Capital* (New York: Currency Doubleday, 1997).

HBS Case: "Working with Your 'Shadow Partner' on Restructuring of the IT Industry (A)," 399-177 (February 11, 2001), prepared by Richard L. Nolan, the William Barclay Harding Professor of Management of Technology.

Chapter 3   How Did We Get Here?

Chandler, Alfred D., and James W. Cortada, *A Nation Transformed by Information* (London: Oxford Press, 2000).

Lewis, Michael, *The New New Thing: A Silicon Valley Story* (New York: W.W. Norton, 2000).

Nolan, Richard L., and David C. Croson, *Creative Destruction* (Boston: Harvard Business School Press, 1995).

Chapter 4   The Value Economy: Following the Market Leaders

On the Business Value of IT (Boston: Harvard Business School Press, 1999).

Saxenian, AnnaLee, *Regional Advantage* (Cambridge, MA: Harvard University Press, 1994).

Tapscott, Don, *The Digital Economy* (New York: McGraw-Hill, 1995).

Chapter 5   You Gotta Believe: Instilling the Critical Nature of Technology into Management

Christensen, Clayton M., *The Innovator's Dilemma* (Boston: Harvard University Press, 1997).

Downes, Larry, and Chunka Mui, *Killer App* (Boston: Harvard Business School Press, 1998).

Hunt, Reed E., *You Say You Want a Revolution* (New Haven: Yale University Press, 2000).

Iansiti, Marco, *Technology Integration* (Boston: Harvard Business School Press, 1998).

Chapter 6   Air Strikes: Merrill Lynch Takes Aim at Charles Schwab

Grove, Andrew S., *Only the Paranoid Survive* (New York: Currency Doubleday, 1996).

Moore, Geoffrey A., *Living on the Fault Line* (New York: HarperBusiness, 2000).

Pottruck, David S., and Terry Pearce, *Clicks and Mortar* (San Francisco: Jossey-Bass Publishers, 2000).

Schwab, Charles, *Charles Schwab's Guide to Financial Independence* (New York: Crown Publishers, 1998).

HBS Case: "Charles Schwab Corporation (A)," 9-300-024 (September 10, 1999), prepared by Nicole Tempest, Associate Director of the HBS California Research Center, under the supervision of F. Warren McFarlan, the Albert H. Gordon Professor of Business Administration.

HBS Case: "Charles Schwab Corporation: A Category of One," 700-043 (October 10, 2000), prepared by Visiting Scholar Tom Esperson from public sources under the supervision of Professor Stephen P. Bradley.

HBS Case: "Merrill Lynch–Integrated Choices," 500-090 (May 18, 2000), prepared by Professor V. Kasturi Rangan and Research Associate Marie Bell.

HBS Case: "OptiMark: Launching a Virtual Securities Market," 399-005 (August 24, 1998), prepared by Professor John Sviokla and Research Associate Melissa Dailey.

Chapter 7   Overcoming Dot Vertigo: The Case of IBM

Cusumano, Michael A., and Richard W. Selby, *Microsoft Secrets* (New York: Simon & Schuster, 1998).

Ferguson, Charles H., *High Stakes, No Prisoners* (New York: Times Business, 1999).

Garr, Doug, *IBM Redux* (New York: HarperBusiness, 1999).

Hammer, Michael, and James Champy, *Reengineering the Corporation* (New York: HarperBusiness, 1993).

Slater, Robert, *Saving Big Blue* (New York: McGraw-Hill, 1999).

HBS Case: "IBM Turnaround" 600-098 (July 21, 2000), prepared by Professors Robert D. Austin and Richard L. Nolan.

Chapter 8   Anatomy of a Dot Com: What Keeps Drugstore.com in the Game

Gilmore, James H., and B. Joseph Pine II, *Markets of One* (Boston: Harvard Business School Press, 2000).

Kanter, Rosabeth Moss, *e-Volve* (Boston: Harvard Business School Press, 2001).

Moore, Geoffrey A., *Inside the Tornado* (New York: HarperBusiness, 1995).

Tapscott, Don, *Growing Up Digital* (New York: McGraw-Hill, 1998).

HBS Case: "Drugstore.com," 300-027 (August 18, 1999), prepared by Richard L. Nolan, the William Barclay Harding Professor of Management of Technology.

Chapter 9   Building the I-Net: The Case of Cisco Systems

Bunnell, David, *Making the Cisco Connection* (New York: John Wiley & Sons, 2000).

Davenport, Thomas H., *Mission Critical* (Boston: Harvard Business School Press, 2000).

Weill, Peter, and Marianne Broadbent, *Leveraging the New Infrastructure* (Boston: Harvard Business School Press, 1998).

HBS Case: "Cisco Systems: Implementing ERP," 699-022 (September 30, 1998), prepared by Doctoral Candidate Mark Cotteleer under the supervision of Professors Robert D. Austin and Richard L. Nolan.

HBS Case: "Cisco Systems: Web-Enablement," 301-056 (March 24, 2001), prepared by Richard L. Nolan, the William Barclay Harding Professor of Management of Technology, and Research Associates Kelley A. Porter and Christine Akers with the assistance of Christina L. Darwall, Executive Director, HBS California Research Center.

HBS Case: "Sun Microsystems and the N-tier Architecture," 399-037 (November 30, 1998), prepared by Richard L. Nolan, the William Barclay Harding Professor of Management of Technology, and Research Associate Kelley A. Porter with the assistance of Christina L. Darwall, Executive Director, HBS California Research Center.

Chapter 10   Act Like a Venture Capitalist: Creating an Action Agenda

Bhide, Amar V., *The Origin and Evolution of New Businesses* (London: Oxford Press, 2000).

Chapter 11   Five Myths of the Internet

Camp, Jean L., *Trust and Risk in Internet Commerce* (Cambridge, MA: MIT Press, 2000).

Evans, Philip, and Thomas S. Wurster, *Blown to Bits* (Boston: Harvard Business School Press, 2000).

Perkins, Anthony B., and Michael C. Perkins, *The Internet Bubble* (New York: HarperBusiness, 1999).

HBS Case: "NTT DoCoMo: The Future of the Wireless Internet?," 701-013 (November 9, 2000), prepared by Professor Stephen Bradley and Research Associate Matthew Sandoval.

Acknowledgments

I am deeply indebted to my network of peers, colleagues, teachers, research associates, students, family, and executives for the ideas and the development of the ideas in this book. I am indebted as well to Kim Clark, the Dean of the Harvard Business School, who supported my research and who has "walked the IT talk" by building an HBS "strategic I-Net," which, in turn, made my teaching and research a much more efficient process. My administrative assistants at HBS, Mary Kennedy, Barbara Link, and Rebecca Moffitt, have skillfully coordinated the myriad of activities required to write, produce, and publish this book. Jeanne Glasser, my publisher, has been an absolute delight to work with, and has made many, many important contributions to the expression of ideas and the writing of this book.

The core foundation of the book is cases on managers in real companies coping with transforming and building companies in the emerging information age. Here I am especially indebted to the executives at Cisco Systems, IBM, drugstore.com, Sun Microsystems, Tektronix, Charles Schwab, Merrill Lynch, Novell, OptiMark, and AOL that allowed us into their companies to develop case studies. With invaluable assistance from my research associates over the past four years, Kelley Porter, Matthew Sandoval, and Christina Akers, we have traveled to these companies, interviewed their executives, and captured their experiences as they compete in the information age.

Pete Solvik, Cisco's senior vice president and CIO, has worked with me from the beginning in developing the Cisco HBS case series consisting of interviews, videoconferences, and participation in class discussions where the Cisco cases were taught. John Morgridge, chairman, and John Chambers, CEO and president, have generously shared their time in capturing key ideas through interviews.

Peter Neupert, chairman of drugstore.com; Kal Raman, CEO; Sean Nolan, vice president and CTO; and Jed Smith, founder, worked with me from the very inception of the idea of drugstore.com right through the implementation of the idea and the building of the company. Russ Seigleman, partner of Kleiner Perkins, my son Sean Nolan's manager while they were both at Microsoft, and investor in drugstore.com, helped me understand what "dev groups" are all about, how they work, and the key concepts of implementing virtual organizations through software.

Eric Schmidt, chairman and CEO of Novell, has mentored me about the future of the Internet. His insights on the Internet and technology are deep, and have had an important influence on my thinking. Also, I appreciate the time that Steve Ballmer, CEO of Microsoft, spent with me during the early idea formulation for the book.

The executive team of IBM including Bruce Herrald, senior vice president for strategic planning; Jamie Hewitt, vice president, support, e-business transformation, and business information executive; and Steve Ward, vice president and previously CIO worked with me on a series of IBM cases. Lou Gerstner, CEO, generously gave of his time and provided his perspective incorporated into the IBM turnaround case included in Chapter 7.

My Harvard Business School colleagues provided a rich venue for debate and discussion. Now for over 30 years, Professor F. Warren McFarlan has been my mentor and closest colleague at HBS. Warren's impressive intellect and razor-sharp insights have continued to help me sort out the really important ideas. Professor Stephen Bradley has been good friend and co-instructor in our second-year MBA course, Competing in the Information Age. During the past decade, Steve and I have jointly edited two research symposia books on the leading managerial issues in the strategic use of IT. Professor Rob Austin is co-chair with me of our HBS Executive Education course for CIOs. Rob and I worked together on the IBM cases, and we developed a working paper on managing IT-based transformation initiatives, which provided the underlying thinking for Chapter 10.

Finally, I am indebted to my family. My wife and best friend, Pamela, has spent countless hours in discussions about the information age, IT, and dot coms. She continues to clarify my thinking and reasoning.

RICHARD L. NOLAN

August 2001

Index